Modern Liberty and Its Discontents

19/20

SLC

Modern Liberty and Its Discontents

Pierre Manent

Edited and translated by
Daniel J. Mahoney and Paul Seaton

With an introduction by
Daniel J. Mahoney

ROWMAN & LITTLEFIELD PUBLISHERS, INC.
Lanham • Boulder • New York • Toronto • Oxford

ROWMAN & LITTLEFIELD PUBLISHERS, INC.

Published in the United States of America
by Rowman & Littlefield Publishers, Inc.
A wholly owned subsidiary of The Rowman & Littlefield Publishing Group, Inc.
4501 Forbes Boulevard, Suite 200, Lanham, Maryland 20706
www.rowmanlittlefield.com

PO Box 317
Oxford
OX2 9RU, UK

British Library Cataloguing in Publication Information Available

Library of Congress Cataloging-in-Publication Data

Manent, Pierre.
    Modern liberty and its discontents / Pierre Manent. Edited and
translated by Daniel J. Mahoney and Paul Seaton. With an introduction
by Daniel J. Mahoney.
        p. cm.
    Includes bibliographical references and index.
    ISBN 0-8476-9087-3 (cloth : alk. paper). — ISBN 0-8476-9088-1
(pbk. : alk. paper)
        1. Liberty. 2. Liberalism. 3. Conservatism. 4. Political
science—History. I. Manent, Pierre. II. Mahoney, Daniel J. III. Seaton, Paul.
IV. Title.
JC585.M474   1998
320—dc21

98-4323
CIP

Printed in the United States of America

♾ ™ The paper used in this publication meets the minimum requirements of
American National Standard for Information Sciences—Permanence of
Paper for Printed Library Materials, ANSI Z39.48–1984.

Contents

Modern Liberty and Its Discontents: An Introduction to
the Political Reflection of Pierre Manent   1
Daniel J. Mahoney

Part One: Reflections on an Intellectual Itinerary   31
  • The Truth, Perhaps   33

Part Two: Essays in the History of Political Philosophy   45
  • Toward the Work and Toward the World:
    Claude Lefort's *Machiavelli*   47
  • Democratic Man, Aristocratic Man, and Man
    Simply: Some Remarks on an Equivocation in
    Tocqueville's Thought   65

Part Three: Christianity and Politics   79
  • Charles Péguy: Between Political Faith and
    Faith   81
  • Christianity and Democracy: Some Remarks on
    the Political History of Religion, or, on the
    Religious History of Modern Politics   97

Part Four: Understanding Totalitarianism   117
  • Totalitarianism and the Problem of Political
    Representation   119
  • Aurel Kolnai: A Political Philosopher Confronts
    the Scourge of Our Epoch   135

Part Five: Democratic Individualism   149
  • On Modern Individualism   151
  • Recovering Human Attachments: An Introduction
    to Allan Bloom's *Love and Friendship*   161

Part Six: Thinking and Acting Politically   167
- Raymond Aron and the Analysis of Modern
  Society   169
- De Gaulle as Hero   173
- Democracy without Nations?   185

Part Seven: Reflections on Strauss, Nature, and History   197
- Strauss and Nietzsche   199
- On Historical Causality   209

Part Eight: Liberalism and Conservatism Today   215
- Liberalism and Conservatism: The Transatlantic
  Misunderstanding   217

Index   231

About the Authors   239

Modern Liberty and Its Discontents: An Introduction to the Political Reflection of Pierre Manent

Daniel J. Mahoney

The crisis of communism did not resonate with explosive consequences in Paris in 1989—the year of the great antitotalitarian revolution in the "other Europe"—but rather in 1974 with the publication of Aleksandr Solzhenitsyn's ideological bombshell, *The Gulag Archipelago.* With that event, one can date the end of the ideological hegemony of the Marxist vulgate in French intellectual life and the beginning of the renaissance of non-Marxist and non-"existentialist" political philosophizing in that great custodian of European culture. The work of an earlier generation of non-Marxist French scholars, such as François Furet and Claude Lefort, is increasingly known in the Anglo-American world, but the pathbreaking work of a younger generation of "neoliberal" thinkers is just beginning to be noticed in the United States.

This book is an introduction to the work of one of the most serious and penetrating of the new French political theorists, Pierre Manent. It consists of fifteen of his essays written between 1983 and 1997. These essays address a remarkable range of subjects: the Machiavellian origins of modernity, Alexis de Tocqueville's analysis of democracy, the political role of Christianity, the nature of totalitarianism, the character of modern individualism, and the future of the nation-state. In addition, there are penetrating reflections on the significance of such philosophers and statesmen as Charles Péguy, Charles de Gaulle, Raymond Aron, Aurel Kolnai, Allan Bloom, and Leo Strauss. But what unifies these diverse writings is a meditation on the nature of modern freedom and the permanent discontents that accompany it. This essay serves as a general introduction to the political thought of Manent, placing the essays within the context of his work as a whole and his analysis of the nature of modern liberty and its effects on the integrity of the human soul.

Manent, born in 1949, was for many years maître de conférences at the Collège de France and since 1992 has been a teacher at the École des Hautes Études en Sciences Sociales in Paris. He is, among other

1

things, a former assistant to the great French anticommunist political thinker Raymond Aron (who initiated the French rediscovery of Tocqueville and of non-Marxist political analysis in the 1950s and 1960s), an independent-minded scholar who has contributed to the revival of liberal (in the older and larger non-American sense) political thought in France, a former editor of and current contributor to the important "neoconservative" journal *Commentaire,* and a serious Catholic deeply influenced by the work of Strauss. Moreover, it is in no small part due to his efforts, as well as those of François Furet and Jean-Claude Lamberti, that Tocqueville's writings are now widely recognized in France as an indispensable guide for understanding modern history and society as well as a rich theoretical alternative to discredited Marxist-inspired critiques of liberalism.

Manent is the author of *Naissances de la politique moderne: Machiavel, Hobbes, Rousseau* (1977), *Tocqueville and the Nature of Democracy* (1982, 1996 in translation), *An Intellectual History of Liberalism* (1987, 1994 in translation), and the two-volume anthology with commentary entitled *Les Libéraux* (1986). Manent has written numerous articles on such thinkers as Joseph de Maistre, Karl Marx, Leo Strauss, Raymond Aron, and Carl Schmitt, as well as on various topics and issues in the history and philosophy of politics.[1]

Manent's work judiciously combines historical studies, philosophical reflection, and political-cultural analysis. At the center of his work is an effort to grasp the meaning of "our liberal destiny."[2] Manent is particularly concerned with the effects of modern democracy on the maintenance and sustenance of substantial human ties. While his writings are sometimes quite demanding, they are also remarkable examples of lucid and concrete philosophical writing. Manent avoids abstract analysis and addresses the effects of democratic individualism on "the moral contents of life," on serious religiosity, sustained political judgment, and the full range of human attachments and affections, including a coherent sense of national identity. While eschewing any traditionalist or reactionary rejection of liberalism, Manent nonetheless stands apart from the current crop of non-Marxist French political thinkers by his considered refusal to idolatrize "individual rights" as the spiritual lodestar of modern society. He is a liberal conservative (we might say a "neoconservative" with appropriate sensitivity to the distinctive French context) who appreciates the dependence of democratic societies on premodern moral capital and on qualities of human nature that are presupposed, but not sufficiently cultivated, by a liberal political order. Nor is Manent a typical adherent of the "social sciences," which, in their claim to scientific rigor, dominate the study of human affairs in the academy. In his latest work, *The City of Man* (1994, 1998 in translation),[3] Manent brilliantly explores the origins of the modern social sciences, which he argues are located in a fundamental, dogmatic, and unsustainable abstraction from the question of the nature of man.

The Theological-Political Problem

Manent's view of liberalism is thoroughly nonideological and avoids the dogmatism that too often characterizes both defenders and critics of bourgeois society. His work includes intelligent, critical, and sympathetic accounts of the major liberal, nonliberal, and antiliberal theorists, from Machiavelli to Rousseau, Marx, and Schmitt. His aim is to understand the origins, nature, and consequences of the liberal project. This deliberate enterprise arose as a self-conscious response to Europe's "theological-political problem"—a problem coextensive with European politics since the fall of the Roman Empire. The problem facing Europe was diagnosed with particular acuity by Marsilius of Padua and Dante, two Christian Aristotelians of the thirteenth century who wished to defend the independence and integrity of the profane world from ecclesiastical despotism exercised in the name of the highest goods of man.[4]

But Marsilius and Dante were precisely "Aristotelians"; they wished to defend the goods of the temporal and natural realm against the superintending claims of the priests who represented the supernatural realm. Manent brilliantly shows how the strategy of "ostracism" pursued by the Christian Aristotelians of the Renaissance was inadequate to the radicalness of the theological-political problem. Precisely because it depended upon a hierarchy of human or profane goods, the defense of the autonomy of the political, of the "regime," was inherently vulnerable to the claims of the church and its representatives that the supernatural completed and perfected nature.

The modern response to the theological-political problem was to reject the Dantean-Marsilian as well as the Thomistic solutions (i.e., to reject all versions of what Hobbes called "Aristotelity"). The modern enterprise entailed the construction of a new notion of sovereignty in which power and opinion and nature and law were firmly and irrevocably separated.[5] Both the mixed regime of Aristotelian political theory, which aimed at balancing, mixing, and "doing justice" to the variety of human goods, and the old regime with its estates and its ecclesiastical establishments were to be replaced by the modern representative state. This state represents individuals, not "spiritual masses," and grounds itself not in any questionable and potentially despotic opinion about the "good" but in the very certain reality of mankind's bodily need.[6]

In *An Intellectual History of Liberalism*, Manent follows Strauss in
seeing Machiavelli as the architect of the modern enterprise, the thinker
who first delineated the possibility of a politics closed to the good, of a
politics that could be utterly self-contained because it is closed in on
itself.[7] Machiavelli explicitly denies the possibility of a common good
because he denies that human beings have access to a hierarchy of goods
that stands above or moderates partisan claims. Manent shows how
Machiavelli rewrites and radically transforms the classical mixed regime.[8]

The people and the great, the many and the few, remain the substance and material of political life for Machiavelli as well as for the
Aristotelian tradition. But there is a vital and striking difference. For
Aristotle, partisans are partisans precisely because the claims of justice
that motivate and justify their actions are partial or incomplete. For the
mixing, sifting, weighing, and balancing of partisan claims to occur, there
must be a standard of justice outside partisanship—whether that be the
"best regime" or the well-balanced soul of the philosopher-political scientist—to guide the mixing of civic, human, and moral goods. For Machiavelli, in contrast, the few and the many are absolutely enclosed within
their respective "humors." Machiavelli eliminates the "dialogic" dimensions of political life, the discussion about political goods that characterizes the practical ideal of classical political science.

He replaces Aristotle's sublime impartiality that does justice to the
truth inherent in the partial claims of both democratic and oligarchic
partisans, as well as the less politically influential but nonetheless
weighty claims of virtue and wisdom, with a radical partiality that "despairs of arriving at the universal, and which contents itself with offering to the human will, the objective of a liberty which is always to be
won, within the limits of society or history" (see his essay "Toward the
Work and Toward the World: Claude Lefort's *Machiavelli*" in this volume). Machiavelli formulates the distinctive moral stance of modernity
that recognizes the radically indeterminate character of human freedom
built upon the stern requirements of natural and social Necessity. This
dialectic of human willfulness and Necessity marks all of the fundamental
currents of modernity and is at the origin of modern man's unshakable
conviction that human freedom consists of a perpetual "flight from evil"
rather than a humanizing pursuit of natural or supernatural goods.[9]

Following Strauss, Manent recognizes the transvaluation of values that
characterizes the Machiavellian analysis. Machiavelli builds upon the sure
foundation of the people—the people who merely wish to be left alone.
The people's "goodness" is simply negative; it consists of the fact that
they do not wish to oppress or be oppressed. Machiavelli's analysis is
both proto-democratic and proto-bourgeois, because for all his empha-

sis on the "glory" of the prince, the prince can do nothing great or lasting without the solid cooperation of the security-seeking people—one might say that the only workable or reasonably stable polity is a bourgeois one. A polity conducive to the needs of human beings is based not upon a positive notion of the human good but on the democratic and morally neutral foundation of the people. To realize such a political solution, one must learn from Machiavelli the fundamental lesson about the "fecundity of evil." Machiavelli's rendition of the manner in which Cesare Borgia established civil order in Romagna and thereby left the people "satisfied and stupefied" powerfully reveals the political order as an "alchemy of evil, a never complete suppression of fear through fear."[10] As Strauss put it, the foundation of all politics is in "terror" and not "love."

In his work, Manent traces the modifications that liberalism undergoes on essentially Machiavellian foundations. Thomas Hobbes constructs a sovereignty based on the radical separation of power and opinion, an "absolute" sovereignty that guarantees the security and property of individuals. Hobbes's "Leviathan," with its artful overcoming of the state of nature, is "the institutionalization of the memorable performance of Cesare Borgia in Romagna."[11] Manent shows how all the subsequent great liberal and antiliberal thinkers were post-Machiavellians whose politics responded to the human circumstances made possible by liberal modernity. Their theorizing and diverse political prescriptions presume the base, the prior existence of the modern "solution" to the theological-political problem.

Modern Individualism

According to Manent, the deepest threat to the integrity of the human being brought about by the modern project is the gradual but revolutionary and ceaselessly unfolding separation of the "individual" from the moral contents of life. (This, Manent suggests, is the "democratic revolution" whose providential and inevitable character filled Tocqueville with "religious dread.") The modern individual in fact is a person who is connected, as all social beings are, to social organisms and intermediate institutions that continue to provide some of the motives of human thought and action. But families, churches, and other intermediate associations and social bodies that embody substantive opinions about the human good have an increasingly diminished status in the formal or political life of democratic peoples. For a long time, the radical character of the sovereign representative state that represented individuals with their rights—and not what Marx called the "material and spiritual elements" of society such as propertied elements, family, religion, and the "knowledge" of philosophers and priests—was obscured by what Manent, following Marx, calls the "bourgeois ideology." This "conservative liberal" ethos melded democratic representation and prescriptive tradition in a mixture that obscured the transformative character of the *democratic* revolution (and thereby humanized and moderated it). Conservative liberals such as François Guizot falsely believed that the democratic revolution could come to an end, that an end of modernity or history could preserve both formal liberty and the natural superiorities and moral contents of life in a happy and unprecedented coexistence (see especially the essay "Totalitarianism and the Problem of Political Representation" in part four of this volume).

But whereas the democratic state presupposes the spiritual and material elements of society, it does not formally and therefore genuinely represent them. It depoliticizes and therefore tends to relativize the opinions that are the basis and reflection of the natural and common world. Only our rights to have and privately defend and "exercise" our opinion have a political status. The substance of our opinions is relegated to the private realm of civil society where it remains a matter of personal "conscience," with no direct or visible political consequences. This lack of political status, this relegation of the contents of life to a private realm of protected rights, cannot help but transform and diminish the contents and motives of human life. They "are 'presupposed' by the liberal representative state. In order for there to be religious freedom, there has to be religion, to have economic liberty, there must be an economy. [But] presupposition . . . is the weakest form of affirmation" (see "Totalitarianism and the Problem of Political Representation").

As a result of this process, the human being becomes more and more of an "individual" and increasingly inhabits a kind of civil state of nature where free and equal individuals are supposed to coexist, dependent on and agreeing on only their possession of individual autonomy and the requirements for protecting it. The goal established by the most radical and self-conscious modern thought is for human beings to become ever freer because more unconnected beings. We moderns are "condemned to be free" and that sentence, the source of the distinctive pathos of modern thought, is also a blow struck at all forms of social authority understood as "heteronomous" domination. Important currents of modern literature reflect the ambition of modern thought to unmask the illusory character of human bonds (a point forcefully made in Manent's essay "On Modern Individualism" and in his introduction to Bloom's *Love and Friendship* in part five of this volume). But Manent makes clear that this ambition is based on a willful and unjustified refusal to confront the inescapable question of what human beings have in common. Aristotle was right to affirm that human beings are "political animals" precisely because it is the city or political community that allows men to fulfill their natural propensity "to put in common actions and reasons" (*Nichomachean Ethics* [1126b11–12]: see also "Democracy without Nations?" in part six of this volume).

In contrast to the Aristotelian affirmation of a common good, the logic or nature of democratic modernity is to assert the radical primacy of the will, of the individual exercising his or her rights with no necessary connection to the contents of the moral life. The radical separation of what Manent calls "power" and "opinion," so central to the modern constitutionalism of Thomas Hobbes and John Locke, paves the way for the pure freedom, diagnosed by Hegel in the *Phenomenology of the Mind,* which turns out to be a pure Negation, the willful annihilation of the spiritual and material elements of society in the name of an unencumbered autonomy or individuality.[12] In the Jacobin and Bolshevik effort to create "a new man" wholly freed from the inheritance of the past and willing only his own freedom, one sees the radicalization and "perfection" of modern liberty, a liberty that is "pure because without motives" or human content.

The two totalitarianisms of the twentieth century, Nazism and communism, are simultaneously reactions against and intensifications of modern individualism. Despite their repeated claims to be harbingers of a new kind of community and a new kind of individual both were "actually unprecedentedly virulent promoters of . . . the absence of the natural human bond" ("On Modern Individualism"). They, of course, go far beyond modern liberalism in their effort to forge human ties that have no natural or traditional supports. They aim to destroy or replace prosaic bourgeois society, but at the same time they reveal the impossibility of the project for a freedom divorced from any or all natural or social determination. The totalitarianisms thus embody the self-destruction of Machiavellian modernity.

This self-destruction of modern liberty was not anticipated by the first liberals. They believed they were freeing Europe from the fanaticism of "pious cruelty." They believed they were making possible the comprehensive enlightenment of human society. Manent has argued that liberalism has fundamentally failed to understand itself. The early modern liberals were convinced that a new political science could construct a civic artifice, a sovereign state, and a "civil society" that would liberate human beings from the civic controversies engendered by the clash of religious opinions and from the danger of a state of nature where the natural rights to life, liberty, and security are threatened by aristocratic pretensions and oppression and by the scarcity characteristic of premodern economic life. Liberalism, however, has paradoxically created a social condition approximating a civil state of nature whose free and equal individuals are increasingly cut off from both the moral contents of life and the minimum requirements of even liberal citizenship. As Montesquieu astutely observed about the English of his times, they are more "confederates than fellow citizens."[13]

Tocqueville and Democratic Individualism

Tocqueville was the most profound student and critic of this humanity-threatening "individualism." It is from his work that Manent draws powerful insight and inspiration in analyzing the strengths and weaknesses of modern democracy. Many American neoconservatives draw comfortable conclusions from Tocqueville's work, finding in his analyses powerful arguments about the dignity and sobriety of a properly constituted liberal democracy. They are not, of course, wrong. Tocqueville *is* a friend of moderate liberal democracy. Manent, however, differs from many American neoconservatives in that he explicitly recognizes Tocqueville's serious reservations about the democratic order. Like Tocqueville, and unlike some of his contemporary admirers, Manent is fully aware of the profoundly radical character of the democratic society based upon liberal premises.

The founders of liberal modernity explicitly rejected any notion of a common good. They intended and promoted the radical separation of power and opinion. They wished to privatize and diminish, although not eliminate, the contents of human life. In other words, they began with a deliberate political neglect of the soul and its claims. The soullessness of modern democracy, much noted by its "cultural" critics from both the left and the right, was a deliberate part of the design of liberal democracy. Today, thoughtful people cannot help but ask, What in liberal democracy is worthy of the commitment and rational assent of those who care about the integrity of the human soul?

To answer this question, it is necessary to turn, at some length, to Manent's analysis of Tocqueville and democratic individualism in his remarkable *Tocqueville and the Nature of Democracy*. Manent begins with the "naive" presupposition that Tocqueville's elaboration of democracy can explain us to ourselves.[14] By confronting Tocqueville's elaboration of democracy, democratic citizens can gain an appropriate distance from the omnipresence of democratic categories and hopes without abandoning their commitment to the preservation of the democratic order or their belief in its real and abiding justice. They are thus able to stand at a distance from what Manent calls the "democratic dogma," without ceasing to be measured friends of democratic liberty. In this spirit, Manent summarizes Tocqueville's teaching in a terse and evocative formulation: To love democracy well, it is necessary to love it moderately.[15]

But what is this democracy whose nature Tocqueville unfolds and that Manent's book attempts to articulate for us? One must begin by clearing up one potential source of confusion in any discussion of modern democracy. For Tocqueville, democracy is not, as in the Greek or Aristotelian view of politics, a political regime in an eternally unchanging cycle of political orders available to man as man. It is, rather, a new human and social dispensation, characterized by "equality of conditions" where the place and efficacy of socially rooted and politically authoritative "influences" and "contents of life"—what American political scientists call "social capital"—are displaced by an all-encompassing hypothesis of radical freedom and equality. (This theme is developed at length in the essay "Democratic Man, Aristocratic Man, and Man Simply: Some Remarks on an Equivocation in Tocqueville's Thought" in part two of this volume.)

Three intertwined "generative principles" bring this about: a new egalitarian social state, the doctrine of the sovereignty of the people, and the dominance of public opinion in a democratic order. In the end, these formulations, although initially vague and abstract, suggest the same, extremely concrete, explanation: Modern democracies are dominated by an *opinion* that affirms that the only legitimate form of obedience is obedience to oneself or obedience to oneself through a majority will that represents the individual in his undiminished sovereignty. Tocqueville brilliantly established that this dogma of "the sovereignty of the people," the "generative principle of the republic," is "the same which directs the majority of human actions." (This theme and quotation resurface repeatedly in these essays.)

When we understand that the principle of "the sovereignty of the people" is applied to every aspect of the social order, then we can begin to appreciate fully the novelty and radicalness of the distinctively modern democratic order. Manent's analysis is subtle, refined, measured, and true to the nuances of the Tocquevillian elaboration of democracy. Manent shows that, for Tocqueville, the democratic understanding of man is based upon a profoundly true insight about the conventional sources of aristocratic authority and influences. Tocqueville proclaims the comparative "justice" and "naturalness" of the democratic idea and political order. But this is only part of the truth about democracy and man.

Here Manent restores greater depth and perspective to the current accounts of Tocqueville and corrects the standard view of him as a cautious and measured, but unabashed, partisan of liberalism and liberal democracy. Manent shows the paradoxical character of democracy and of Tocqueville's approach to it. Undoubtedly just, democracy profoundly threatens the cultivation of intellectual *eros,* the articulation and manifestation of the civic and manly virtues, and even the ability of individuals to act together or upon each other (i.e., to *influence* each other within society). At its extreme limits, democracy creates an apolitical, apathetic individualism that risks dissolving the social and civic bonds into a "dis-society."[16] Because the democratic dogma is based on an abstractly true, "purely formal," and "dizzyingly empty" abstraction, it threatens the nurturing and sustenance of those excellences that give *substance* to individual freedom and choice.[17] Democracy, moreover, exalts in an exaggerated and potentially enervating manner the real, but limited, "virtue" of mildness or "humanity." In Manent's succinct formulation, "democracy embodies nature in a way that puts nature in danger."[18]

In the closing chapters of *Democracy in America,* Tocqueville highlights the danger of a democratic, or tutelary, despotism that arises when the nature of democracy is unchecked by a sovereign "art of liberty." Friedrich Hayek and other contemporary classical liberals have rightly highlighted Tocqueville's fear of an oppressive, managerial, bureaucratic state that formally represents the general will but saps free individuals of individual responsibility, economic initiative, and personal prudence. This is certainly one feature of Tocqueville's analysis of "democratic despotism," but it is only one aspect. Manent places it in its broader and proper perspective: Tocqueville understands democratic despotism to entail a despotism of mildness or softness itself.[19] This "despotism" comprehensively undermines the associative, civic, and intellectual capacities of democratic man.

Democratic despotism is precisely *soft* despotism, marked, to be sure, by an egalitarian centralized state but made possible by the disarming of the soul by a dogma that recognizes only the legitimacy of sovereign, rights-bearing individuals and of the state that speaks for them. This dogma publicly delegitimizes those groups, bodies, activities, or authorities that are required to give content, direction, scope, and firmness to the individual and collective activities of people. It weakens the *public* character of mediating or intermediate structures.

However, despite his sometimes chilling diagnosis of the dangers of democratic despotism, Tocqueville is no partisan of hardness or cruelty à la Nietzsche or the proto-fascist right.[20] Democratic mildness undoubtedly humanizes life, eliminating the cruelties of aristocratic conventions and providing a place for natural sentiments, especially within the bosom of the family. But even the family is radically transformed by the democratic principle. The ties between parents and children are democratized and thus made "sweeter" and more "natural," but they risk finally being thoroughly democratized in a manner that dissolves them or empties them of substance altogether.[21] The family risks becoming a "contractual" arrangement devoid of sufficient hierarchical or authoritative influence. Hence, democracy completes its revolutionary work, pitting nature against nature.

So what do Manent and Tocqueville recommend? Are we left to contemplate and to bemoan the paradox of democracy as an order where nature inexorably undermines itself? Is there a political alternative to modern democracy that offers a way out of this seemingly cruel impasse? The answer is both no and yes. For Manent and Manent's Tocqueville, justice and prudence demand unhesitating loyalty to liberal or constitutional democracy. In his moving concluding section of the book, Manent criticizes democracy's two main enemies: its stubbornly unreflective reactionary opponents and its far more numerous and therefore dangerous "excessive or immoderate friends."[22]

The reactionaries who reject the progress of democracy "do not know what they are doing or what they want." They fail to appreciate the ways in which their own thoughts and sentiments have been transformed by the democratic tempest. Their dream of a reactionary utopia, where "natural and necessary inequalities" are restored, is paradoxically based upon a democratic prejudice that allows them to exaggerate their knowledge about the true nature of human beings. In the French and European context, Manent clearly highlights the once significant, but now minuscule, band of reactionaries who failed to heed Tocqueville's advice that the aristocratic party should educate democracy by correcting its faults and by working to preserve those predemocratic "contents of life" that democracy threatens but that are indispensable to its well-being. "It is true that democracy is in a very real sense the enemy of human grandeur, but the enemies of democracy are much more dangerous enemies of this grandeur."[23]

The excessive friends of democracy are its most dangerous and disingenuous enemies. They claim to be merely friends of real liberty and genuine equality. But they fail to realize that liberal democracy is compatible with the "nature" of man precisely because it limits itself to protecting formal liberty and not to using government to actualize the democratic dogma in every aspect of personal and social life. The obstinate desire to realize the democratic abstraction, without respect for those compromises, inheritances, and persisting natural and conventional inequalities that characterize liberal democracy, is precisely an invitation for the unprecedented modern expression of despotism that we call totalitarianism. Just as modern democracy as a social state cannot be classified within the classical cycle of regimes, so totalitarianism is an eminently modern and "democratic" phenomenon whose magnitude, perversity, and humanitarian pretensions radically distinguish it from premodern tyranny.

Tocqueville shows that there is one alternative for friends of human liberty and dignity. They must exercise an art of liberty whose central feature is the deliberate cultivation of a science of associations, a political art that preserves local liberties and mediating structures between the "sovereign" individual and the "central power" and that gives freedom and moral support (but not state establishment) to a religion that sets limits to unencumbered human willfulness.

One of the strengths of Manent's sobering analysis is that he clearly adumbrates the unfinished and unfinishable character of this noble and necessary art. This recognition can help restore a sense of measure to our sometimes inflated contemporary political expectations. For American conservatives who are natural recipients of Tocqueville's teaching, a salutary inference can be drawn. There can be no permanent conservative "revolution" that will cure the democratic propensity toward disassociation, radical individualism, and reliance on the impersonal power of a central government that alone claims to speak for the "general will." Nor should conservatives forget that American religion is already an at least partially democratized religion, as Manent brilliantly shows in his analysis of the transformation of Puritan America into liberal America.[24]

Despite the brilliance of its analysis, *Tocqueville and the Nature of Democracy* is marked by a perhaps excessive note of pathos and a tendency to underestimate liberal democracy's own internal resources. These internal resources are more evident when one analyzes modern democracy through the lenses of Aristotelian regime analysis rather than by accepting its own grandiose claims at face value. Despite his adamant opposition to all forms of modern progressivism, Manent is sometimes insufficiently skeptical of modernity's claims that it has succeeded in remaking the fundaments of human and political life. Despite the desire of its architects to found a new order of human things and not another regime in the age-old cycle of political forms, modern democracy nonetheless retains some of the characteristics of a political order and hence fails in its efforts to transcend the natural order altogether. I do not think that Pierre Manent would finally disagree with this formulation. My reservations, then, have more to do with rhetorical emphasis than with the

substance of the matter. And as we shall see when we analyze Manent's
The City of Man, one of the great strengths of his approach is precisely
the way in which it combines a trenchant critique of historicism with a
refusal to succumb to an over simplified and dogmatic antihistoricism.
It does so, in part, because it recognizes that democratic man has complex and somewhat attenuated relations with man *tout court*. (We will
return to this theme, which is at the heart of all of Manent's work, later
in the essay.)

The Virtues of Liberalism

Despite a tendency to overstate the formal or abstract character of
modern freedom, Manent surely recognizes that it is not only political
liberty and the inherited moral capital of the premodern era that serve
to "humanize" modern and democratic life. Manent does not deny that
liberal democratic modernity has its own strengths and its own not in-
considerable resources that serve to maintain a respect for the "natural
order of things" (although he emphasizes this more in his politically
oriented essays than in the more theoretical *The City of Man*, which
emphasizes the remarkable audacity and "unnaturalness" of the modern
project). The self-interest and emphasis on economic utility that are the
motives, the fuel, and the justification for the abstraction called
the market are not merely abstractions. Interest and utility are rooted
in the natural world, even if the *homo economicus* of capitalist
theory is a product of the civil society created by the liberal separation
of power and opinion. "Invoking *interest*, liberals founded their construction on a possibly abstract principle. . . . [They have] some illusions
about the lucidity of the man who 'searches for his interest,' but they
designate a powerful and universal resort of human action."[25] As important, a market order with its appeal to the free, self-interested activities
of economic man replaced an economic and social order of arbitrary
command that too often oppressed and offered little opportunity to the
poor—that is, to the vast majority of human beings throughout history.
The market, then, for all its narrowing of the human soul to a realm of
utility, remains, however problematically, a *human* order rooted both in
nature and justice. The same cannot be said about the socialist effort to
restore the order of command in a "democratic" manner so that real as
opposed to merely formal freedom can be established. To put it in a
nutshell, liberal capitalism is not an "ideology" in the sense that Marxist socialism is with its dream of a different logic of history, society,
and economy.[26]

Manent writes respectfully about the "Lockean circle of utility and representation."[27] In a "Lockean" regime, there is an absence of fanaticism, of an effort to remake or transform the essentials of human nature. In such a regime, political representation is an instrument aimed at guaranteeing the rights of citizens. These rights serve not only to attenuate the power but also to defend and sometimes embody the spiritual and material contents of life. Real human needs and activities, especially commercial ones, are protected and represented in a representative commercial regime. "The act of representation finds its motives in the ordinary life of each person within civil society."[28] By representing civil society, the political life of a liberal regime represents more than abstract, autonomous individuals. It represents real human needs and activities; it represents the life embodied in the "commerce" and "culture" of civil society.

Manent, accordingly, has a very rich appreciation of what some scholars have termed *commercial republicanism.* He is a great admirer of both the prudent constitutionalism and the commercialism of thinkers such as Montesquieu, Benjamin Constant, and Frédéric Bastiat.[29] He readily accepts the argument of Montesquieu that commerce can have a softening and humanizing effect on political life and human mores and tastes. He appreciates the necessity and the brilliance of the constitutionalist construction of the separation of powers formulated by Montesquieu in the eleventh and nineteenth books of *The Spirit of the Laws* and is sympathetic to the Constantian and Tocquevillian criticism of the tyrannical propensities of an unmitigated popular sovereignty.[30] He has also written that as radically a "democratic" thinker as Thomas Paine was saved from Jacobin fanaticism because he had an appreciation for commercial utility and because he refused the ideological "suspension" of natural sentiments.[31] Manent, then, is genuinely appreciative of the "humanity" and "decency" of the liberal regime.

But he also learned from Tocqueville, among others, that humanity, decency, and "softness" are not the only or highest human virtues. He believes that humanitarianism can undermine liberty itself by weakening the civic and "severe" virtues (e.g., the capacity for political deliberation, the willingness to punish criminals, and the ability to recognize and if need be fight enemies), thereby undermining what he calls, in a particularly felicitous phrase, the "instinct of political existence" itself.[32]

The very real virtues of liberalism are, simultaneously and paradoxically, its very real vices. The humanitarianism of modern liberals can degenerate into relativism and a universalized despotism of soft, enervated souls, whose chief manifestation is the democratic despotism outlined by Tocqueville. Manent, I believe, can be characterized as what he himself has termed a "sad liberal."[33] He appreciates the pacification of religious and civic strife that liberalism has achieved; is appreciative of its civic and political liberties and the unprecedented prosperity it makes possible; is aware of its decency and humanity yet profoundly alert to the ways in which the unqualified victory of its principle threatens the liberty and dignity of human beings. Apolitical individualism, moral relativism, a failure to recognize the existence of foreign enemies as well as the intrinsic wickedness of totalitarianism, and the lack of spiritual independence and pride culminate in the "tyranny of public opinion" and are all effects of the public soullessness that was deliberately constructed by the philosophical legislators of the bourgeois liberal order.[34]

Manent has analyzed at length and with subtlety the ways in which modern totalitarianism is a form of representative, or democratic, politics wherein the party and the party-state through the intermediary of the nation or revolution claim to democratically represent the true sources of authenticity or legitimacy. But he understands the ways in which totalitarian "representation" also entails a decisive and unparalleled break with the principles and mores of European civilization (see "Totalitarianism and the Problem of Political Representation"). While rejecting a "Constantian" view—so attractive to progressive-minded intellectuals and social scientists—that reduces totalitarianism to an atavism or anachronism of a premodern past, Manent also appreciates the chasm, the gap of principle and practice, that separates liberal and totalitarian modernity. For this reason, he criticizes the partisans of liberal capitalism, such as Hayek, for too closely identifying the providential or tutelary state (which is the product of the expansion of the welfare and administrative responsibilities of the modern state) with the totalitarian party-states of the twentieth century. (As his essay "Liberalism and Conservatism: The Transatlantic Misunderstanding" makes clear, he also believes that the welfare state, kept prudently within the bounds of a social market economy, can remind citizens of commercial societies that there are other human motives than those of individual freedom and subjectivity that need to be socially recognized in a decent society. The welfare state, as long as it does not aim to institute a restrictive system of command, can be a political "instrument of self-obligation," a reminder that our freedom operates within a context of mutual obligations that are not reducible to market or contractual relations.) Regardless, any simple identification of totalitarian and tutelary "despotism" ignores the ideological and revolutionary character of twentieth-century communist and national socialist totalitarianism. Manent writes in his commentary on *Les Libéraux*:

> These new totalitarian regimes do not situate themselves any more, at least the Russian and German ones, in the prolongation, even the extreme prolongation, of this or that trait of European politics that liberals had the habit of denouncing (protectionism, collectivism, etc.). They mark the rupture of the tradition of civilization. However, the liberals . . . accustomed to seeing man under the traits of homo economicus, or of the law-abiding citizen, risk being, more than the conservative or socialist, helpless before the new figures which are the militant of the totalitarian party, the functionary of the secret police, the ideologue.[35]

Manent notes one of the most disturbing political phenomena of the twentieth century: the inability of most liberals to understand and appreciate the singularity, the civilizational "rupture" that totalitarianism entails. Either many liberals succumbed to radicalism by emphasizing and admiring the rational and progressive features of communist societies, or they underestimated the sheer surreality and suffocating absurdity of communist practice. There were, of course, notable and noble exceptions.

The Influence of Aron and Strauss

One such exception was Manent's teacher and colleague (on the review *Commentaire*) Raymond Aron. Manent has written several fine appreciations of Aron's work that center around three central points of Aron's philosophical reflection: his critique of Marxism and historicism, his unfailing grasp of and opposition to totalitarianism, and his political and nondoctrinaire liberalism.[36] Manent's portrait of Aron emphasizes that while accepting the principles of the liberal and modern worlds, Aron incarnated the premodern virtues of prudence and political reason. At the theoretical level, he formulated a philosophy of "politics and history" that attempted to liberate citizens and statesmen from the yoke of necessity or the tyranny of systemic theoretical determinism. Aron worked to demystify the power of Marxist historicism. In doing so, he wished to restore the political world of choice and responsibility to citizens and statesmen.

Manent admires the greatness of the Aronian enterprise, a greatness easy to misunderstand now that "the power of the fascination of communism has dissipated."[37] Manent's beautiful description of the grounds of the Aronian opposition to the "lie" at the core of Marxist-Leninist ideology deserves to be quoted at length. It reveals the ways in which the communists' efforts to restore the connection between power and opinion entail a perversion and destruction of civic and human life, precisely because the claims of communism are not rooted in concrete human life but are ideological and mendacious abstractions. Manent lucidly summarizes the Aronian critique of Marxist-Leninism:

> The idea comes to the service of power, power to the service of the idea, in a new relationship which defines communism: the men who have taken power in 1917 are not men who have taken power, they are "representatives" of the Russian proletariat, avant-garde of the world proletariat, itself the avant-garde of humanity upon the march; the measures that they decide are not good or bad political, social or economic measures: they "construct socialism" . . . "produce a new man." It is these word games—word games with such murderous consequences—that Aron has always refused to enter. He has always refused to communism the privilege of human "extraterritoriality" that it has consistently claimed for itself.[38]

Above all, Manent admires Aron because he is the model of the man of political reason. He refused to acquiesce in the ideological distortion of reality. He knew that liberalism had enemies and that the liberal regime had to be protected against both its immoderate friends and its ideological enemies. Aron knew that the progress associated with liberal institutions and practices would not put an end to the need for political judgment or civic virtue. Aron was a political scientist who equitably judged the human world, upholding liberal principles but refusing to neatly fit human and social needs and passions into some doctrinal straitjacket. Aron's political science was characterized by a taste for human things, by a sense of the "amplitude and diversity of the human world."[39] Manent's measured defense of the welfare state and his reservations about the doctrinaire tendencies of Hayekian liberalism owe much to Aron. At the theoretical level, Manent's philosophical analysis in *The City of Man* of the coexistence of modern individualism with the enduring political nature of man builds on Aron's emphasis on the interpenetration of *process* (the new transforming features of modern life such as technology, industrialism and democratic individualism) and *drama* (the persistence of politics and the continuing need for prudence in the new modern context). In *The City of Man*, Manent develops, at the level of the history of political thought, an important theme of Aron's political sociology (see especially the essay "Raymond Aron and the Analysis of Modern Society" in part six of this book). Yet their philosophical standpoints, as well as their evaluations of liberal democracy, are, in some important respects, quite distinct. Aron was a conservative-minded liberal while Manent is a conservative who opposes any "reactionary" rejection of modern democracy. The practical conclusions of the conservative liberal and the liberal conservative are often indistinguishable, but in their deepest bearings they belong to distinct, if overlapping, spiritual families.

Aron remained more sanguine than Manent about the prospects for liberal democracy in part because he believed that it had relatively healthy and durable moral foundations. Hence their somewhat different evaluations of the danger posed by Tocqueville's "democratic despotism." (See the opening essay "The Truth, Perhaps." But it is also worth noting that Aron moved closer to Manent's position in one of his final works, *In Defense of Decadent Europe*.[40]) But despite these differences, the liberal Aron was, for Manent, in some important sense, a premodern orator and educator. Through his scholarship and journalism, he helped preserve the political contents of the moral life. The personal and intellectual influence of Aron on Manent should not be underestimated.

The classical character of the work of another "model" and inspiration for Manent, the political philosopher Leo Strauss, is much more explicit. Manent appreciates much better than the fevered critics of "Straussianism" that Strauss, the partisan of classical political philosophy, is a friend of liberal democracy. This is because Manent recognizes the classical distinction between theory and practice: in the classical understanding, theoretical radicality can and ought to coexist with practical sobriety.

Manent is a believing Catholic. But he has learned from Strauss, the Hellenic Jew, that the investigation of the complex relationship between liberal "rationality," the Christian religion "with its relation of affinity to and opposition to liberalism," and the "order of human things," the "natural order," must be based on political philosophy and natural reason.[41] He understands the danger of a "political theology" that obscures the natural world and exaggerates the political wisdom to be discerned from Scripture or strictly theological reflection. Manent, in the spirit of Thomas Aquinas, is open to philosophers who study nature from a nontheological perspective, such as Aristotle, Montesquieu, Aron, and Strauss. This is also why Manent places so much emphasis on recognizing and respecting the moral, as opposed to the simply religious, contents of life. Only by recognizing the natural world—the world inhabited by faith, philosophy, family, politics, statesmanship, and art—can the tensions and ambiguities, the demands and conflicts of human life be recognized in their density and amplitude. (The essays on Charles Péguy and Aurel Kolnai in this volume illustrate Manent's sympathy for Catholic thinkers who appreciate the created dignity of a common world rooted in the *givenness* of reality, thinkers who welcomed the "carnal" or temporal foundations of Christian faith.) Finally, Manent agrees with

Strauss and Bloom that a nonhistoricist political philosophy and liberal education provide the best and most immediate access to such a restoration of the natural world.

However, a subtle difference exists between Manent and Strauss, a difference that qualifies Manent's "Straussianism." Strauss appears to be a Platonic rationalist, an exegete and philosopher whose works aim at a nonhistoricized view of the fundamental alternatives of politics and philosophy, philosophy and revelation. But Strauss is less interested, finally, in rehabilitating the moral contents of life (although he wishes to recover the presedimented and preideological political world) than he is in showing the superiority and superior rationality of the Socratic way of life within that world. Manent is a partisan of the natural world in all its complexity; Strauss is ultimately a partisan of the possibility of philosophy, of the life of rationality.

Doing Justice to Nature and History

Manent follows Strauss in rejecting "the history of being"—to the extent that human beings remain human their future, like their present and past, will be a political one (see the essay "On Historical Causality"). He knows that the beginning of all sensible political reflection is the commonsense notion that a "human nature" is available to reason and experience. But Manent's awareness of the modern modification or transformation of human beings, what he calls the *modern difference*, leads him to question Strauss's recourse to the sempiternity of "nature" and the "permanent human questions."[42] Strauss himself recognizes that modernity has the character of a self-radicalizing project and that this project obfuscates the original Greek understanding of the relationship between nature and convention. Manent believes that Strauss does not draw the necessary conclusion: "There is something unnatural about this movement away from nature described so well by Strauss."

In *The City of Man* Manent investigates the question of man in relation to this *modern difference*. In doing so, he aimed to interpret "the modern movement, the condition of modern man, in accordance with a triangularization which takes seriously the ancient, modern and Christian poles" of Western experience. "And it is by taking seriously the Christian pole" that he is "able to escape from the alternatives of Straussian 'naturalism' and Heideggerian 'historicism,' while preserving the phenomena of nature and history" (for the previous quotation, see "On Historical Causality"). In *The City of Man*, Manent presents a penetrating and faithful phenomenology of modern consciousness in order to address the question of man in light of the modern modification or transformation of human beings. He grapples with the fundamental theoretical and practical dilemma confronting any effort to make sense of modern consciousness. Modern man remains a man, he retains some real relationship to man *tout court* ("simply"). Yet, his nature appears to be suspended in some kind of unexplainable limbo or located at least in part in an unavailable and definitively historical past.

Modern man then lives under the power or illusion of history. He experiences historical consciousness; he believes himself above all to be a historical being; he feels and is dominated by the sentiment of historicity. The modern difference is then essentially tied to a new "authority of history"—an authority that remains virtually unchallenged in all the theoretical and political camps of modern life.[43] Manent's book is accordingly a profound, historical, and philosophical investigation and reflection on the modern difference, on the origin, foundation, and work of that new authority, history, and the way in which it transforms, deforms, and coexists with the old human nature, with the substance, motives, and ends of human beings.

As we have suggested, Manent takes up and renews the problem of nature and history, of natural right and history, and in doing so he builds on the pioneering researches of Strauss. Drawing widely on Strauss's analyses of the quarrel between the *ancients* and the *moderns*, Manent delineates as fairly and accurately as possible a *phenomenology* of the modern difference. And, like Strauss, he recognizes the centrality of the theological-political problem to any adequate comprehension of the human situation. He treats the theological-political problem in a manner that is indebted to but finally diverges from Strauss's approach, however. He is more attuned to and sympathetic to the Christian accounts of nature, creation, and law and to the place of Rome and all that it represents in the premodern presentation of and contestation about the human things. Strauss attributed the vitality of Western civilization to the fundamental and irresolvable tension between Athens and Jerusalem.[44] For Manent, in contrast, the invigorating moral and political tension that defines and sustains the vitality of the West is the conflict between humility and magnanimity—between the heroes of Plutarch and the *Imitatio Christi* heralded by Thomas à Kempis, between greatness of soul and humility before that which is divinely responsible for every human excellence. According to Manent, the city of man—the city of "history," the "atheistic city"—is an effort to put an end to the tension and dialectic between greatness and humility, to literally "flee" any rigorous demands of a natural or created order, to flee the motives or contents of our nature.

Manent is, as I have argued, less a partisan of *philosophy* than of the moral phenomena or moral contents that the city of man ignores, transforms, and relegates to the private, idiosyncratic realm of civil society. But he recognizes that the democratic revolution (the revolution described in different but complementary ways by Hegel and Tocqueville), the revolution that emancipates the human will (Hegel) or the sovereignty of man over himself (what Tocqueville calls "popular sovereignty"), does endlessly transform human beings. It gives man a *history*. Man becomes modern man, democratic man.

The sentiment of the modern difference, of democratic or modern man as the reflection of a "new humanity," must be confronted with the utmost seriousness if one is to do justice to the phenomena. And Manent is, above all, interested in being scrupulously attentive to the phenomena as they come to sight in all their complexity and imprecision. A genuine science of man and society must do justice to the democratic revolution, to the seemingly endless transformation of human life under the aegis and empire of the human will. Modernity understands itself as the emancipation or triumph of the will, of its liberation from the framework of human ends, substance, or finality.[45] And yet Manent believes that a genuine phenomenology of modern consciousness must recognize what Horace recognized, that nature despite the most powerful efforts of the human will always returns, and what the French Catholic poet-philosopher Charles Péguy articulated with characteristic beauty: "Homère est nouveau ce matin, et rien n'est peut-être aussi vieux que le journal d'aujourd'hui." ("Homer is new this morning and nothing is perhaps as old as today's newspaper.") A true science of man must give "voice to the sentiment of our shared nature across the modern difference" (see "The Truth, Perhaps"). How can we moderns remain faithful to the claims of human universality? How can we sustain our very humanity while remaining faithful to the modern difference, a difference that threatens to erode or overcome that very universality? Manent's book, his penetrating researches and analyses, culminates in this paradoxical and arresting claim: the modern experience and sentiment of history, the work of human sovereignty, of the emancipated will, is very real indeed, but the moral authority of history is a "bombastic illusion," in fact, "the most bombastic illusion that has ever enslaved the thinking species."[46]

Can an illusion be productive of so many results? The city of man, the atheistic city, is derived from an illusion, but it is the illusion on which modern man has made or constructed himself. It is a "sincere feeling" that defines the consciousness of modern times.[47] Yet it is a sentiment that can finally provide man only with a negative and ultimately self-refuting criterion: we must flee the law we are given by nature or God for a law that we have made for ourselves. And in the name of history modern man perpetually flees the law that he has made for himself, for law and tradition risk becoming a new kind of servitude, a new kind of limit. Modern man must flee every heteronomy, every authority, every claim of *phusis* and *nomos*: under the protective dispensation of history he must become the maker of himself. Under the authority of history, in this new city of man, "the nature of man is his principal enemy."[48] To become truly human, to be free or autonomous, modern man risks his very humanity.

Manent shows the artificial or constructed and therewith distorting character of the modern consciousness of the self. It is impossible completely or successfully to flee our nature and the dialectic of nature and law that is constitutive of our humanity and human dignity, but the effort to do so creates a new world, the modern world, which is neither Christian nor Greek, where neither magnanimity nor humility rules.

In the first part of his book, entitled "The Consciousness of the Self," Manent investigates the three pillars of modern consciousness: "The Authority of History," "The Sociological Viewpoint," and "The Economic System."[49] To comprehend clearly each of these massive shapers and determinants of the modern self-understanding, Manent turns to the origins of these new perspectives in the serious thought of the seventeenth, eighteenth, and nineteenth centuries. He does so not only because the origins of phenomena help reveal their nature but also because these approaches, which form the modern consciousness of the self, approaches that we take for granted, which seem as natural as the morning sun, were the deliberate products of thought. Modern consciousness, then, is not the result of an inexorable process of history or a mysterious dispensation of fate. Rather, it is the free creation of a human project, the result of a new empire governing the souls of men.

The City of Man is remarkably successful in its efforts to show the inadequacy of either naturalism's or historicism's efforts to account for the meaning of the modern difference. It corrects Strauss by showing that this question cannot be considered without the most attentive consideration of Christianity's role in generating a distinctively modern consciousness that challenges the claims of both nature and grace. It develops Strauss's own insight about the character of modernity as a *project* and refuses an antihistoricism that claims against the evidence, that all fundamental human and political problems were known to the Greek philosophers because they had discovered the problem of nature in its essentials. But the book is less successful in integrating the modern difference with the enduring features of the human condition: Manent emphasizes the relentless dynamic of the modern flight from the conflicting claims of nature and grace, of magnamity and humility, but he does not adequately explain how man's continuing character as a political animal, who lives in communities where men "put in common actions and reasons," affects the outcome of that effort. Is the consciousness of modern men shaped simply by modern thought, or do powerful strands of classical and Christian thought, and perhaps more important, of spontaneous human nature, work to humanize and naturalize the inhumanly abstract modern enterprise?

As I suggested earlier in this essay, I do not believe that Manent would fundamentally object to these objections. But it is in his occasional essays (many of which are collected in this volume) where Manent is addressing such theoretical-practical questions as the place of religion in modern life, the experience of totalitarianism, the role of love and friendship in contemporary life, and the future of the nation-state, that he most successfully integrates his Aristotelian (and commonsensical) affirmation of the permanently political character of human life and his recognition of the "mutated" character (to borrow Raymond Aron's term) of modernity. This is not surprising: the interpenetration of the old and the new and the simply human is most fully grasped through concrete phenomenological analysis. Perhaps *The City of Man* succeeds in highlighting the *problem* of the modern difference more than the coexistence and interpenetration of modern man and man *tout court* because it is phenomenological at a certain level of abstraction—it takes its bearings primarily from the effects of modern theory on the human soul.

Thinking and Acting Politically

Manent's analysis of the modern difference is never a merely theoretical or abstract concern. It is rooted in a concern for the human order of things, for the sustenance of the greatness inherent in the moral contents of life. This is what animates Manent's "practical" political commitment. For twelve years, Manent was coeditor of the neoliberal (Americans would say neoconservative) review *Commentaire* founded by Aron in 1978. His historical studies and scholarship, as well as his occasional pieces in *Commentaire*, can be associated with the liberal revival (in both politics and political theory) that has taken place in France since the mid-1970s. The antitotalitarian liberalism of *Commentaire* has less in common with the liberalism of Hayek than with the sensibility of Aron—a liberalism grounded far less in economic theory than in an appreciation of the prudential and political reflection of Montesquieu, Constant, and Tocqueville and in a taste for and defense of the moral and political prerequisites of the liberal order. The regular presence of Bloom's work in *Commentaire* revealed the affinity of its editors for a liberalism that is based on something much firmer than academic theorizing about reciprocity and rights and the merely formal requirements of a democratic order (Manent was, in fact, the French translator of Bloom's *Love and Friendship*; see "Recovering Human Attachments: An Introduction to Allan Bloom's *Love and Friendship*"). In France, it seems that reflections about the integrity of the human soul or the humanly and socially debilitating consequences of value and cultural relativisms are not automatically dismissed as elitist and antidemocratic. A "libéralisme triste" inspired by Tocqueville can accommodate the "Straussian" enterprise with its critically sympathetic engagement of Lockean life and politics in a way that an American liberalism obsessed with rights and the "maximization of equality" apparently cannot.

Manent rarely writes specifically about contemporary politics. But in two essays contained in this volume—"On Modern Individualism" and "Democracy without Nations?"—and in several "Letters from Paris" published in the London-based journal *Government and Opposition*, Manent has made clear both his approval of the contemporary European and French liberal revival and his opposition to a technocratic economism that promotes the dissolution of France and Europe into a homogeneous administrative state, a "Europe-Behemoth" where national variety and sovereignty are slowly eroded.[50] A touch of "Gaullism" is apparent in Manent's voice: a simultaneous recognition that modern societies are no longer capable of true greatness and that they need to be reminded of the possibilities for national self-respect and the analogues of national grandeur that are possible even in the era of world economic "interdependence" and European integration.

Today, modern civic societies are self-absorbed. They wish to contemplate themselves; they desire to escape arduous political existence. Manent is not a utopian. He does not wish society to aspire to more greatness than it can sustain. He recognizes that "acknowledgement of the exigencies of the world market and the acceptance of European obligations" constitute the "alpha and omega"[51] of contemporary European politics.

But the partisans of the contemporary European project do not sufficiently appreciate that the political community in the form of the nation-state is the framework within which democracy operates. The nation-state may be in some important respects antiquated, but in that case it needs to be succeeded by a new political framework that fulfills the indispensable political function of "putting something or having something in common," first of all "a certain territory and a certain population." But the construction of the emerging European "community" is torn between two rival notions of the future, one aiming at the "depoliticization of the life of peoples—that is, the increasingly methodical reduction of their collective existence to the activities of 'civil society' and the mechanisms of 'civilization'"—and the other supporting "the construction of a new *political* body, a great enormous European nation." Manent believes that the "political vacuity" of the new Europe is revealed by its refusal to define its boundaries and by its desire for "indefinite expansion." This refusal to define itself territorially goes hand to hand with its inability to act forcefully—that is, politically—in the world. Europeans believe that "passionate attachment to place" is folly, and they were impotent, even incredulous, when faced by the ferocious interplay of such attachments in the form of the war in the former Yugoslavia. Europeans hide behind an "unreal communication that pretends to be real, as if the unity of humankind had already been realized through such superficial ties." The reconciliation of France and Germany in the 1950s and 1960s, in contrast, reveals that a "tradition of common European action" based upon the political cooperation of nations is a living possibility rooted in the concrete experience of European peoples. But the larger political purposes of the nation-state need to be cultivated by statesmen who know that the common ties of citizenship are based on something more substantial than commercial ties (which, after all, are subpolitical and transnational) and such vagaries as "cultural identity" and "communication." (The quotations in this paragraph are all drawn from "Democracy without Nations?")

In words clearly aimed at the technocratic-administrative vision of European unity promoted by the most vociferous of contemporary Europeanists, Manent reminds us that the malaise of contemporary French and European society has its roots precisely in the failure of the European political class to nurture the sentiment of national political existence. He writes:

> They [the market and European integration] are certainly the alpha and the omega. But one must be able to repeat the rest of the alphabet: every political community, France, as well as Britain and Germany, wants its own existence to be recognized. One is not doing one's duty as a French, British or German politician when one uses one's credit exclusively to announce to the electors that they are destined to be dissolved in the world economy or in a Europe-Behemoth and that, in addition, they must rejoice at this destiny.
>
> Nations, no more than individuals, want to die. They are, however, ready to recognize the inevitability of their fate if those who lead them know how to speak of the nobility of the ultimate sacrifice and the hope

of a later renaissance. De Gaulle was the last statesman who knew how to speak of France to France.[52]

Manent is an admirer of de Gaulle's statesmanship, especially his intransigent and magnanimous defense of national sovereignty and liberty in June 1940 and his "founding" of a self-respecting presidential Republic after 1958. De Gaulle's "mission" to both France and the democratic world was to sustain a sense of national and personal honor in an era when human grandeur was threatened by both totalitarian fanaticism and the erosion of political life and of moral seriousness in democratic societies (see the essay "De Gaulle as Hero").

On the political level, de Gaulle was a statesman who powerfully illustrated the efficacy of forceful political action but who self-consciously rejected the radical voluntarism of modern political thought. Despite a certain romantic bravado, he was fundamentally classical and believed that "self-affirmation and the affirmation of the nation—two affirmations equally imperative with [him]—are not separable from the recognition of an 'order of things' or from a 'nature of things' which is objective and which obliges men in the two senses of the verb, oblige."[53]

De Gaulle embodied the greatness of political existence. He challenged a tendency of modern societies to degenerate into civic decadence or to succumb to economic preoccupations. Today, his vision of a "Europe des patries" stands as a permanent challenge and alternative to the reigning vision of European integration.

Besides his penetrating investigation into the character of our liberal and modern destiny, in addition to his clear, insightful, and often original historical studies, Manent's work contains a respectful challenge to the complacency of liberal theory and society. Refusing to flatter liberalism, he attempts to humanize it, to remind it of the "better angels of its nature." He reminds contemporary liberals that the statesmanlike prudence of Aron, the spiritual profundity of Tocqueville, and the patriotic nobility of de Gaulle all coexisted with and enriched the democratic legitimacy that defines the modern era. He reminds us that we need not accept the soulless character of the public square as either our own personal destiny or the eternal fate of modern society. Despite the "irresistibility" of the democratic revolution, the human order of things persists.

Notes

Parts of this introduction originally appeared in somewhat different form in *Perspectives on Political Science* (Fall 1992) and *The Public Interest* (Summer 1996). They are used here with permission.

1. For a representative sample of Manent's work see, in addition to the essays in this volume, *Naissances de la politique moderne: Machiavel, Hobbes, Rousseau* (Paris: Payot, 1977); *Tocqueville et la nature de la démocratie* (Paris: Fayard, 1993, previous editions from Paris: Commentaire-Julliard, 1982), translated as *Tocqueville and the Nature of Democracy* (Lanham, Md.: Rowman & Littlefield, 1996); *Les Libéraux*, volumes 1 and 2 with a preface, "Situation du libéralisme," and short essays and commentaries on liberal thinkers from Milton to Jouvenel (Paris: Hachette, 1986): *Histoire intellectuelle du libéralisme: Dix Leçons* (Paris: Calmann-Lévy, 1987), translated as *An Intellectual History of Liberalism* (Princeton: Princeton University Press, 1995). See also the essays by Manent in *New French Thought: Political Philosophy*, ed. Mark Lilla (Princeton: Princeton University Press, 1994), pp. 123–33, 178–85.

2. See Manent's penetrating introductory essay, "Notre Destin Libéral," to the French translation of Heinrich Meier, *Carl Schmitt, Leo Strauss et la notion de politique: Un Dialogue entre absents* (Paris: Commentaire–Julliard, 1990), 7–12.

3. Pierre Manent, *La Cité de l'homme* (Paris: Fayard, 1994), translated as *The City of Man*, with a foreword by Jean Bethke Elshstain (Princeton: Princeton University Press, 1998).

4. Manent, *An Intellectual History of Liberalism*, 3–12, especially 10–12.

5. See Manent, "Situation du libéralisme," in *Les Libereaux*, 11–16, especially 31–35.

6. See Manent, "Situation du libéralisme," 13.

7. Manent, *An Intellectual History of Liberalism*, 10–19.

8. Manent, *An Intellectual History of Liberalism*, 15–17.

9. Manent, *The City of Man*, chapter 1, especially 47–49, and 203–5.

10. Manent, *An Intellectual History of Liberalism*, 19.

11. Manent, *An Intellectual History of Liberalism*, 19.

12. Manent presented this argument in a "Post Scriptum à Propos de Deux Révolutions," delivered at a colloquium on the French Revolution sponsored by the Olin Program for the Study of Constitutional Government at Harvard University in April 1989. It appears as a "Postscript Concerning the Two Revolutions" appended to his article "The French Revolution and French and English Liberalism" in *The Legacy of the French Revolution*, Ralph C. Hancock and L. Gary Lambert eds. (Lanham, Md.: Rowman & Littlefield, 1996), 70–75.

13. Montesquieu, *The Spirit of the Laws*, book 19, chapter 27. See Manent's remarks in *An Intellectual History of Liberalism*, 63–64.

14. See Manent's "Preface to the 1993 French Edition" in *Tocqueville and the Nature of Democracy*, xi–xiv.

15. Manent, *Tocqueville and the Nature of Democracy*, 132.

16. Manent, *Tocqueville and the Nature of Democracy*, 12, 124.

17. Manent, *Tocqueville and the Nature of Democracy*, 126.

18. Manent, *Tocqueville and the Nature of Democracy*, 79.

19. Manent, *Tocqueville and the Nature of Democracy*, Chapter 5, 47–52, and *An Intellectual History of Liberalism*, 111.

20. Manent, *An Intellectual History of Liberalism*, 112.

21. Manent, *Tocqueville and the Nature of Democracy*, 69–76.

22. Manent, *Tocqueville and the Nature of Democracy*, 130.

23. Manent, *Tocqueville and the Nature of Democracy*, 129.

24. Manent, *Tocqueville and the Nature of Democracy*, 93–96.

25. Manent, "Situation du libéralisme," 1:20.

26. Manent, "Situation du libéralisme," 20–24.

27. Manent, "Postscript Concerning the Two Revolutions" in *The Legacy of the French Revolution*, 75.

28. Manent, "Postscript Concerning the Two Revolutions" in *The Legacy of the French Revolution*, 75.

29. See his comments in *Les Libéraux* on Montesquieu (1:218–22, 248, 266–69), on Constant (2:66–72, 94–96), and on Bastiat (2:226–27,261).

30. Manent, *An Intellectual History of Liberalism*, 53–64, 84–87.

31. Manent, *The Legacy of the French Revolution*, 70–71.

32. Manent, "Situation du libéralisme," 40.

33. Manent, *Les Libéraux*, 2:379–80.

34. Manent, *Les Libéraux*, 2:379–82 and "Situation du libéralisme," 39–49.

35. Manent, *Les Libéraux*, 2:381–82.

36. See Manent's essay "Raymond Aron éducateur," *Commentaire* (February 28–29, 1985): 155–68. The essay appeared in English in *European Liberty* (The Hague: Martinus Nijhoff, 1983), 1–23 and in *In Defense of Political Reason*, ed. Daniel J. Mahoney (Lanham, Md.: Rowman & Littlefield, 1994), 1–23. See also the notices in *Les Libéraux* 2: 424–25, 447–48, 466–67.

37. Manent, *Les Libéraux*, 2:447–48.

38. Manent, *Les Libéraux*, 2:447–48.

39. Manent, *Les Libéraux*, 2:467.

40. See Raymond Aron, *In Defense of Decadent Europe*, with a New Introduction by Daniel J. Mahoney and Brian C. Anderson (New Brunswick, N.J.: Transaction, 1996).

41. Manent, "Notre destin libéral," 11–12. See also his critique of de Maistre's "providentialism" in his introduction to Joseph de Maistre, *Considérations sur la France* (Brussels: Complexe, 1988), vii–xviii.

42. On the Straussian interpretation of the Platonic "ideas" as "permanent human questions" see especially Thomas L. Pangle's provocative introduction to Leo Strauss, *Studies in Platonic Political Philosophy* (Chicago: University of Chicago Press, 1983), 1–26.

43. Manent, *The City of Man*, 11–49.

44. See, in particular, Strauss's essay "Jerusalem and Athens" in *Studies in Platonic Political Philosophy*, 147–73, and "Progress or Return" in *An Introduction to Political Philosophy: Ten Essays by Leo Strauss,* ed. Hilail Gilden (Detroit: Wayne State University Press, 1989), 249–30.

45. Manent, *The City of Man*, chapter 5, "The Triumph of the Will," 156–83.

46. Manent, *The City of Man*, 205.

47. Manent, *The City of Man*, 205.

48. Manent, *The City of Man*, 204.

49. Manent, *The City of Man*, 11–108. The second part, "The Self-Affirmation of Modern Man," consists of three chapters entitled "The Hidden Man," "The Triumph of the Will," and "The End of Nature" that trace modern philosophy's "desubstantialization" of human beings, or the displacement of the idea of human nature by a self made or affirmed through a self-conscious "flight" from the demands of nature and grace.

50. Manent, "Letter from Paris," *Government and Opposition* (Summer 1990):317–20.

51. Manent, "Letter from Paris," *Government and Opposition* (Summer 1990):319.

52. Manent, "Letter from Paris," *Government and Opposition* (Summer 1990):319.

53. Pierre Manent, "Foreword" to Daniel J. Mahoney, *De Gaulle: Statesmanship, Grandeur and Modern Democracy* (Westport, Conn.: Praeger, 1996), xii–x. This quotation is drawn from viii.

Part One

Reflections on an Intellectual Itinerary

"The Truth, Perhaps" is Pierre Manent's self-description of his work to date, at least in its main lines and major moments. For over twenty years, Manent has meditated on the modern world and its inhabitant, the modern human being. Aided powerfully by political philosophers, ancient and modern (including Leo Strauss), he has investigated the fundamental political elements, structural and dynamic, of this world, as well as the thoughts, feelings, and self-interpretations that define modern consciousness. The author's account of his intellectual itinerary (which originally appeared as part of a symposium on the work of the "new generation" of French philosophers) reveals the powerful illumination one can derive from attentive consideration of political phenomena as well as from a searching engagement with our predecessors in the effort to think about our modern condition.

The Truth, Perhaps

Pierre Manent

1992

The questions from *Débat* show me that the investigations I have been conducting for the past twenty years can appear to a well-disposed observer to belong to philosophy. I would not have said so myself. I am even more doubtful of my right to put on its noble tunic since my first intention was not properly philosophical. More exactly, if philosophy were a central element of the situation that I wanted to understand, nothing guaranteed that being the problem it would also be the solution. But what situation and solution are we talking about?

The Modern Development

We cannot know ourselves without first understanding our situation. And we cannot achieve either without first recognizing ourselves as "moderns." We must affirm the "modern difference" in order to identify ourselves: it is part of our self-understanding. It is certainly possible to evaluate the amplitude, radicality, and the meaning of this difference in very different ways. One can even hold quite opposite judgments about it—one, for example, can be "progressive" or "antimodern." But as soon as this difference is recognized, thought no longer can choose its subject; a tear is introduced into the tissue of the human community, which it is necessary but also perhaps impossible to repair. In what way and to what extent does being a "modern" man differ from being simply a "man"? In a certain way all of *modern* philosophy is a commentary on this difference. But where did the difference originate?

It seems that it came first from philosophy itself. The latter, during the course of the seventeenth and eighteenth centuries, elaborated the

---

This article originally appeared in French in *Débat* (November–December 1992) and appears here with permission.

project of reforming European religion, politics, and society in accordance with reason or philosophy itself. To be modern, in its simplest and at the same time most august definition, is to live according to reason. This movement inspired the numerous and often happy transformations of life that characterize the progress of Enlightenment. Politically, it culminated with the French Revolution, the first and unique attempt to establish the human order on the sole foundation of reason. Theoretically, it found its complete expression in Hegel's work; the latter puts forth the essentially rational, and thus the essentially satisfying character of the modern state. After the *Principles of the Philosophy of Right*, published in 1821, political philosophy will have no systematic expression, or even a truly coherent one; no other philosophy will attempt to tie closely its interpretation of the philosophical life to a complete analysis and evaluation of the human world and, above all, of the political world. Philosophy turns away from the state, it turns away from its own work. Is this simply because it is "satisfied"? This is doubtful if one observes how, quite to the contrary, Sören Kierkegaard and Karl Marx, Friedrich Nietzsche and Martin Heidegger revolt against the purportedly rational order of Enlightenment in the name of faith or of action, of creation or of thinking. Is it not philosophy itself that— contemplating its work, suspects that it was bad, even very bad? One might retort that Kierkegaard and Marx, Nietzsche and Heidegger cannot represent philosophy because they attack philosophy or the reason that undergirds modern politics. This is undoubtedly true. But if the most vibrant and powerful expressions of thought turn away from philosophy, how can the latter, and the political order founded on it, claim to be satisfactory?

To be sure, another response is available. The authors I just mentioned can be dismissed as extravagant and dangerous geniuses, born out of the tumults, excesses, and oppositions spawned by the modern democratic movement. But all that belongs to the past. Today the rational order reigns from Los Angeles to Vladivostok. One is left with a major difficulty, however: the docile inhabitant of this "rational" order thinks in the same way as do its enemies. He thinks, for example, that man "creates his values." The nice high school student and the committed bureaucrat think the same thing as Nietzsche. The rational order harbors and perhaps foments the negation of reason. Therefore, does living according to the modern difference mean living according to reason or living according to the denial of reason? Apparently it means both.

These reflections discouraged me from seeking the illumination of our situation in the first place from what Heidegger called the "gigantomachy" of Western metaphysics. It was more urgent to reconstruct an exact chronology. The difference that I was attempting to understand, whatever its ultimate meaning, distinguished between a before of prejudice and an after of reason. And as soon as the distinction appeared between epochs, an epoch was in fact *made*, one where the subjective combined with the objective in a singular fashion, singularly auspicious for investigation. My first task then was to reconstruct its exact chronology, the precise articulation of the modern movement of becoming modern, being conscious of it, and willing to be modern. This required a work of history and the historian.

At these words certain sharp minds will no doubt object that I am guilty of historicism! The blow hurts when it hits its target, but does it really reach its target? I simply asked when, how, and with what emphasis was such an intellectual and moral position advanced for the first time? When was the modern project or point of view, if there is such a thing, first formulated? What transformations and qualifications did it subsequently undergo? Finally, was it replaced by another so-called postmodern point of view?

It seemed to me that these questions could and should be raised. They obey the same impulse and have the same legitimacy as investigations concerning the history of madness or of prisons, or the history of totalitarianism or of ideology.[1] More specifically, one becomes more aware of the necessity of this work by observing the confusion that prevails where it is neglected, where the difference skips nonchalantly along the chronological chain. For example, since one of the fundamental traits of modernity is the separation of political power and religion, nothing is more important than to know exactly when and how the political critique of religion was decisively accomplished. It is necessary to know when and how atheism for the first time came to support a political project. Those who dismiss this inquiry, or who conduct it unseriously, or even find in it something vaguely unworthy of scientific interest— like trailing a suspect down dark streets—end by writing intellectual histories in which nothing really happens. The political authors who are essential to our investigation, especially Thomas Hobbes, John Locke, and Jean-Jacques Rousseau, are only seen in the "context" of their time, particularly the religion of their time, without any thought that a first rank mind could liberate itself from the conventions of its time, and think and will something completely novel. In this way one cannot truly appreciate how these supposedly more or less "Christian" philosophers, especially the good "Calvinist" Locke, enthroned political atheism! Very often, therefore, those who today expound the great books understand them less well than those who burned them three centuries ago.

Because it was a matter of history and because we first of all sought for a chronology, it was of prime importance to be sure of the point of departure. It is here, at the beginning, that one must proceed smartly. I found this point of departure in the work of Machiavelli. This was, of course, a reassuring commonplace.

Machiavelli immediately was considered as the contemporary or the principal predecessor; and historical retrospection often accorded him a very important role in the elaboration of the modern point of view on the human world. However, this point of departure—itself a first result of the investigation—became less conventional in light of the interpretation that guided me.

I began to study seriously Machiavelli's work after having caught my breath on an island of friendship, serenity, and good cheer: Raymond Aron's seminar. Aron too had been fascinated by Machiavelli, but political exigencies had led him to confront the "Machiavellianism of the twentieth century" rather than the work of the Florentine itself. A philosopher who distrusted philosophy because it had scarcely been lucid about the twentieth century, he saw that I began the study of modern political philosophy with more hopes than he thought prudent. However, only taking thought of what could assist me the most, he told me to read Leo Strauss. Henceforth, I was on my way.

The modern age is characterized by a strange interpenetration between the concept and event, between intellectual and political history. Because of this, it was necessary first of all to elaborate exactly the conceptual content of modern politics. And it was reading the political philosophers, from Machiavelli to Montesquieu, from Rousseau to Tocqueville, that brought me the most light. This point does not entail the adoption of any methodological approach, of any position on "causality" or any appeal to "in the final analysis": neither Weber nor Marx. If this procedure imposed itself on me, it was simply because read attentively, with the passionate attention paid to them by Strauss, the texts of these philosophers provide us a convincing phenomenology of the political and moral life of the last three centuries. Moreover, from the works of certain of these authors, Hobbes in particular, we can extract in a strikingly clear way the architecture and the movement, the static and the dynamic, of our political regime. Let us briefly turn to this point.

One can agree without too much difficulty as to the principal elements of the modern regime, namely, liberal democracy (they are legible in our institutions as well as books). All legitimacy is founded on individual or collective consent; men possess equal rights; law is sovereign; the state is distinct from society and is the latter's representative instrument. Where better is it given to read the irresistible dynamism of the conjunction of these elements, to trace the history they contain, than from the route that runs from Hobbes to Tocqueville? This history begins with Hobbes, who was the first to deduce rigorously all political obligation from the sole consent of the governed. At the end of this route, Tocqueville, with a mixture of fear and admiration, saw that this principle organizes not only the visible political institutions but also reconstitutes the most intimate metabolism of men's lives in the American democracy. In this philosophical path one is able to discern the ambiguities of absolutism (necessarily caught between conservation and emancipation and between authoritarianism and individualism), and those of liberal democracy (necessarily caught between the promotion and the critique of representation, between the emancipation of the individual and the imposition of a uniform rule). And it is here that one appreciates the seemingly rational irresistibility of the passage from one to the other. It was this political history, which at the same time is an adventure of reason, that I attempted to recount in composing the intellectual history of modern politics.[2]

In studying this segment or vector that leads from Machiavelli and Hobbes to Tocqueville, from absolutism to democracy, I accomplished the easiest part of my task. It is in this dynamic sequence that the intellectual and political articulations are the most salient, and their correspondence the most obvious. At this point verification is the easiest. Thornier is the understanding and appreciation of the origin and the end (if we, in fact, have arrived there) of the movement.

Democratic Man

Let us begin with the end, our democracy, which of the two is best known to us. It occasioned one of the most singular phenomena in the history of political thought. At the beginning of this regime an observer without a particular intellectual formation, basing himself on no particular scientific discipline (and unable to be claimed by any), gave it an exact and exhaustive description. Better yet, the more that generations pass, the more that democracy grows in extension and comprehensiveness, the more Tocqueville's analysis grows in truth. Of course, this is a claim that must be proven. Here we are in a domain where proof is extremely difficult to find. Or rather, every attempt at scientific verification or falsification is useless here. Is the analysis correct? Tocqueville's reader, who is also a citizen of a democracy, can only look around and within himself, dialogue with the mirror that is offered to him, deliberate and evaluate, and, if he is sufficiently sure of his judgment, conclude. In such a procedure, one sometimes discovers oneself close to another who initially seemed far away or suddenly in disagreement with someone formerly close: in the Tocquevillian description of "democratic despotism," which seems to me to be full of truth, Raymond Aron saw a kind of myth, striking to be sure, but very far from describing our experience. In any case, I attempted to expound the coherence and amplitude of the phenomenology of democracy, to show how Tocqueville unfolds before our eyes the "nature of democracy."[3]

If Tocqueville is right, modern democracy has a nature. It acts in the same direction and perpetually transforms the life of men who more and more become "democratic men." The difference about which I spoke at the beginning, the modern difference, is not an ethereal will-o'-the-wisp, a poetic object that first of all attracts our imagination; it is realized and institutionalized in a regime that has a nature. And the rupture it introduces is so abrupt, the novelty it brings so radical, that in contrast all of its predecessors, as different as they were, from Greek democracy to the French old regime, appear to be simple species of the same genus, of what Tocqueville calls "aristocracy." Concerning the two regimes governing human life, aristocracy and democracy, he goes so far as to write that they are like "two distinct humanities." Tocqueville was not drawn to such a conclusion by a philosophical system, or a religious conviction, or by a partisan political position; he was led to it by the acuity and amplitude of his observations. In his high-level naïveté, his evaluation of democracy always appeared more convincing to me than, for example, those of Marx or Nietzsche, who also were quite alive, in their distinctive ways, to the modern difference. It remains true, however, that in leaving us with the division of humanity into two distinct humanities Tocqueville leaves us before an abyss.

The most important question to us—what is man?—thus takes on an unprecedented character and urgency. Man as man, is he "aristocratic man" or "democratic man" or some "third man" such as communist man or the "Superman" who would be able to achieve the reconciliation and transcendence of the first two? About the latter, Tocqueville—unlike Marx and Nietzsche—says nothing.

What makes the question so urgent is also what gives us a novel access to the question. The division between the two humanities, between the old and new man, reveals a double determination of man where one necessarily presupposes the other. The new man presupposes the old one and, as such, affirms him. In willing to be modern, modern man affirms the division and nonetheless does not cease to be the old man and to recognize him as such. This division is thus proper to man, with this dual and unequal affirmation. To be sure, this interior situation and self-understanding can be seen as contradictory. And not only is one not mistaken in pointing it out, but the exploration of these contradictions and the ironies of modern man's situation and self-understanding constitute one of the most interesting and exquisite of the registers of modern moral life. Benjamin Constant is perhaps the most brilliant virtuoso of this register. But these ironies do not stop democracy from producing its effects, which conform to its nature. In fact, it is the contradiction or the division about which I am speaking that provides the impulse and direction in accordance with which "modern" man displays his own point of view, the properly modern point of view on the human world.

Such an assertion, with this degree of generality and abstraction, does not claim to convince. It even appears to assume the exorbitant presupposition that modern man defines himself by a single point of view. But everyone knows that what is characteristic of the modern mind is its multiplication of points of view, each one defining a "domain" or "field" of research. There are as many sciences of nature as there are points of view on nature, as many human or social sciences as there are points of view on man or society. To be sure, I could respond that to consider the human world as the material for points of view is to submit it to one arbitrary point of view, to the principle of the point of view. Heidegger has some very cogent developments on this subject.

But I also believe that the primordial division of which I am talking is endlessly defracted, not only in the different points of view that define the theoretical attitude of modern man but also in his practical attitude where the "effectual truth" of democracy is located: in modern man's definition of himself as the being with rights. It is here that the reader must take as credible very great assertions and must accept my promise to justify them soon in what I will call here a sketch of "the phenomenology of modern consciousness."[4]

The City of God and the Earthly City

Earlier I spoke of the political history of the last three centuries as a vector oriented toward and leading to democracy. What is central to this history, what makes it precisely a history with a meaning (and which gives the different historicisms their *almost* irresistible plausibility), is the rational and really irresistible connection of its phases, from absolutism to representative democracy, and then to a democracy ever more democratic. One must account for this radicalization. This is the great "phenomenon" that theory or interpretation must "save."

The currently dominant view, put in academic terms, is that the vaguely Hegelian historicism prevalent today saves the phenomenon by main-

taining that in the "rational" society or the liberal and democratic regime we know, we are essentially satisfied. Humanity has henceforth
rejoined its essentially democratic nature, or is at least essentially friendly
to democracy. But if our democracy is "according to nature," why did it
take such a long history to get to it?

It is here that generally appears what one will allow me to call the
deus ex machina of the historical interpretation of democracy: the "secularization" of Christianity. If we have had to wait so long to attain the
only legitimate regime—modern democracy, founded on the equality of
all citizens, and even of all men—it is because Christianity (itself breaking with but basing itself upon the imperfect universalism of Judaism)
was first established and then disestablished; equality before God became equality in the world. To be sure, this schema can be the basis of
very learned and illuminating considerations on our history. But as it is,
it suffers from a major weakness. One of two things must be true. One
possibility is that Christian revelation is true. If this is true, the essential fact remains the soul's relationship with the true God. Then democracy, assuming that it derives from Christianity, is only a consequence,
perhaps a happy one, but more likely an ambiguous one as are all human things. In any case it is subordinate to the truth of Christianity itself. Or the Christian religion is false. Then, far from democracy being
its result or consequence, it is the Christian religion that would be the
first, imperfect, and alienated experience of democracy. Religion, then,
would not explain democracy since democracy explains itself. The approval that the notion of secularization enjoys is owing to the fact that
its scientific aura allows us to escape an intellectual and spiritual decision that is finally unavoidable.

But it is necessary to formulate the prescientific kernel of truth underlying the secularization thesis: democracy does, indeed, have "something to do" with Christianity. But this relationship can also be one of
opposition, a polemical relationship, rather than one of causality or of
proximity. Today we forget how important the polemical relationship
between Christianity and democracy was and remains. How can one
overlook the fact that at least during its period of combat and establishment—that is, during the greater part of its history in continental Europe—the liberal democratic movement saw in Christianity an enemy,
even *the* enemy? History is written as if one had never heard Voltaire's
sardonic voice. We might sum up the problem by saying that modern
democracy appears to be both the realization and the negation of Christianity. This formulation at least has the merit of warning us that even
if we are successful in our search, the solution will not be simple and
linear and will of necessity be dialectical.

Let us return to the beginning point of the democratic vector, to the thought of Machiavelli and Hobbes. For them it is emphatically a question of liberating men from the political power of religion. Today one says rather glibly that this enterprise contains nothing intrinsically or fundamentally antireligious because the political order is only one domain among the plurality of human domains. This, of course, ignores the possibility that the political domain is really the generative principle of the human world. Leaving this question behind, I will simply note that in order to liberate men from the political power of religion it was necessary to limit the power of religion over their souls. And for this purpose it was insufficient to deliver them from the fears of Hell. It also was necessary to deliver them from the attraction of the very idea of God.

In its initial impetus the modern movement implied and bore a critique of the idea of God. As unique as the idea of the one God may be, it is also at the head of numerous other ideas; it is the center of a magnetic field both spiritual and intellectual. One cannot overthrow or "deconstruct" it alone. To stop it from immediately reconstituting itself, one must invalidate or at least decisively weaken many other ideas that appear to be unconnected with it, or that even seem to rival it rather than support it. I have in mind, for example, the idea of nature. This latter, as elaborated by Greek philosophy, had worked to deliver men from the fear of punitive gods: it contributed to the intelligibility of a world to which the God of the philosophers was indifferent.

Does it fulfill the same office with Christians? Certainly not! The idea of God is now too strong, as the technical vocabulary of Christianity itself indicates: God is "super-natural." Therefore, in order to liberate himself from the "supernatural," modern man cannot rest content with becoming "pagan" again. It is not enough to affirm or reaffirm nature. This latter is henceforth exposed to being outbid or trumped by the supernatural. If nature is good, even very good, the supernatural is necessarily better, because it is infinitely good. If the earthly city provides natural goods, the heavenly city, which the church prefigures, dispenses supernatural goods that are incomparably superior to the former. Thus, between these two cities the contest is unequal as long as the earthly city remains "natural." Therefore, if the critique of the supernatural is going to achieve its political ends, (i.e., if it aims to exclude in advance any possibility of being trumped), it must entail a critique of nature. The critique of Christian revelation implies the critique of pagan politics and philosophy. *Tantae molis erat. . . .*

The dialectic is, in fact, doubly complicated. A critique of pagan politics and philosophy is already contained in Christian revelation, more precisely in the critique of paganism this revelation introduced. The lo-cus classicus of this critique is the one leveled by Saint Augustine in *The City of God*. The Machiavellian critique of Christianity, the origin of the modern vector, constantly intersects with the Augustinian critique of paganism and of sinful humanity, sometimes overlapping with it, or at least superimposing itself on it. I believe that this web merits being disentangled with care: this double critique delineates and produces the dialectical circle from which the modern moral and political develop-ment cannot extricate itself. It is at the source of the perpetual move-ment and the apparently endless radicalization of democracy.

If I were using the language of philosophy, I would be tempted to say that in this way a third way is limned between historicism and its enemies. My purpose, however, is not at all to establish or to refute any philosophical position. I simply wanted to give expression and a solu-tion to the following difficulty contained in modern experience: if we adhere without any reservation to the modern experience of history, then man becomes at this point so different from himself that his very hu-manity is put in danger. If, on the other hand, we hold firm to the rec-ognition of human universality, if we give voice to the sentiment of our shared nature across the modern difference—*Homère est nouveau ce matin*[5] ("Homer is new this morning")—we then risk becoming unfaith-ful to modern experience. One could say that modern men have a knowl-edge of human nature that is invincible to any form of historicism and that we have an experience of history that is invincible to any antihis-toricism. In short, we are too natural for what we have of the historical, too historical for what we have of the natural.

Yet it seems to me that the positions taken in this century by the philosophers who have established the terms of the debate on the rela-tionship of nature and history are not faithful to the equilibrium of this uncertainty and that they do like the Frenchman in the capitol who threw his sword on the scales: sure enough, it tipped. Without a sword in Rome, and not exactly a historian or a philosopher, with my divisions and my dialectics, I scrutinize and I mend the human difference. At the end of the road, I still hope to find the truth, perhaps.

Translated by Daniel J. Mahoney and Paul Seaton

Notes

1. This is a clear reference to the "genealogies" of Michel Foucault and, rather closer to Manent, to the accounts of the intellectual origins of communism provided by Alain Besançon (editor's note).

2. See Pierre Manent, *Histoire intellectualle du libéralisme: Dix Leçons* (Paris: Calmann-Lévy, 1987). *An Intellectual History of Liberalism*, trans. Rebecca Balinski (Princeton: Princeton University Press, 1995) (editor's note).

3. See Pierre Manent, *Tocqueville et la nature de la démocratie* (Paris: Commentaire-Julliard, 1982; revised with a new introduction, Paris: Fayard 1993), *Tocqueville and the Nature of Democracy* (Lanham, Md.: Rowman & Littlefield, 1996) (editor's note).

4. This work appeared as *La Cité de l'homme* (Paris: Fayard, 1994). It was published in English in 1998 as *The City of Man* from Princeton University Press (editor's note).

5. This phrase is Charles Péguy's (editor's note).

Part Two

Essays in the History of Political Philosophy

In "Toward the Work and Toward the World: Claude Lefort's *Machiavelli*," Manent pays homage to the interpretive achievements of two of his fellow thinkers on modernity who appreciate the fundamental centrality of Machiavelli in this enterprise. Leo Strauss and Claude Lefort, in different ways, illumine Machiavelli's "work" and the "world" he helped to articulate and to bring into being.

Manent's appreciation, however, is not untempered by criticism. Lefort has put his finger on a basic problem in Strauss's advocacy of classical political philosophy over and against modern thought: how does Christianity figure into the equation? And against Lefort's alliance of political philosophy and the people or democracy, Manent invokes Aristotle's impartial umpiring as a model of political science that retains its equilibrium vis-à-vis the elements of the city.

But Aristotle's judicious phenomenology of politics needs to be supplemented by an awareness of the distinctively *modern* characteristics of the modern democratic regime. Manent suggests that Tocqueville is the single best analyst of our modern democracy in its specific traits. Manent's consideration of modernity is thus inextricably a continuous meditation on the Tocquevillian corpus. Yet, here, too, admiration does not preclude the discovery of problems in this illuminating and essential author. Manent's critical reflections focus on Tocqueville's own deepest attachment, liberty. Both modern democracy itself and modern liberal theory fail to appreciate the intrinsic value and "charms" of liberty and thus undermine its exercise and prospects. Manent shares this Tocquevillian concern. But Tocqueville's account of this higher sort of liberty convinces him less. In "Democratic Man, Aristocratic Man, and Man Simply: Some Remarks on an Equivocation in Tocqueville's Thought," he ventures an alternative rendering of this liberty and its appearance in democratic times. In these essays, textual exegesis serves an exact, ample understanding of ourselves and the world.

45

Toward the Work and Toward the World: Claude Lefort's *Machiavelli*

Pierre Manent

1993

I no longer remember if the pavement of the old hotel on rue de Tour-non was smooth or uneven, but I do remember that Raymond Aron's seminar was held there. It was there that I first heard Claude Lefort. He spoke to us about Machiavelli. The exact subject of his presentation escapes me today. I only recall his eloquence and my discomfort as a newcomer. He had just published *The Labor of Machiavelli's Work* (*Le Travail de l'oeuvre Machiavelli*[1]), or he was about to do so. At that time I fluttered around Machiavelli like a butterfly around a flame. The conjunction of philosophy and politics, the connection and the conflict between politics and religion, were then my overriding concerns. I plunged into the lengthy work.

> Jamque rubescebat stellis Aurora fugatis
> Cum procul obscuros collis humilemque videmus
> Italiam. Italiam . . .
>
> Already, stars shining, the sun grew red
> when far off and obscure we saw low lying
> Italy. Italy . . .

Twenty years later, more seasoned and freighted, I have just repeat-ed the same voyage. And from it I bring back these notes.

Le Travail de l'oeuvre Machiavelli (*The Labor of Machiavelli's Work*) appeared during the time of the ascendancy of the human sciences. Their general sterility was not yet established, or at any event it was not ac-

This essay originally appeared in French in *La démocratie à l'oeuvre: Autour de Claude Lefort*, edited by Claude Habib and Claude Mouchard (Paris: Édi-tions Esprit, 1993), and appears here with permission.

knowledged. Claude Lefort, reviewing certain of the "exemplary interpretations" of Machiavelli, criticizes what he called the "positivistic interpretation" (*TOM*, 187), particularly that of A. Renaudet, an otherwise intelligent and scrupulous historian. He shows how, by assuming and exercising an exorbitant sovereignty that his personal modesty would not allow him to gage or even to become aware of, the historian places Machiavelli, as an object of explanation, under the light of and in dependence on two things he believes he knows and supposes are known. These are, on one hand, the history of Italy and on the other, Machiavelli's psychology (i.e., the states of soul held plausible for a high functionary in disgrace). These two explanatory principles are complete fictions. The history of the Italian cities and the meaning of this history are as uncertain as the meaning of Machiavelli's work. The former depends on the latter as much as the latter does on the former, if only because the Italy of that time would not have the same color for the historian if Machiavelli had not written what he did. As for Machiavelli's psychology, we do not know anything about it that can be usefully separated from his writings to designate it as the explanatory cause of his writings. He concludes: "Thus the joining of two unfounded observations . . . passes for science" (*TOM*, 187).

Lefort's analysis here is even more interesting in that it does not entail an abstract "critique of historical consciousness," but rather has a concrete and "eminent" object, namely, Machiavelli. At the same time it is generalizable, although Lefort does not do so explicitly or willingly to every text as such. Charles Péguy recommended and practiced the method of these "eminent cases."

If philosophy has been pushed farther and farther from the public square, far from the center of the city, toward the beautiful precincts of formalism, or, further yet, toward the forests of Being, it is, among other reasons, because this center has been occupied by the competent, quantifiable, interdisciplinary volubility of the human sciences. Rare are the philosophers who have attempted to recapture and to liberate the public square by analyzing the methodical misunderstanding characteristic of the aforementioned sciences. Lefort belongs to this group. Reading Lefort's *Machiavelli* today, I think of what Péguy wrote about the modern historian in his *Zangwill,* and it seems to me that by very personal routes the refined phenomenologist joins hands, on important points, with the fiery and profound poet.[2] Leo Strauss's ambition was certainly to recover the original meaning of political philosophy, and therewith that of philosophy as well as of politics. Lefort was one of the first in France to grasp the importance of his work. In his *Machia-*

velli, he renders him the homage of a beautiful discussion. It will introduce our subject.

Lefort and Strauss approach Machiavelli's work with the same principle of reading. They both affirmed that one must first of all ask the work itself for particular signs or indications of its specific intelligibility; one forfeits the opportunity of understanding Machiavelli if one does not read him first of all as he wants to be read. This principle is espoused, however, by the two writers for different reasons, and they derive quite different consequences from it. In Strauss's eyes this principle is tied to a certain "art of writing" and should be understood in a rigorous manner. In Lefort's case it is connected to the labor of all interpretation and cannot be understood rigorously because no author is the master of all the significance of his work. What the two do share suffices, however, to place them strictly apart in the distinguished but variegated band of Machiavelli interpreters.

It is strange that this principle of reading, at least as a principle, which of course can be applied erroneously even by Lefort or Strauss, should be mentioned sometime with irony, or more often passed by in silence (along with the interpretations that illustrate it). These interpretations are so obviously more interesting than the others that with even a moderated confidence in the progress of Enlightenment one would expect to see them dominate, or at least be an object of emulation, in the domain of Machiavelli scholarship. If this is not the case, it is no doubt because this principle of reading obliges the historian (i.e., the modern reader) to strip himself of his sovereignty, which is so hidden but also so clear, and to agree to learn something from the author he is reading by entering into philosophical dialogue with him. It would become impossible, then, even for a Hercules of the South Sea, to produce a transhistorical and transatlantic "Machiavellian moment" joining Aristotle and Thomas Jefferson.[3]

On this point of greatest proximity, Strauss and Lefort remain nonetheless rigorously separated, as I noted earlier. This common principle of reading—marked by sharp attention to the phenomenon of the text—takes on a different meaning with the two authors. Lefort judges that if it "is necessary to interrogate the contradictions, omissions, and digressions within the horizon or context of the search for the truth," we are not obliged "to postulate that the discordances and slips of the discourse are always the result of an intention." The Straussian postulate is "tied to a conception of philosophy as a teaching, or of the philosopher as master," which Lefort denies. In his eyes, these characteristics of the discourse launch us on an indefinite quest that, precisely, if we are philosophers, we cannot claim to conclude (*TOM*, 290–91). And this is exactly what Strauss claims to do by extracting Machiavelli's teaching and then judging it. Strauss judges this teaching in the name of the teaching of classical Greek philosophy and concludes that Machiavelli represents not a progress of enlightenment but an "obfuscation" because his thought no longer has a place for itself. It no longer has a place for philosophy. Lefort thus directs against Strauss's position a sharp and profound critique. Fixing on the Straussian claim that Machiavelli "is unable to give a clear account of his own doing,"[4] Lefort is astonished that the American political philosopher "devotes almost 100 pages to demonstrate that there is not a word, or a missing word, or a silence that wasn't the result of a decision." He continues: "How can one say that Machiavelli rigorously conducts his discourse and that at its most profound level is unaware of its meaning?" (*TOM*, 292). What makes the difficulty so pressing is that Strauss underlines the speculative grandeur of Machiavelli and does not hesitate several times to call him a "philosopher."[5] Yet how can one be a philosopher and philosophize and ignore what one is doing and be unaware that one is doing it?

It is true that Strauss proposes a qualification of this judgment when he suggests that Machiavelli perhaps brings less an obfuscation of philosophy than a transformation of its meaning, and philosophy now comes to the service of the passions of ordinary men and thus combines the functions of philosophy and those of religion. Thus, it does not contribute any advance in knowledge, but it merely divulges what the ancient philosophers hid from the crowd. Strauss's judgment is severe: "Machiavelli does not bring to light a single political phenomenon of any fundamental importance which was not fully known to the classics."[6] Lefort feels that he is authorized to summarize Strauss's position as such: "What is *new* is divulgation" (*TOM*, 296). Thus comes to the forefront the other "novelty" to which the Machiavellian novelty responds—the novelty of Christianity. Moreover, with an extraordinary ingenuity and in an often convincing manner Strauss shows us how the Machiavellian discovery is intimately organized by the critique of the authority of the Bible. Lefort comments:

> However, once more the contradiction is only displaced. If it is true that Machiavelli's principles are not new except with regard to the situation created by the power of the Christian Church, was not this power new? Or must one believe that nothing proclaimed in Christian discourse was unknown to Greek philosophy? Strauss is silent on this not insignificant question. (*TOM*, 297)

One is impressed by the sureness with which Lefort puts his finger on the weak points, or in any case the invisible premises, of Strauss's thought.

Between Strauss and Lefort, Machiavelli is the *bone of contention*. The disagreement bears inseparably on the interpretation of Machiavelli's thought and on the understanding of political philosophy as such. It is impossible here to enter into the details of the interpretations of Lefort and Strauss or to present a studied comparison of them. At least we should introduce the profound truth of this statement of Lefort: "The reestablishment of the truth about Machiavelli concerns *here and now* the establishment of the truth about politics" (*TOM*, 131).

An excursus will allow us to grasp more precisely the impact of the statement.

Political philosophy, philosophy, and politics were "born in Greece." Plato, Aristotle, and Thucydides explored the public space with an amplitude and precision that even those least nostalgic for classical philosophy or for "ancient liberty" can hardly fail to admire. And if anything was lacking in the experience and thought of the Greeks, it seems that the long and singular history of Rome is there to supply it. In short, granted that local color changes, climates differ, and the comparative state of technological development is markedly unequal, we must still ask, What do we today have to say about or know about politics that the Greeks and the Romans did not say or know?

If we turn to modern political philosophy—as abundant, rich, and impressive as it is—to try to grasp the essentials of modern political life, we are struck by its singularly abstract character, which distinguishes it in so trenchant a fashion from classical political philosophy. The proof of this is the decisive role played at the decisive moment by the central abstraction: "the state of nature," matrix of "the individual" and of his "rights," and the "rights of man," the spiritual heart of modern politics.

While ancient political philosophy is first of all the analysis of the experience of the Greek city, modern political philosophy is first of all, in theoretical terms, a hypothesis and thus, in practical terms, a project and, in moral terms, a hope. This project, hope, and enterprise have obtained, all said, an extraordinary result: the construction and consolidation of modern democracy on both sides of the Atlantic. However, a sort of uncertainty or anxiety shadows this triumphant march. The most clear-sighted or perceptive of the moderns have understood or felt that all the practical successes in the world do not remove from the hypothesis its status as a hypothesis. These informed spirits then ask themselves if modern man lives, and lives more and more, in accordance with the democratic hypothesis or convention, what is its underlying *experience*? Only if one can draw the contours of an experience proper to modern man can modern politics be said to be truly founded, and thus capable finally of shedding its status as an hypothesis.

Of course, it could happen that the experience thus brought to light might furnish motives for dissatisfaction with the democratic convention, and even for revolting against it: the modern experience could appear as the friend and support for the democratic hypothesis but also as its enemy. The experience that has generally appeared as belonging to modern man, because it was discovered by him, is that of *history*. Now, as one knows, historicism in its different versions, for whom "man is an historical being," has been claimed by both the friends and the enemies of democracy.

Whatever may be the case with the "experience of history," whether it be a discovery or an invention, historicism appeared late in the development of modern philosophy, no earlier than the middle of the eighteenth century. We are therefore left with the obscure but strong sentiment that the modern experience antedates the discovery of history, or that it antedates its thematic presentation by the philosophy of history, or that there is a modern experience more radical or original than the experience of history.

Now, if we can experience the greatest uncertainty over what is "for the first time" or what is "truly" modern, we have no doubt over what is ancient: the pope and emperor, St. Thomas and Frederick II, Canossa and Anagni. The modern, whatever it is, appears when this order is contested. One knows that the radical questioning of the medieval organization showed itself in the political and religious domains at the same moment, with Luther and Machiavelli. But it is Machiavelli who interests us here. He did not construct a system. What he says appears as little abstract as life itself: anecdotes, portraits, witticisms and *bon mots*. It is a world of thought and sentiment very removed from us (what is César Borgia to us?). It is another world, and yet, enigmatically, it is somehow our world. Our task is to remain faithful to this experience. However, frightened by it, many readers hasten to cover Machiavelli's work with the reassuring cloak of abstraction; thus, the shock of the reading is explained and neutralized. The troubling secretary of the Seigneurie counts only as a founder or precursor of political science. Of course, he is a bit overheated—that is understandable, but there is no reason to trouble ourselves, because we now have the habit and mastery of this science. We social scientists are *in control*.

But philosophers, or merely readers who are a bit sensitive and perceptive, do not sleep quite so easily on the pillow of science. They sense that something decisive concerning modern politics, the meaning of our situation, is at issue in and between the lines of Machiavelli. But what?

Precisely because modern political philosophy is so abstract, it seems that one could not apprehend it in a concrete perception, a phenomenon

that contains simultaneously the fact and its meaning. Ancient philosophy, in contrast, lends itself to such a perception. We can say that the
phenomenon of Greek politics is the congregation or assembly on the
public space with the pregnant tautology that man is a political animal
as its accompanying commentary. Or one might prefer the more developed formulation: man exercises and deploys the powers of his
nature in political activity. In short, the thought of ancient politics mo-
bilizes, if not necessarily, at least naturally, an ontology of nature, which
is what the ontology of Aristotle is par excellence. The ontology of nature
and the phenomenology of the assembly in the public square belong to
one another.

Now, when we read in Machiavelli that "men ought to caress or slay,"
when we observe that by far the longest chapter of the *Discourses* is
devoted to conspiracies,[7] when we seek in vain to sketch the outline of
the image of the Machiavellian prince, to whom it is recommended that
he remove from his nature all real attachment to the good in order better to manifest the appearance or to refuse to do the good, according to
the necessity of the case,[8] we feel that we have entered into a political
element quite different from the Greek city, which is, to put it succinct-
ly, *what it appears to be*. Troubled and anxious, but also full of eager-
ness, we set out in search of the phenomenon brought to light, but also
withdrawn or hidden by Machiavelli, that stigmatizes as outmoded or
naive the ancient phenomenon. Only if this hunt succeeds will the ultimate validity of modern politics be acknowledged, since we will have
rejoined the experience that is the source of its abstraction.

Claude Lefort brings together all of this when he writes that Machiavelli sketches "a new ontology" (*TOM*, 425). Surprisingly, and apparently exorbitantly (who would dream of making the harsh Florentine a
"shepherd of Being"?), this proposition quite simply goes to the heart
of the matter. As contested, refuted, ridiculed, and pronounced dead as
it has been, there has been but one positive ontology—that of Aristotle.
If modern politics wants to be truly founded, it must be founded on an
understanding of being fundamentally different from that of Aristotle.
This is why the Machiavellian political phenomenology strikes us by its
radical strangeness and novelty. Here we have, if not the proof, at least
the sign that a new ontology is at work, which the good reader must
take it as his task to uncover.

To discover the meaning of Machiavelli's work is to recover the
implicit ontology of modern politics, the ontology that has been veiled
perhaps at the same time it was explicated in the great systems from
Hobbes to Hegel that subsequently formulated the modern political

project. This, I believe, is the significance and import of Lefort's affirmation to which we instinctively gave our agreement: "The reestablishment of the truth about Machiavelli concerns *here and now* the establishment of the truth about politics."

The interpretation of Machiavelli, because it is not separable from the explication of the "new ontology," entails that the interpreter and his reader find themselves or move in a sort of gray zone, located between the ancient and the new ontology. The same proposition and the same sequence of thoughts can take on very different colors, depending on whether one sees in it a "modification," an "internal critique," a "polemical reversal" of the ancient ontology, or rather an opening, perhaps still uncertain and not fully self-conscious, toward the new one. The interpreter's approbation as well as his critique become equally difficult and demand extremely extended and meticulous considerations. It would be to facile to hide behind this difficulty, though, and to limit the commentary on the commentary of Lefort to the sincere affirmation of its powerfully illuminating and suggestive character. Instead, I would like to sketch a discussion.

In a first approximation that remains necessarily at the level of generality, Lefort underlines that Machiavelli criticizes the ontology of essence or substance, of nature, of the continuity or primacy of repose, finally, of order, and substitutes an ontology of accidents, of history, of movement and of disorder. Not only is this opposition formulated by Machiavelli himself, and in terms clearly if discretely metaphysical, but it also is expressed and "stylized" in an emblematic, historical form in the contrast between Sparta and Rome, between the city founded by a sovereign legislator, remaining intact for eight centuries within the limits of its territory and persevering in its order, being, and essence, and the other city that reinvents itself ceaselessly, enlarging its empire as luck, accidents, and disorder would have it.

As tempting as the recommendation to follow the example of Rome rather than Sparta might be, however persuasive the suggestion to prefer the new to the ancient ontology, it appears that Machiavelli's affirmation of a hierarchy of political courses of action (one must build on something which is thus founded in some way or another on "Being") leads back to the supremacy of the ancient ontology at the very moment one rejects it. It appears that the durable palladium of the old ontology—the principle of non-contradiction—is still capable of exercising its influence and that the Machiavellian attack is destined to be defeated at the fortress of necessity.

Lefort does not allow himself to be disconcerted, and he responds quite directly to the objection:

It will not work to object to Machiavelli that in the absence of a standard it is impossible to make a judgment about political conduct, or to compare different forms of power. This objection only weighs against a naive empiricism which leaves unchanged the ancient ontology. It is true that Machiavelli cannot denounce the *defects* of a regime, since he has renounced the model of a regime without defects. But it does not follow that the only thing left is empirical observation, that for him there is only the prince's defeat, sanctioned by his loss of power or death, the dissatisfaction of the people or the State's enslavement. In the critique of experience he discovers that in each situation there is a *required* political course of action. (*TOM*, 426)

Put in these terms the response is at once convincing and deceptive: convincing, because if the action to be taken is rigorously determined by the situation, the classical elaboration of the "best regime" is effectively deprived of relevance, deceptive, because "the exigencies of the situation" most often depend on the nature of the regime that confronts it. In fact, different regimes and different ideas of the political order can emerge in response to the same situation. The same defeat in 1940 led to the emergence of both Pétain and de Gaulle.

The notion of situation thus appears to be underdeveloped. It is of weak ontological alloy. It is an advantage when it is a matter of criticizing the ancient ontology, but it is a handicap when one wants to establish a new one. Aware of this difficulty, Lefort attempts to augment the ontological tenor of the notion of situation. A little later he writes:

There are more or less rich situations where political action is of a more or less greater import, where virtù sees a more or less great career open before it, where the implantation of power is more or less profound, society more or less free and vibrant—in short . . . there are degrees of Being. (*TOM*, 428)

With these last words the temptation is great, of course, to exclaim that Lefort, even before one makes the request, has handed over the weapon with which "to extinguish" him, or at least "to assure oneself" of him, since, to shore up the new ontology of the situation, he ends by appealing to the most "conservative" principle not only of Greek but of scholastic ontology, "degrees of Being." I have nothing more to ask of you says the conservative, magnanimous in his victory. "There are degrees of Being." I have never said anything but that. It is futile, you see, to attempt to escape the venerable embrace of Aristotle and St. Thomas.

As understandable as this conservative reaction might be, it cannot end the discussion. It is not strictly true that the affirmation of "degrees of Being" is equivalent to classical ontology. What is decisive in this context is the relationship between "the degrees of Being" and human desire. To what extent can man appropriate the ontological difference, to what degree is membership and participation in the "good regime" an ontological perfection of the citizen? Or more simply: to what extent does man *qua* citizen–participant in a "good whole"—become a better citizen and man because the whole in which he participates is better? It is here I believe that Machiavelli, interpreted by Lefort, breaks effectively with ancient ontology. According to Machiavelli, human desire is of two sorts. There is no whole, or rather the whole itself is divided— in fact, it cannot be understood or experienced except as divided. Of all of Machiavelli's commentators, Lefort is the one who draws the most radical consequences from what Machiavelli has to tell us about social division. It is in or through this division that the "new ontology" finds its experience and its phenomenon.

Let us recall the Machiavellian thesis. Every political body is composed of two parts: the people and the Great. Each part is moved politically by a "humor" or a "desire": the Great have the desire to command and to oppress the people, the people the desire not to be commanded or oppressed. The people's desire is thus "more decent" than that of the Great. The prince—more generally, the political agent—will base himself on the people rather than the Great, since the former "want not to be oppressed," while the latter only consent to the power of the prince in order "to be able to satisfy their appetite in his shadow."[9]

It is certain that the tendency or tone of the argument is clearly "democratic." And Machiavelli is very conscious when he underlines the virtues or the capacities of the people that he is contradicting the entire tradition of political thought, *tutti gli altri istorici, tutti gli scrittori.*[10] The point where the radicality of his reinterpretation of the social world especially manifests itself is his reevaluation of the relationship between conservation and acquisition. The tradition was "conservative" for the reason that the desire to conserve what one has—the desire of possessors, therefore—was naturally a principle of order and stability, while the desire to acquire—that of the people—was necessarily a cause of disorder and instability. Machiavelli on the contrary affirms that the desire of those who possess is more dangerous, or more "disordered," because "the fear of loss excites the same violence as the desire to acquire, and in addition the solicitude to conserve what one has prompts one to want to obtain ever more" (*TOM*, 478).

We glimpse now why Lefort sees in Machiavelli's political radicality the sign of his ontological radicality, why in his eyes the two run together. It is insufficient to say that Machiavelli is revolutionary or inaugurates a revolution in political thought because, while until then authors had "aristocratic prejudices" and were "for the Great" and "against the people," he is the first who is "for the people" and "against the Great." It is even less adequate to say, in a more elegant fashion, that Machiavelli effected "a transvaluation of values" and substituted "democratic" for "aristocratic" values.[11] What must be done is to unpack the anthropological and ontological import of what Machiavelli tells us about acquisition and conservation.

Aristotle's ontology is "conservative" because it is an "ontology of having, of possession": the fundamental human movement is to appropriate goods and the Good.[12] The quality or character of a man and a citizen is proportionate to the amount and quality of the goods he possesses. Now, to be sure, we must distinguish external goods such as property from internal goods such as the virtues. But as different as they may be, and though the latter are intrinsically more noble than the former, both are elements of the supreme human good, which is happiness. It is good to have because what one has is the good or a good. The city is the place where, and the organ or instrument by which, men appropriate, together and separately, the different human goods, and especially happiness and justice.[13] Such an ontology naturally gives the advantage to those who have property or virtues, who of course are not necessarily the same people. But they have in common the fact of having; in this sense, the ancient ontology is politically conservative and aristocratic.

If, as Machiavelli maintains, those who have less the happiness of having than the fear of losing what they have always want more because their appetites have been whetted rather than fulfilled, then the fact of having—as a source of dissatisfaction rather than of satisfaction— no longer can provide the vital principle of the city. And the city no longer can be defined as the place and instrument for the appropriation of goods and the Good. The Good and goods no longer can be the element for the satisfaction and simultaneous coexistence of the needs and desires that are born in the city. In short, for man in the city there can be no autarchy or self-sufficiency.

Moreover, the ontology of appropriation fails to grasp the meaning of the social division at the very moment when it affirms the difference between those who have and those who do not. The "conservative" position is false when it says that all men desire the same things, except that some have them and others want them. It is wrong because it masks what Machiavelli uncovers: there are two kinds of desire, not two desires for the same things, nor even two desires for different things, but two desires that are different, even irreconcilable. According to Lefort classes do not exist as classes, not so much because some have and others do not—as important as this "empirical" difference may be—but because they do not exist as such except in relation to each other. They "do not exist except in their confrontation, revolving around the issue which for one involves oppressing, for the other resisting oppression" (*TOM*, 385).

When Machiavelli states that the desire of the people is "more honest" than that of the Great, he speaks the "conservative" language of the old morality: he suggests that the people are both more moderate and more just. But the course of his thought shows us how useless these laurels are for social virtues. It is not its relative rectitude that makes the people's desire so salutary in the eyes of the philosopher. It is because it is a completely different desire from that of the Great. It is the Great who already possess, who desire positively to acquire. They truly desire to have because they know what it means to possess. At the same time that they show the error of Aristotle's ontology. Their having, Machiavelli reveals, is a principle of disorder rather than order, but they nonetheless lend plausibility to Aristotle's ontology. It is partial to them because it is partially true about them. In this sense it is their "ideology." It is the people's desire—which Aristotle's ontology has no place for—that moves us out of these categories. On this decisive point, we should let Claude Lefort speak:

> In the two works of Machiavelli, the *Prince* and the *Discourses*, human desire, involved and at work in the universal conflict of the classes, shows itself to be irreducible to the appetites for power, wealth and honors; in as much as it consists in the refusal to be commanded and to be oppressed (i.e., the people's desire), one must agree that no object furnished its measure, that it detaches the subject from every particular position and disposes it to an unlimited demand. This demand appears to be of such a nature that satisfaction cannot be obtained by one without it reemerging in another; or that beyond any eventual redistribution of property, prestige or power, the same power of negativity is maintained. (*TOM*, 722–23)

Thus, in the supposedly full world of the Aristotelian city the people's desire causes a void, interjects indetermination, and exercises the work of the negative. It endlessly reignites division and liberty because it always wants something other than what it eventually obtains—such and such a "redistribution," such and such an "improvement"—because it is the desire "of a power that would be at the same time non-power" (*TOM*, 386). One can say therefore in the conventional language Machiavelli resorts to with the intention of communicating a revolutionary meaning, that the people are more honest, more constant, wiser than the

Great; one can even retain the old *vox populi, vox Dei.*[14] These propositions do not have empirical or even statistical validity. The claims
of the people—are they more often more reasonable than not, or vice
versa? It would be an ideologue who says they are more reasonable!
But these propositions indicate an ontological truth: it is by means of
the people's desire that the being of society asserts that it is stronger
than all the haves, by the people's desire society exists more as society,
it is by it that society's being causes and makes known its difference
and its excess vis-à-vis all given reality. It is thanks to it that "there are
degrees of Being."

One then sees how thinking about politics, how political philosophy,
shares something with the people's desire for liberty:

> It puts at stake [like the people's desire], although at a distance from its
> *action,* the question of the being of the city: a question covered up at the
> place occupied by the prince and his discourse. (*TOM,* 729)

Here we see combined—in a legitimate complicity—the interpretation of Machiavelli, the new ontology, and democratic radicalism, perhaps even revolution. Hence, the great book of Claude Lefort finds its
amplitude, profundity, and coherence.

What keeps me from being completely persuaded? It is the fact
that Lefort does not think that philosophy can be impartial. To be able
to think authentically about politics, the philosopher deliberately
must attach himself to the people's point of view and to their desire.
I believe that philosophy can and therefore ought to transcend this
partiality.

Now, according to Lefort, philosophy's point of view is certainly not
the same as the people's. He knows that the latter's desire for liberty
retains an irremovable connection, on one hand, to the desire for vengeance, and on the other, to the desire for security. But finally it is in
the hostile distance between itself and the Great that the people recognize and establish between it and the established order of powers, that
philosophy finds the space for the critical distance it takes toward the
established sciences and dominant discourses. The social division is the
condition of possibility for political philosophy, whose working out is
inseparable from the activity of the people's desire. Thus, political philosophy accompanies the democratic movement during the course of its
history, at least since the Machiavellian revolution.

It seems to me then that modern political philosophy is more partial
to the people than classical political philosophy ever was toward the
Great. One might say that partiality toward the people is really impar-

tiality since the people are, tendentiously, the whole of society or the city. But this is the naive and "ideological" democratic point of view that Machiavelli and Lefort have refuted radically by demonstrating that the social division was *constitutive*: the city takes its form and its life from the confrontation of the two irreconcilable desires. No, here there is a partiality, and one that is simply assumed or asserted. Is it too much to say that with Machiavelli modern political philosophy decides to be partial—for a part, and a party of the theological-political body—and that it never has reconsidered this original decision even when it revolted against certain of its consequences?

Whatever may be the case with this point, it seems to me that philosophy can recognize the social division without being obliged to adopt the point of view of one or the other part. And it seems to me that this is what Aristotle succeeds in doing, when he explicitly treats the social division in book three of the *Politics* but in a more impartial manner than Machiavelli does in either the *Prince* or the *Discourses*. Of course, this is not the place to justify this assertion. But at least I can suggest that Aristotle's political philosophy does not allow itself simply to be reduced to the ontology of the degrees of being.

The partiality of Machiavelli's interpretation is indicated already when he defines the Great's desire without concerning himself with what the Great *say* about it. He ratifies without comment the point of view of their enemies. And he violently reduces the *two* desires to animality by designating them as *umori* (humors). Aristotle's impartiality is indicated in the fact that he takes very seriously what both *say*. He scrupulously reproduces, to examine them carefully, the opinions of both the democrats and the oligarchs about justice. Each one is partial, to be sure, but they "touch" the truth.[15] The desires of the classes speak: it is this speech that we must sift through in order to free the truth and to deliver ourselves from partiality.

Someone might retort that the procedure that distributes the parts of justice—the partial ideas about justice—to the parts of the social body is too simple. Aristotle knows well that partiality consists in the fact that a partial idea takes itself for the whole. But this means that it contains a certain idea of the whole, that it thus has some real relationship with it. Aristotle's critique consists in showing that these incompatible ideas of justice do not adequately encompass the idea of the city, that before being incompatible with each other each one is incompatible with the complete idea of the city. The implicit city of the oligarch, as well as that of the democrat, is not truly a city. For example, according to Aristotle, the oligarchic idea supposes or implies that the city is merely a commercial enterprise, a limited partnership where influence is proportionate to one's capital investment.[16] Who can say that Aristotle is partial to the haves?

Aristotle's impartiality shows itself also in the fact that he gives great attention to those who are not truly a part of the city and yet who deserve to govern it: The "virtuous" or the "capable." To be sure, as soon as they play a political role, these, by themselves, or, more likely, inside one or the other of the two camps, become a part of the city. Aristotle shows very well he is not even partial toward the impartial.[17]

Aristotle considers, with a great deal of acumen and respect, the democratic point of view. He sees quite clearly that there is a certain way in which what is democratic about a city makes it a city. The people accomplish as a part of the city what it accomplishes as a whole, namely, the integration of the different human goods.[18] In the world of the Greek cities where the poor effectively could command and oppress the rich, he sees the people's desire not to be commanded or oppressed: the idea of the city implicit in the people's desire is that of "a defensive alliance against injustice."[19] It is true that he does not see there the work of the negative but simply an incomplete idea. But one must pay great attention to this idea, as well as to those of the oligarchs, the virtuous, and the other significant elements in the civic conversation.

Someone might object that this admirable impartiality nonetheless presupposes the affirmation of an ontological referent "exterior" to the city, the "natural ends" in virtue of which Aristotle judges the ideas of all the parties to be partial. These "natural ends" of the city imply a hierarchical, normative nature, the fulcrum or pivot of the conservative ontology I myself just sketched a moment ago. Thus, the free debates of the agora become almost irresistibly the articles of the *Summa*.

Let me brave a last, brief remark. The human mind left to its own resources only has two possible referents or standards, those of nature and history. Lefort, more explicitly than Machiavelli, chooses history, as the history of negativity, the history of liberty. But since he knows better than anyone the ambiguities of the desire of liberty, its oscillations between vengeance and security, he cannot exclude or deny that this desire might become an enemy of itself and turn against the people, that the democratic movement might evoke a new domination or a domination of a new kind. He needs a positive standard in order to confirm that the people's desire here and now continues the authentic work of negation. He needs a referent that does not pass away. Claude Lefort himself recognizes that "there is consubstantial to the time that passes a time that does not pass" (*TOM*, 64). This is a beautiful definition of nature.

It was important to Aristotle to be free in the city, but it was also more important to him to be free from the city, not in the sense of the "idiotic" retreat into private pleasures but in the grasp or understanding of the universal order of "human things." If Machiavelli signals and introduces an obfuscation into philosophy, this consists in the partiality that despairs of arriving at the universal and that contents itself with offering to the human will the objective of a liberty that is always to be won, within the limits of society or history.

I do not believe, however, that Claude Lefort is captive to democratic partiality. If he committed himself to the exploration of Machiavelli's work, it was to find the original issue or emergence of modern liberty, which wells up from the self-conscious social division between the Great and the people. But it also was to have emerge from an exemplary work a science of the text and the world—"this science which grows ever more obscure" (*TOM*, 67). Thinking about politics is thus no less a "restoration" than a "revolution." It is a restoration, by way of the text, of the complexity of the world.

Translated by Daniel J. Mahoney and Paul Seaton

Notes

1. Claude Lefort, *Le Travail de l'oeuvre Machiavelli* (Paris: Gallimard, 1972), hereafter cited as *TOM*.
2. For a fuller account of Péguy's critique of modern historical consciousness, see "Charles Péguy: Between Political Faith and Faith" in part three of this volume.
3. This is a clear reference to the influential work of J. G. A. Pocock, who assimilates the supposed "civic republicanism" of Aristotle, Machiavelli, and some of the American founders. See Pocock, *The Machiavellian Moment* (Princeton: Princeton University Press: 1975) (editor's note).
4. Leo Strauss, *Thoughts on Machiavelli* (Chicago: University of Chicago Press, 1978) 294.
5. Strauss, *Thoughts on Machiavelli* 10, 294.
6. Strauss, *Thoughts on Machiavelli* 295.
7. Machiavelli, *Discourses on Livy*, book 3, chapter 6.
8. Machiavelli, *The Prince,* chapters 15 and 18.
9. Machiavelli, *The Prince*, chapter 9 and *Discourses,* I, chapters 4, 5, and 16.
10. Machiavelli, *Discourses*, I, 58.
11. From the beginning of his work, Lefort warns that the notion of values is of no help because it can be used for every purpose.
12. See the beginnings of both the *Politics* and the *Nicomachean Ethics.*

13. This ontology will be taken over by the Catholic Church, which will propose a new good: God Himself. In the church and by the church it is God Himself that men appropriate.

14. See, for example, Machiavelli, *Discourses,* I, 58.

15. Aristotle's *Politics*, book 3, chapter 9, 1280a9ff.

16. Aristotle's *Politics*, book 3, chapter 9, 1280a25–32.

17. Aristotle's *Politics*, book, 3, chapter 10, 1281a25–35.

18. In this context, Aristotle judges that the multitude is the better judge of the work of musicians and poets, because one person judges one part of the work, the other another, and all judge the whole (*Politics*, book 3, chapter 11, 1281b5–10). What modern democrat would go so far?

19. Aristotle's *Politics*, book 3, chapter 10, 1280a30–35.

Democratic Man, Aristocratic Man, and Man Simply: Some Remarks on an Equivocation in Tocqueville's Thought

Pierre Manent

1990

I would like to draw your attention to an at once serious and revealing difficulty in what François Furet has aptly called Alexis de Tocqueville's "conceptual system."[1]

The Originality of Tocqueville's Conceptual System

To grasp clearly what is original in Tocqueville, it is natural and necessary to indicate, even if very briefly, the approach of his contemporaries with whom he is most naturally compared.

My main example will be the French philosopher, historian, and statesman François Guizot, whose Sorbonne courses at the end of the Restoration were passionately followed by Tocqueville.[2]

Guizot's strength lies in the competence and assurance with which he employs tested, available, and inherited categories. These are essentially and explicitly those of French and Scottish eighteenth-century authors: categories such as civilization, the middle classes, and representative government. More implicitly, he also has recourse to much hoarier concepts dating from antiquity, such as that of the mixed regime. By his confident use of traditional notions drawn unequally from both the Enlightenment and the ancients, Guizot illustrates his thesis of the essential continuity of European civilization. And even if he gives an extremely refined analysis of the new relations connecting the modern state and modern society, one that we have again learned to admire,[3] he does so by employing the well-established conceptual idiom of *representation*.

Now let us consider Benjamin Constant, who embodies within French liberalism restlessness or irony in as striking a way as Guizot does assurance or satisfaction.[4] To be sure, Constant is unequaled in displaying the paradoxes, contradictions, and ironies of modern politics and society. But his conceptual equipment is as traditional as Guizot's; he perhaps expends even less effort in reworking it and rendering it rigorously consistent with his personal vision. Like Guizot's, Constant's thought is dominated by the idea of representative government. And even if he did not appreciate the place of that idea in the thought of Montesquieu, he formulated quite clearly and fully the "Scottish" idea of the contrast between successive ages of war and of commerce.

Leaving the liberal circle, let us turn to Karl Marx. We see that he, too, shares the "Guizotian" vision of a political history that develops in correspondence with social history and "represents" it.

It is here that we come to my point of departure. Tocqueville eludes, although he does not reject or refute, the categories common to Guizot and Constant, the categories of "liberal sociology." These are the categories of the dominant self-interpretation of modern politics—of the interpretive circle within which Marx himself remained caught. In particular, how can one fail to note that Tocqueville never thematizes the notion of representation, even if as a matter of course he makes use of it in his description of American institutions? (The word representation only occurs one time in the chapter and paragraph titles of *Democracy in America*, which are quite numerous and frequently rather long.) More precisely, the only basic reflection he expresses concerning representative government (he formulates it twice) ends by denying to representation any durable political effectiveness.[5] How, then, does he proceed?

Tocqueville has recourse to the notion of democracy, whose origin is found in Greek politics and thought where it signifies a political regime. It is to be observed that the word and the notion had not recovered or acquired credibility at the time of the elaboration of Enlightenment philosophy and politics because it was attached to a too disordered, insufficiently rational, too "harsh" and, in a word, too "inhuman" phase of human history, one that had been surpassed thanks to the progress of civilization and of representative government. Civilization and representative government are what distinguish the modern commercial republic from the ancient warrior democracy, to the advantage of the former in the eyes of the dominant liberal school. It is to be remembered that the American and French revolutionaries declared they founded representative republics and not democracies.

Of course, by using this term, in one sense Tocqueville only follows the example of his contemporaries—under both the Restoration and the July Monarchy everyone spoke of "democracy." But better than anyone else he enables us to see the singularity of this usage: the name of a political regime comes to designate a "generative principle . . . that regulates the greater part of human actions."[6] A political concept comes to designate something we can provisionally call "metapolitical."

Is this idea of democracy clear? And to begin with, is it distinct? It cannot be distinct unless there is something other than democracy, another thing that one can name. That is aristocracy. Tocqueville interprets human history and comprehends the order of political things by means of the pairing of democracy and aristocracy. And even if he does not account for the generative principle of aristocracy, even if he does not confirm that it has one, even if aristocracy appears to us to be sketched rather less positively than negatively as the antitype of democracy, it is nonetheless clear that it, too, is a "metapolitical notion." Like democracy, it envelops all the aspects of human life. This polarity is so marked and so determinative that it seems that to live in democracy and to live in aristocracy are two essentially distinct expressions of the human condition. In a manner of speaking, it is to belong to two distinct humanities without relation to each other. In the "General View of the Subject," which closes volume two of *Democracy in America* and thus the work as a whole, Tocqueville writes the following with respect to aristocracy and democracy: "They are like two distinct humanities, of which each has its particular advantages and disadvantages, and goods and evils proper to it . . . these prodigiously different societies are incomparable." There is thus a "democratic man" whose features (I dare not say whose nature) Tocqueville describes with as much amplitude as precision. The portrait of the "aristocratic man" is less complete and at the same time more composite; it stands forth nonetheless with salient characteristics. But where is man *simpliciter*? What does Tocqueville answer when we ask him, what is man, neither aristocratic nor democratic man, but simply man, man "in all the truth of his nature"? Does he even respond?

The pairing aristocracy–democracy contains a perhaps deceptive symmetry. Democracy in the metapolitical sense, in the Tocquevillean sense, can be conceived and presented as a "generalization" or a "universalization" of democracy in its original political sense, the maxims of the "citizen" becoming those of "man" in all his roles. Tocqueville says exactly this on the previously cited chapter (see note 6). He writes:

> In the United States the dogma of popular sovereignty is in no way an isolated doctrine unrelated to habits or the totality of dominant ideas; on the contrary one can conceive of it as the last link of a chain of opinions which envelop the entire Anglo-American world. Providence has given to each individual the degree of reason necessary for him to be able to

direct himself in the things that exclusively concern him. This is the great maxim upon which civil and political society rests in the United States; the father of the family applies it to his children, the master to his servants, the township to those it administers, the province to the township, the state to the provinces, the union to the states. Extended to the whole of the nation it becomes the dogma of the sovereignty of the people. Thus in the United States the generative principle of the republic is that same that regulates the greater part of human actions.

Democracy thus has a generative principle that we are able to know. As I stated earlier, Tocqueville never revealed to us the "generative principle," if there is one, of aristocracy. And how could he, since aristocracy for him covers simultaneously the Greek city, Rome, the European old regime, modern England, and perhaps even the Indian tribes? But what, then, is this genus that includes species that previously were considered incompatible? Does Tocqueville, practicing an improvised and maladroit "division," simply label as "aristocracy" everything that is not democracy? However, if his division is so poorly conceived that it appears to be barely plausible, why is it as fruitful as it is?

Democracy, Nature, and History

One might suggest that, by defining aristocracy and democracy as "regimes of humanity" rather than as political regimes, Tocqueville only recovers the original Greek meaning of the notion of regime and moreover the meaning of politics. For Aristotle, as well as for Plato and Thucydides, there corresponds to each regime a human "type" and, in this sense, a "distinct humanity." But besides the fact that the Tocquevillean regimes correspond only partially to a part of the "Greek" regimes, one consideration obliges us to distinguish them rigorously. The Greek regimes are affected by an essentially "cyclical" history, a history that is circumscribed and regulated by *nature*.

In contrast, Tocquevillean democracy bears or implies a process, an *indefinite history*. This is even the prime motive of the inquiry conducted in *Democracy in America* and the main wellspring of its *pathos*: one does not know where democracy is taking us. Of course, Tocqueville tells us in the *Author's Introduction* to the work that he crossed the ocean in order to discover the "natural limits" of democracy: "There is a country in the world where the great social revolution of which I speak seems to have nearly attained its natural limits." Even without underlining in too emphatic a fashion the precautions Tocqueville here takes—"seems," "nearly" (quite significant precautions and reservations in the context where the author gives a summary of his results, and the increase in knowledge obtained by his voyage)—one must note that in numerous other passages Tocqueville writes that even in America "democracy has surpassed all of its former limits"[7] or that "there is something precipitous, I almost could say revolutionary, about the progress made by society in America."[8] In short, the American example ought to guide our action, and it can temper, without completely abolishing, our "terror." However, it cannot, like the Greek idea of "nature," give us a knowledge that closes the horizon of possibilities. "Where are we going, therefore? No one can say; we lack the terms of comparison."[9]

To be sure, for the Greeks themselves there is a history of the Athenian democracy, a process or a progress, but this progress is circumscribed by the limits of politics and of human things. The "democratic party" or the "extreme people"[10] or the Salaminian rowers[11] were quite capable of acquiring even more power, and Athens itself, under their impetus, or to make room for them, was quite able to expand the range of its domination. There comes a moment, however, when the eternal nature of political and human things asserts its empire and punishes the immoderation of Pallas Athena's city. At that time, Athens leaves the scene of history. Thucydides' history thus unfolds a tragedy.

In Tocqueville's democracy the power of democracy is not the power of man over man, or the power of one party over another, or it is so only very secondarily and provisionally.[12] It is rather the power of man over himself: more and more actions, more and more sentiments, more and more thoughts, come to live under the democratic regime. And it seems that this process of the conquest of man by democracy is both irreversible and indefinite. Putting before us the Athenian democracy and the Spartan "aristocracy," Thucydides displays two possibilities of human nature actualized and pushed to their limits in the greatest conflict known to Greece. These two possibilities, however, are always ("aei") possible, that is, always at least potentially copresent in human things as two subtly but radically different modulations of the same humanity. In contrast, the Tocquevillean aristocracy and democracy are two successive and exclusive versions of humanity (we do not dare to speak of "the same" humanity when Tocqueville himself speaks of "two distinct humanities"), where one has definitively defeated the other and will continue to increase its victory.

In Tocqueville's view, aristocracy had to yield its place because, despite its merits—and the aristocratic man has many features he invites us to appreciate and to admire—it was essentially unjust, founded in the final analysis on force.[13] Democracy possesses an assured status because it is essentially just.[14] Once men are in possession of justice, a justice in which the great majority have an interest, it is hard to see how historical progress could "turn back," that is, how men could renounce the "gains of democracy." But if democracy is just, it is because it conforms to man's nature or situation. One would be right to suppose, therefore, that it is an eminently stable state. Why then does it unleash a continuous, unending process of radicalization? More exactly, why does the "passion for equality" grow even when conditions become more equal?[15]

Here we touch one of the most important points of Tocqueville's diagnosis, which prevents us from simply saying that for him democracy is "in conformity with nature." If men naturally "hunger and thirst" for justice, why do they have an even greater "hunger and thirst" for justice, that is, democracy, when they have more and more democracy, that is, justice? Hunger is not naturally insatiable.

Increasing our perplexity, Tocqueville next teaches us that this process of equalization, taking on ever more amplitude, risks ceasing to be just, of moving toward a new form of injustice by oppressing or sterilizing the higher parts of the soul.[16] Must we say that democracy is too just for the majority of men ever to renounce it, but also too unjust to leave to certain men the place or power or prestige that would allow them to reverse the historical movement? But this last "injustice" is itself also just because this overturning of democracy, if *per impossible* it were possible, would mean the restoration of aristocracy, thus of injustice. Or is justice itself subordinated to the opposition between democracy and aristocracy? As these give birth to "two distinct humanities," are there then two "distinct justices"? But at no point does Tocqueville affirm or even suggest this. In fact, the very idea of subordinating justice and truth to a political partiality, even a majoritarian one, caused him horror.[17] But can he truly escape from such a conclusion?

I do not wish to show Tocqueville mistaken or lacking, nor do I desire "to complete" or "to perfect" him. Rather, I am attempting to discern the meaning and import of this division of humanity into two "regimes of humanity" and to this end to specify in particular the use he makes of the notion of nature.

The Nature and the Art of Democracy

To follow Tocqueville, we must note here that he adds another "division" internal to democracy to his initial division between democracy and aristocracy. He distinguishes in a quite trenchant manner between the *nature* and the *art* of democracy. Its nature, its "instincts," push it blindly toward ever greater equality, even at liberty's expense; its art preserves liberty. Notice that I say "preserves." In treating the relations between democracy and liberty, Tocqueville endlessly repeats the same double affirmation: on one hand, democratic man naturally desires and has a taste for liberty, on the other, if he must choose, he naturally will prefer equality.[18] In the context of democracy, liberty appears to him to be threatened. This menace is redoubtable, but it is possible to ward it off: "The Americans have shown that it is not necessary to despair of regulating democracy, with the assistance of laws and mores."[19] This last formulation is even more striking because it is found in the first volume of *Democracy*, published in 1835. (Reviewing the second volume in 1840, Saint-Beuve could write, "Monsieur Tocqueville carries the cross of democracy.") It is the democratic art that allows us to ward off the threat and not to despair of democracy.

The democratic art is employed to prevent democracy's nature from oppressing or sterilizing man's nature. In this context Tocqueville designates an opaque moral and social being, democratic man, who is at once nature and will, or whose nature is to will ever more equality. How, and according to what criteria and in the name of what principles, can we enlighten and regulate his "instincts"? What bit will be strong enough to master this impetuous, blind steed, or what prod will be sharp enough to animate this obtuse and obstinate cow? Tocqueville, as everyone knows, multiplies his recommendations.

First of all, let me say a word about religion. By its origins and perhaps by its essence, it is external to democracy; this is why it can regulate democracy. It says to democratic man's liberty, to his envy, and to his disordered passions, you will not go any further! And this circumscription of liberty is, in fact, a consolidation of it. However, if, as in Europe, religion remains strictly external to democracy, religion will not be democracy's restraint but its enemy. To be able to moderate and not combat democracy, religion must adapt itself to democracy. On the other side of the coin, democracy must appropriate religion for itself. From this, it seems to me, comes a fundamental hesitation or ambivalence about democracy's relation with religion: One must fear that the "pantheism" natural to democracy might come to destroy the religious nature of man[20] and that the reciprocal adaptation of religion and democracy might ultimately mean democracy's triumph over religion. Was not this final fear already contained in Tocqueville's initial and apparently so "promising" observation: "Puritanism was not only a religious doctrine; it also overlapped on several points with the most absolute democratic and republican theories"?[21]

In contrast, there is no hesitation with respect to the democratic art, since it is a matter of taking advantage of a division internal to democracy.

In what does this democratic art consist? To what are its good effects owing? In what is its goodness situated? Let us take the exemplary case of associations. The art constructs or re-creates the social bond that in aristocratic societies was given with the hierarchy of families (and which the democratic equality of conditions has eroded). This construction or reconstruction—because it is deliberate, setting in motion the free initiative of equal citizens—can be judged superior to the "natural" bond furnished by aristocracy, whose ultimate foundation, we must never forget, resides in force. In aristocracy the social bond is both suffered or at least received, and unequal; in democracy it is free or deliberate, and equal. Democracy thus appears to have a double advantage.

But Tocqueville simultaneously presents associations as a never ending effort to overcome the disassociation introduced by democratic equality and to preserve the "civilization" threatened by what one might call democratic "nomadism": "the Anglo-Americans arrived fully civilized on the soil their posterity occupies," but the diminution of "individual influences" due to extreme democracy puts this civilization itself in danger.[22] In short, the associative effort appears to be more of a remedy to a new malady than the discovery or invention of a new good. As Tocqueville emphasizes several times, by means of the democratic art, democratic man learns or is reminded that he is not alone on the earth and that he has fellow citizens. What a paradoxical necessity it is to have to instruct individuals that they are parts of a community in a society in which the sentiment of human resemblance, especially in the form of pity, is so strong! The elimination of aristocratic inequality and constraint, felicitous in themselves, translates into a lessening of the visibility and presence of the social bond.

I cannot delve here into the most difficult question raised by the contrast drawn by Tocqueville between an inherited social bond and a constructed one. A bond produced by liberty is obviously preferable to one submitted to by constraint. But, on the other hand, the more that a bond is conceived and experienced as freely and sovereignly instituted, the more it runs the risk of being less and less a bond, of having less and less the nature of a bond. A bond freely constructed and instituted is by definition a bond that could not have been. It soon will be *experienced* as being able not to be, as not being a bond. If we suppose that humanity lives by means of the various bonds that attach men to each other, the more these bonds become democratic, the more humanity will live with the awareness of the contingent or arbitrary character of the bonds that constitute it. Its "human tenor" will tend, therefore, to diminish.

The Love of Liberty

How can one approach these questions without knowing what the principle of the democratic art is, without knowing its wellspring in the human soul, the passion or virtue that animates and sustains it? Tocqueville does not make this decisive question a theme. He treats it in passing, responding to the circumstance; the only time that he comes to a stop before it (in *The Old Regime and the Revolution*) he has recourse to pathos:

> I have often asked myself where is the source of this passion for political liberty which, in all ages, has caused men to do the greatest things humanity has accomplished, in what sentiments it is rooted and nourished. . . .
>
> What in all ages has attached liberty so strongly to the heart of certain men are its own features, its own charm, independent of its benefits, it is the pleasure of being able to speak, to act, and to breathe without constraint, under the sole government of God and the laws. Whoever seeks in liberty anything other than itself is made to serve. . . .
>
> Do not ask me to analyze this sublime taste, one must experience it. It enters of itself into the great hearts that God has prepared to receive it; it fills them; it inflames them. One must not try to make it comprehensible to the mediocre souls who have never felt it.[23]

This quite beautiful "elevation" surprises us. Liberty, and therefore one can suppose, the art of democratic liberty, has its natural wellspring in a grace granted to a few. It is an immediate gift of God that eludes both art and reason; it cannot be analyzed. Love of liberty here has a foundation that is clearly and emphatically inegalitarian and thus antidemocratic; the exaltation of "great hearts" and the disdain for "mediocre souls" certainly does not belong to the "instincts" of democracy. But do they belong to its art?

I do not believe that one can minimize the importance of such a declaration, one unique in the published work of Tocqueville,[24] who himself stresses that it is the fruit of a lifetime's meditation. Nowhere as clearly as here does he attribute a natural basis to his political doctrine. Do we finally grasp here the natural basis common to aristocracy and democracy, the *tertium quid*, the *humanum commune* that overcomes their "division"; do we finally grasp "man simply," *homo simplex*?

To know the answer to the question, we should put this "love of liberty" to the test in each of the great Tocquevillean "regimes."

It appears difficult to find it or to make a place for it in democracy, because its characteristic inequality so directly contradicts democracy's basis. One could say, of course, that it provides the "homeopathic" dose of aristocracy that is necessary for every political organization, even the democratic one. For example, in Thomas Hobbes's social contract, which is so emphatically egalitarian, it is necessary for a few, out of pure generosity or greatness of soul, to take the risk of beginning the process of disarmament and alienation of one's rights in the state of nature. But there, too, it is the case that once the first step is taken, and the example given and followed, that Leviathan has within itself all the means to persist in being without the support of this generosity, which Hobbes tells us is "too rarely found to be presumed on."[25] And in a democratic society, the noble pride of the "great hearts," so difficult to hide according to the testimony of Tocqueville's contemporaries, would be a permanent challenge or defiance to the passion of equality. This passion would satisfy its envy by depriving these men of political careers worthy of their ambition and in accord with the country's true interests.

However, the nondemocratic love of liberty is no more at home in aristocratic societies. Aristocratic liberty is the "enjoyment of a privilege"; it is a noble version of "egoism"; it is inseparable from a proud domination over those who are not free.[26] Aristocratic liberty is not pure, and it does not have the idyllic flavor of the liberty eloquently praised in the above-cited passage. One would have great difficulty to indicate a historical experience, an aristocratic political experience, that corresponds to the Arcadia sketched by Tocqueville. In fact, he neitherlindicates nor even suggests one with any clarity. Thus, at the very moment when we believe we have grasped him, this *tertium quid*, this *humanum commune*, this *homo simplex* eludes us. This third man, this pure lover of liberty, does not appear to be common to both aristocracy and democracy except to the extent that he does not find a place in either regime.

The reader will wonder why I have taken so much time on the "conceptual status" of this "love of liberty." It is because this love as a passion or disposition of the soul played a very small role, to say the least, in the thought of the founders of liberalism. The "rights of man" are rooted in the necessity of self-preservation. In the liberalism of the seventeenth and eighteenth centuries liberty is a means and an effect much more than an intrinsically worthwhile end. This is even true with Montesquieu. It is true that he wrote about the English, "This nation would love enormously its liberty, because this liberty is true" (*The Spirit of the Laws*, book nineteen, chapter twenty-nine). But if one takes into account the context of this remark, one sees that this love of liberty of which Montesquieu speaks, on one hand, is an impatience with everything that would threaten liberty, on the other hand, it is a certain knowledge of its benefits. But these are precisely the two things that Tocqueville says liberty is not when it is truly loved for its own sake. It seems to me that with Tocqueville liberty becomes, as we say today, a *value*, and it is this that I am attempting to get at.

At the risk of violating the most salutary rule of historical interpretation, in my conclusion I would like "to understand Tocqueville better than he understood himself" by suggesting that far from appearing "in all ages" as God provides, this pure love of liberty is rather a quite singular but very interesting aspect of the life of democratic societies.

Democratic Spirituality

Democratic society is basically satisfied and it has good reasons to be so. But this satisfaction expresses itself in something that resembles dissatisfaction. There is in the democratic desire "to improve one's condition" a frenzy that resembles dissatisfaction. In an analogous way, the sympathetic recognition of human similarity in democratic society is also the envious desire for an ever greater human resemblance. As for the dissatisfaction of well-born souls, it has as its flip side a satisfaction characterized by an exquisite bitterness: no longer able proudly to appropriate power as a privilege but also unable to consent to the "social power" of the "majority" or of "public opinion," they taste the pure love of liberty. Thus, the elect of nature accede to pure nature.

The "elevation" that Tocqueville displays in honor of liberty could without any problem be employed in honor of another deity, of another "value." In fact, democratic convention and the social project of democracy detach the different human experiences that, until then, bound them to one man's power over another. Now the "old" experiences, such as art, literature, love, and religion, attain an unprecedented purity, a truly "ineffable" one, since no "common sense" or "common world" any longer makes them communicate among themselves or allows men to communicate among themselves concerning them. This is precisely the "new experience" democracy brings. In this sense democracy, which provides solid satisfactions for the great majority, also has "mystical" satisfactions for the few. The latter are perhaps even more separated from the majority than they have ever been: No communication is possible between the vulgar prose of commercial society and the ineffable experiences of the few.

Tocqueville nowhere sketches the profile of *Homo simplex*. The polarity between democracy and aristocracy (i.e., everything that preceded democracy) remains at the end of the inquiry what it was at the beginning. The "division" never leads to any "unity." This is because, in the end, democratic man is divided as follows: He is preoccupied with distinguishing and separating in his experiences, with an ever more refined chimerical scrupulousness, what had been affected by aristocratic inequality, by man's power over man, and what can be defined and experienced as pure nature. This is really neither the egalitarian nature of democracy nor its liberal art but rather its *work*. For reasons one can easily guess, this work is endless.

Translated by Daniel J. Mahoney and Paul Seaton

Notes

1. See François Furet, preface to Alexis de Tocqueville, *De la Démocratie en Amérique* (Paris: Garnier-Flammarion, 1981), 7. The preface is entitled "Le système conceptuel de le *Démocratie en Amérique*."

2. For Manent's reflection on Guizot's role in the history of modern liberal thought, see *An Intellectual History of Liberalism*, chapter 9, "François Guizot: The Liberalism of Government" (Princeton: Princeton University Press, 1995), 93–102. Guizot's 1828 lectures at the Sorbonne, assiduously followed by Tocqueville, are available again in English. See Guizot, *The History of Civilization in Europe* (London: Penguin, 1997). On Tocqueville and Guizot, see Larry Siedentrop's introduction to the above-mentioned edition, xxx–xxxiii (editor's note).

3. See François Guizot, *De la peine de mort en matière politique* (1822) (reissued, Paris: Corpus des philosophes français, Fayard, 1986) and above all *Des moyens de gouvernement et d'oppositions dans l'état actuel de la France* (1821) (reissued, Paris: Belin, 1987; introduction by Claude Lefort).

4. See Manent's chapter on "Benjamin Constant and the Liberalism of Opposition" in *An Intellectual History of Liberalism*, 84–92. See also Constant, *Political Writings*, ed. Biancamaria Fontana (Cambridge: Cambridge University Press, 1988) (editor's note).

5. "[A]lthough the form of the government is representative, it is evident that the opinions, prejudices, interests, and even the passions of the people cannot find any durable obstacle which would prevent them from being translated in the daily direction of society" (*Democracy in America*, [hereafter *DA* I]; part 2, chapter 1), and "It is true that the representative system was almost unknown in antiquity. In our day, popular passions show up with more difficulty in public affairs; one can be sure, however, that the representative always will end by conforming himself to the mind of those who have sent him and

that they will cause their inclinations as well as their interests to prevail" (*DA* I, part 2, chapter 5).

All translations from Tocqueville are our own. Rather than citing any particular translation of *Democracy in America,* we have cited each quotation from *Democracy* by *DA* followed by volume number, and volume part and chapter, for easy reference to any editions of the book. Manent's references are all drawn from the two-volume edition of *De la Démocratie en Amérique* published by Gallimard in the *Ouevres Complètes de A. Tocqueville* (Paris: Gallimard, 1951).

6. *DA* I, part 2, chapter 10.
7. *DA* I, part 2, chapter 5.
8. *DA* I, final chapter.
9. *DA* I, author's introduction.
10. Aristotle, *Politics,* 1277b.
11. Aristophanes, *The Assembly of Women,* verse 38.
12. *DA* I, part 2, chapter 2: "On parties in the United States."
13. *DA* I, final chapter.
14. See Tocqueville's *État social et politique de la France avant et depuis 1789,* in *L'Ancien Régime et la Révolution* I, (Paris: Gallimard, 1952) 62–63.
15. *DA* II, part 2, chapter 13 and part 4, chapter 9. Here our author writes, "It is thus natural that the love of equality ceaselessly grows with equality itself." I do not understand why this is "natural."
16. *DA* II, part 1, chapter 10; part 3, chapter 19; part 4, chapter 6.
17. *DA* I, part 2, chapter 7.
18. The following is an excellent example: "I think that democratic peoples have a natural taste for liberty; left to themselves they seek it, they love it and they see with pain when someone deprives them of it. But for equality they have an ardent passion, insatiable, eternal, invincible; they want equality in liberty, and, if they cannot have it, they still want it in servitude" (*DA* II, part 2, chapter 1).
19. *DA* I, part 2, chapter 9.
20. *DA* II, part 1, chapter 7.
21. *DA* I, part 1, chapter 2. [On this question, see "Christianity and Democracy" in this same volume (editor's note).]
22. See successively *DA* I, part 2, chapter 5 and chapter 9, and *DA* I, part 1, chapter 3.
23. Tocqueville, *L'Ancien Regime,* book 3, chapter 3.
24. See however *DA* II, part 2, chapter 1.
25. Thomas Hobbes, *Leviathan* (ed. Michael Oakeshott, selected and with an introduction by Richard S. Peters) (New York: Macmillan, 1962), part 1, chapter 14, 111 (editor's note).
26. See Tocqueville, *État social et politique,* 62.

Part Three

Christianity and Politics

"Christianity and Democracy" retraces the various, necessarily inadequate "solutions" proposed and actually established to the problems posed by the Christian churches to the political order of the Western world. Our current solution, the separation of church and state, follows on the heels of previous efforts and their demonstrated inadequacies. Today's "situation" of Christianity in the democratic West has its own strengths and liabilities for both parties. A merely secular democracy, which says nearly nothing publicly or authoritatively about man, increasingly creates a void for its members who seek for greater self-understanding. The Christian church, observes Manent, is uniquely positioned to alleviate this spiritual or interior distress because of its elevated doctrine of man's nature and dignity.

While the church possesses this "dialectical" or doctrinal advantage, it is otherwise at a disadvantage in democratic societies. Democracy's sole principle of legitimacy, the consent of individual men and women, is in some tension with the authoritative, divinely mandated character claimed by the church in its millennial self-understanding. In the liberal democratic West today, the church is tempted by various impolitic inclinations, including the "progressive" desire to adopt indiscriminately the spirit of democracy and the reactionary impulse to reject the modern world. It must resist these and be guided by a prudent assessment of its situation.

Manent, of course, is not the first to consider the relations between the spiritual and the temporal, the church and the city. The great French poet and thinker Charles Péguy was deeply concerned with these issues. In "Charles Péguy: Between Political Faith and Faith," Manent sketches this fiery man's intellectual and spiritual itinerary and deftly highlights his powerful critique of "the modern world" and its guiding lights, "historical and sociological consciousness." Less successful, in Manent's view, is Péguy's analysis of the temporal and the spiritual realms of human and Christian existence. However, in Manent's judgment, Péguy is still quite relevant to our needs and concerns today: he continues to remind us, by means of his famous distinction between "mystique" and "politique," that there is a sacredness proper to political life and that our deliberately desacralized politics have something decidedly unnatural about them.

Charles Péguy:
Between Political Faith and Faith

Pierre Manent

1984

Charles Péguy (1873–1914) is certainly not forgotten. In death, as in life, he remains a controversial figure. A man of passion, he still arouses passion in others. Even today, at least in France, a book on Péguy is almost certain to give rise to polemics. The details of his political, sentimental, and religious life are scrutinized in minute detail. What is most often neglected, what is not taken seriously in this stormy celebrity, is the thinker or, if you like (Péguy would have liked), the philosopher. His views on the city and the church, on Sophocles and on the Gospels, on the modern world and what makes it move, on men and gods, are sometimes very profound and beautiful. So many writers who are greatly inferior to him now occupy a major place in the textbooks of philosophy, sociology, and historiography that it is only fair to deal, even if only briefly as here, with Péguy's thought. He himself would have liked to be considered from this angle: was it not the ambition (one of the ambitions) of his life to finish a thesis on *the place given to history and sociology in modern times?* Although unfinished, the few hundred pages which he left are rich enough to show that he was one of the most penetrating critics of the historical and sociological points of view which dominate modern consciousness.

It is true that he did not make it easy for us. An imperious spirit, fascinating all who knew him, as the many biographies written by his intimates testify, his work was violently personal. No matter what the subject of his discourse, Péguy spoke about himself, interminably, about those he loved and especially about those he hated. Propositions and analyses of universal significance were caught up with arguments *ad*

This essay originally appeared in *Government and Opposition* in the winter of 1984 and is reprinted with permission.

hominem, with detailed descriptions of events which seem minor to us. Uplifting mystical passages often finished up with an insult. Everything that happened to Péguy or touched him nearly had a *weltgeschichtlich* significance for him. A devouring and bitter self-obsession leaves its mark on his work. The reader must make a violent effort to break through this enclosure; but if he is willing to do so, he will discover, at the center of this spirit shrouded in melancholy, a luminous mind, eager to understand and to think.

Fortunately the most important event in Péguy's life and for his work was also of capital importance, not only for the French of his generation but for the Western world ever since. This was the Dreyfus Affair. What he experienced then, what happened to him, was truly *weltgeschichtlich.*

Péguy and the Dreyfus Affair

The fundamental political, human, and spiritual experience of Péguy's life was the evolution of the Dreyfus Affair. It was while observing the transition from militant Dreyfusism to Dreyfusism triumphant that he worked out the main elements of his interpretation of the modern world. The clear political outcome of the victory of Dreyfusism was the formation of a ministry of republican defense and then the establishment of Combism,[1] a system of party domination that Péguy detested. In other words, what the original Dreyfusism had opposed—the coming of a demagogic domination disastrous for liberties—was taking place in the wake of and under the banner of Dreyfusism.

At the risk of seeming to go into unnecessary detail, it is important to sum up briefly the history of Péguy's commitment to the cause of Dreyfus. It was Lucien Herr,[2] librarian of the École Normale, who at the very beginning informed him of the Affair, just as he also initiated Jaurès and convinced him of Dreyfus's innocence. When the great battles began in 1898–1899, Péguy's bookshop in the Quartier Latin became the outpost of the Dreyfusite students, with Péguy himself as the ringleader, in the clashes with nationalist students. It seemed to him then that the Dreyfusite struggle was paving the way for the socialist revolution. While actively engaged in the struggle, he was also writing articles on the Affair, particularly in the *Revue Blanche.* In these articles, he took issue with the army and the church; he feared a sort of French Inquisition: "Will France remain true to her revolutionary past," he asked, "or will she suffer the same fate as Spain?" But already by the end of 1899 or the beginning of 1900, Péguy realized that the Dreyfusite socialists were carrying out a policy which ran counter to the principles they claimed to uphold in the Affair. This helped to bring about his break with Lucien Herr and his group and was the beginning of the slower, more difficult, break with Jean Léon Jaurès which, in the years before the war, led to a paroxysm of hatred in Péguy. He accused these socialists of wanting to control thought and word: "We sense the arrival of the truth of the State, although we have spent twenty months and more in distinguishing and making others distinguish the truth of the state from the truth."[3] Thus, already in 1900 while the Affair was still at whiteheat, Péguy was uneasy; his warnings increased. Ten years later, in *Notre Jeunesse,* he drew up the balance sheet.

For Péguy the Dreyfus Affair was a "predestined affair." It revealed very clearly the value, distinctive, specific, peculiar to an event. "That some events should be of a specific value, should have a specific value, an intrinsic value, is one of the most poignant problems of history. . . . That there should be predestined events. . . . This is the greatest problem of creation."[4] Péguy saw the Dreyfus affair as the event par excellence, the event which is unforeseeable, which neither historians nor sociologists could understand, because they try to find general laws of history, because they make general categories.

In what did the originality, the "predestination," of the Affair lie? It took place at the intersection of three crises: a crisis in Jewish history, a crisis in the history in France, and a crisis in the history of Christianity. It was the culmination of three mystiques—Jewish mystique, republican mystique, Christian mystique. The Dreyfus Affair threw Péguy into the heart of what was to become the central meditation of his life: what is a people, what is a city? And indissolubly linked to these two: what is Christianity?

Ten years' distance from the event had shown Péguy that the significance of the Affair did not lie in the struggle between the official Dreyfusites and the official anti-Dreyfusites. The real dividing line did not run between the political camps; it ran within each camp, between the mystical people and the political people. The opposition between the "mystics" and the "politics" became common currency in France; and in its present usage it expresses the opposition between purity of intentions and generosity of sentiments, on the one hand, and the compromises and maneuvers characteristic of political action in the actual world on the other. In Péguy's work, this opposition was an expression of the radical conflict between "the ancient world, all the ancient worlds" and the "modern world." The rapid degeneration of Dreyfusism was a striking example of the internal logic of the "modern world." The real, original Dreyfusites were "the last": "We were the last—almost the after-last. Immediately after us, another age began, a quite different world, the world of those who no longer believe in anything . . . the world which we will continue to call the modern world . . . the world of those devoid of mysticism. . . . The movement of the derepublicanization of France is at the bottom the same as the movement of its dechristianization."[5]

Later, we shall deal with the way in which Péguy described and interpreted the modern world. But here the central point of his historical vision should be noted. All the great oppositions which give history its momentum, the opposition between paganism and Christianity, between republicanism and monarchy, pale before the fundamental opposition between the modern world and all the others: "the modern world is not only opposed to the *ancien régime* in France, it is opposed, it runs counter to all the ancient cultures, to all the *anciens régimes,* to all the ancient cities, to everything which is culture, to all that is a city."[6]

Thus, Péguy overturned the accepted chronology of French history: "The significant date is not 1 January 1789 between midnight and one minute past. The significant date is situated around 1881."[7] Why 1881? This date marks the beginning of what he called the "primary domination" or, interchangeably, the "domination of the intellectual party." In France, this domination was the result of primary education and the picture it painted of the Revolution. Its method was to divide the history of France into a *before* and an *after.* What defined the central operation of the intellectual party was its specific representation of history which "pretends to ignore the fact that mankind has lasted a long time already"; which invents the convention of an *"ancien régime"* unrelated to reality; and which presents the Revolution as marking the transition from darkness into light. But this is not how things happened. There was of course a break between before and after, but it was a break between the modern world and all the ancient worlds. Here we should sketch the broad lines of Péguy's interpretation of the modern world.

The Critique of the Modern World

What gives its unity to Péguy's intellectual and spiritual history, what underlies his evolution from a very personal socialism to a problematic Catholicism, was his hostility to the modern world, which sometimes, if infrequently, he described as "democracy." Already in *Marcel, Premier dialogue de la cité harmonieuse,* the most "socialist" of Péguy's books, written in 1898, he had rejected the idea of equality, a "bourgeois" and false idea which held that the value of human labor could be calculated: "The division [in the *cité harmonieuse*] is not made according to what we in bourgeois society call the equality of the workers, an equality according to which the workers take equal shares among themselves, because all equality necessarily presupposes the calculation of values and we cannot calculate the value of human labor."[8] More important still, in *Marcel,* he affirmed the independence and the superiority of *nature* in relation to *society,* "the citizens of the harmonious city have not invented the personal beauty of souls and the form of souls; this personal beauty and this form is natural to each soul."[9] It was this very vivid perception of the independence and the preeminence of nature which, in the following years, was to govern the first expression of his opposition—at first purely ideological—to Jaurès. Jaurès had spoken of a "socialist conception" of art. Péguy retorted:

> It would be dangerous if we let it be believed that we have a socialist conception of art. The social revolution will bring about the liberation of art. It will give us a free art, but not a socialist art. . . . We demand that scholars and artists, as scholars and artists, should be in the city, should be independent from the city. We demand that science, art and philosophy be left unsocialized, just because the socialization of the major means of production and exchange, rather of the labour indispensable to guarantee the bodily life of the city, will have given to that city the leisure and the space not to have to socialize what does not appertain to it, but appertains to mankind itself.[10]

Contact with socialist intellectuals aroused Péguy's awareness of the difference between his socialism and theirs. Their politics and ideology, their political practice, and its accompanying theoretical discourse, seemed to him more and more clearly to constitute a *system,* a *metaphysics,* indeed a *materialist* metaphysics. But this metaphysics concealed itself; it appeared as the negation of all metaphysics, as the movement of reality itself. Materialism very early on aroused Péguy's irony: "For philosophers, materialism is one system of metaphysics among a great many systems of metaphysics. Let me describe it briefly by saying that it tends to reduce everything to matter, just as spiritualism tends to reduce everything to spirit. Many people would like everything to be reduced to matter. They do not know what it means, but it pleases them all the same."[11] More seriously he objected: "Unfortunately this reduction does not stand on its own. We have an even more confused and less usable idea of matter than we have of spirit." And he drew this conclusion: "Therefore not only is materialism a metaphysics for the philosopher but materialism . . . is the most untenable of all metaphysics, which at first presents the greatest difficulties and, if truth be told, the most insurmountable impossibilities. "[12]

But what struck him most was that this materialism, this atheism, lived only on what they rejected, that is, on the Christian or perhaps the ancient idea of the world: "Atheism presupposes a God who is denied or gods who are denied and the definition of what is denied."[13] Thus he gradually recognized what was to be for him the fundamental trait, the essence, of the modern world: its parasitical and parodoxical character.

While he was still strongly opposed to Christianity, Péguy saw rising before him a perverse parody of the religion he had rejected, a "religion of reason." His very significant remarks should be quoted at some length:

> Do not let us found, do not let us allow a religion of reason to be founded. . . . We have rejected a religion which commanded us to believe in a personal God, in three persons, . . . do not let us found a religion which would forbid us even to pronounce a name of which we can at least say that it has had some success in the history of mankind. A religion of reason would add all the worst aspects of the rational vices to all the religious vices. This would be a rare accumulation of ordinarily irreconcilable, habitually separated, logically contradictory, vices. Any catechism is unbearable. But a catechism of reason would contain in its pages the most frightening tyranny, at once a parody and a text.[14]

Some years later, when he had been reconciled to Catholicism, he was to be struck by the aspect of parody in the republican ceremonies at the Pantheon. On the funeral of Berthelot he wrote that "they are pursued in their imitation by the idea of the body and of the Real Presence."[15]

Another aspect of the socialist system which aroused his opposition was its vision of history. The socialist claim, expressed by Jaurès in particular, to sum up and crown the whole "history of the human spirit" seemed to him profoundly false and really dangerous: "History is not socialist. It is historical. Philosophy is not socialist. It is philosophical. And a genuine encyclopedia[16] should not be socialist. It is already impossible for it to be encyclopedic."[17] The idea of a "capitalization" of the gains of the human mind seemed to him to run counter to the very essence of intellectual activity:

> The whole economy of philosophical liberty is based above all on this foundation: that one person may be right against every one else and that there may be times when no one is right. . . . It pleases you to represent to yourselves and to us all the great hearts and minds, as bound to the achievement of a continuous advance of human thought, in which each individual would carry on from his predecessor and each predecessor find precisely the right successor. This textbook portrayal does not seem to bear any resemblance to the reality. It does not conform with the ideas

most of the great philosophers have held of themselves and of their philosophy.[18]

Péguy continued to develop the idea that what lay at the root of modern perception was a particular representation of history. To understand "the place given to history and to sociology in modern times" was the speculative undertaking of his life. On this point his reading of Ernest Renan and Hippolyte Taine was to prove decisive.

Taine, who was the exponent of the deterministic interpretation of history in France, wrote a book, *La Fontaine et ses fables,* which seemed to Péguy to be the basic text of modern historical methods. Taine's ambition to explain La Fontaine's genius by the most detailed analysis possible, by an exhaustive analysis—if this is possible—of the circumstances and conditions of artistic creation was for him the clearest expression of the modern representation of history. His train of thought should be carefully followed. When a modern historian has to explain a text, or, more generally, has something to explain—whether a text, an event, a person—his *first* impulse, his decisive impulse, is to *turn away* from his subject in order to make a complete inventory of the "conditions" and "circumstances" of the existence of this subject:

> the modern idea, the modern method comes down essentially to this: given a work or given a text, how do we proceed to know it? Let us start by ignoring the text; above all, let us be careful not to pick up the text or even to look at it, that would come at the end, if it were ever to happen. Let us begin at the beginning or rather because we must be complete, let us begin by the beginning of the beginning; the beginning of the beginning is to find in the vast, moving, universal, total reality, *the exact vantage-point which, though bearing some relation to the text, is the farthest removed from the text.*"[19]

Péguy's objection to this procedure was simple but decisive: this "method of infinite exhaustion" of historical detail presupposes that the historian is a god, an infinite god. For indeed the infinite series of secondary causes—assuming that they can explain what needs to be explained—can be conceived only by an infinite understanding.

Here the paradoxical situation of the modern historian is fully illuminated. At this point the comparison between modern civilization and the two great civilizations—the Greek and Christian—which preceded it becomes inevitable. Both were well aware of man's limitations as man. For the Greeks "it was recognized that man was limited by human limitations, and the historian remained a man." In Christianity, a superhuman place is in one sense given to man—to man created in the image and resemblance of God, and God made man; this is balanced by an acute sense of the misery arising from sin. Hence, in the Christian age the contradictions in the human condition formed the very substance of the dialogue which every individual conducts with himself and with God: "in these civilizations it was recognized that man was a creature and limited to human limits; the historian remained a man."[20]

But once modern man had rejected God without rediscovering the natural limits affirmed by the Greek, he had lost his proper place; since he no longer encounters anywhere any other than himself whom he can respect (nature or cosmos, gods or God), he is no longer able to achieve consciousness of himself:

> When man found himself in the presence of avowed gods, with human attributes, gods who were recognized and so to speak acknowledged gods, he could clearly remain a man; just because god was called god, man could call himself man. By a really novel twist of irony, it was precisely when man believed that he had emancipated himself, when he believed that he had thrown off all gods except himself, that he no longer kept his place as man. . . . Faced with nothing, faced with a zero God, the old pride did its work; the human spirit was unseated; the compass went mad; the modern historian became a god.[21]

Péguy was well aware that such a statement would be derided by modern historians and sociologists; was it not precisely modesty which, on the contrary, characterized the scientific spirit? But he thought that although historians, as individuals, could be modest, the "ancient pride" had taken refuge in the *method;* and because it was impersonal and hidden in the method, the pride of the historian was "enlarged, carried to the limit, to the infinite."[22]

Thus, what formed the horizon, the aim of modern historical method, was the idea or image of a humanity which at last possessed itself, was master of its whole history, of which it would exhaust the minute detail, "having encompassed all knowledge in the universe of its total memory."[23]

One last feature completed the picture; by claiming that *its causes* explained all the workings of genius (in this case the mind of La Fontaine), Taine claimed to know the secret of man and of nature. Having explained how genius is produced, he put man in the position and attributed to him the power to produce it at will. In a word "he plays the role of God, the Creator."[24]

Péguy was aware that since Taine and Renan no historians had revived, at least not explicitly, the vast ambitions of these two, that they had given up the pursuit of infinite exhaustive detail (for how could one produce any work without giving it up?). Nevertheless, deep down, this secret ambition of the historical method continued to govern the modern mind. Herein lies the poignant contradiction: the historical method incapacitates the historian's work, and the historian, in order to pursue his task, must forget the method.

The sway of history over the modern mind is not only expressed in the unbounded pride of the historical method; it is expressed even more in a characteristic feature of modern man, and not only of professional historians—namely the appeal to the judgment of history. What struck Péguy first was the derisory, "childish" character of that appeal. The judgment of history is by definition the judgment of posterity, of those who will come after: now those men "will have the same nature, the same limits, the same weakness, the same incompetence,"[25] as the generation which is appealing to their judgment. This is the "perfect vicious circle." Modern man refuses even to consider that posterity will be no more interested in him than he was interested in the generation which preceded him, that posterity will be sufficiently absorbed in its own problems and that perhaps it too in turn will appeal to posterity, to its own posterity. He imagines that all later generations, all the later generations, will focus their attention on him, he sees them occupied in considering him and judging him. He imagines that they are at his service. And because he sees them in this way, in untold numbers and indefinitely succeeding each other in order to judge him, they seem to him to be masters of a definitive judgment. Péguy certainly saw in this a parody of the last judgment: "Who does not recognize in this so-called definitive judgment, which hides itself and shies away, a tentative, a pitiful, a temporal, a temporary failure of the last judgment?"[26] But this is not what interested him most. What aroused his thoughts was that this seemed to present an "inversion" of the human condition, an inversion which was characteristic of modern man. This "inversion" was the center or target of all Péguy's thought. What he was trying to express cannot be easily summarized, but an attempt will be made to do so here.

The original error of the modern thought or attitude is in some way to have exchanged the respective places of theory and practice, of thought and action, because it no longer understands the radical distinction between the two realms. It is because this distinction was no longer understood, that without people being aware of it, thought was given the attributes of action and action those of thought. Take, for instance, Descartes, founder of modern philosophy, or more accurately of the attitude of modern man toward the world. In his argument "everything is conduct and the will to conduct. . . . And perhaps his greatest invention and novelty and his greatest stroke of genius and of force is to have conducted his thought deliberately as though it were an action."[27] This is why Péguy can write about the *Discours de la méthode:* "It is a programme, alas, and it is almost an electoral programme."[28] Symmetrically, the divinization of history which we have just briefly analyzed implies the absorption of the point of view of action in the theoretical point of view. Modern man contemplates the whole history of mankind as he would contemplate landscape: the essential difference—which forms the essence of mankind—between the past, the present, and the future, is dissolved in the proclamation of "general" laws. The actual time in which the action takes place is transformed into the past, or, more accurately, it is abolished in an intemporal present of the mind which promulgates these laws. Action—above all political action—is undertaken in the name of and according to an intellectual representation of history. It is freedom and the risk, inseparable from genuine human action, which are hunted down by modern intellectualism. As we shall see, Péguy found that this liberty and this risk had been faithfully preserved in Christianity.

Péguy's Christianity

The most natural way to approach Péguy's Christianity is undoubtedly to follow the chronology of his changing attitudes toward Blaise Pascal—whom he considered at one and the same time to be a Christian of outstanding quality and the consummate "thinker." Even before he became a Christian, while he was still very hostile to Christianity he devoted long passages to Pascal. He was very interested in Pascal's "malady"; one can say, I believe, that at that time (around 1900) it was Pascal's malady and his attitude toward this malady that attracted him. And for Péguy that malady was not essentially physiological, it was the "mal de penser," aggravated by the "mal de croire." At this point Christianity both attracted and repelled him. If Christianity was so profoundly conscious of the malady inseparable from humanity, it was because it was itself an expression of it. It is true that it seemed to "have an answer to everything," to integrate and to reconcile all the contradictions of life itself, but that was merely an illusion: "It is only a semblance of life, a distorted image, a strange combination of irrational infinity and of ailing life. I would go so far as to say that it is a fake, a deformation of life."[29] The theme and even the words in which this judgment is couched are the same as those of Friedrich Nietzsche, whom Péguy did not know.

What lay at the root of this general judgment, what caused Péguy's determined rejection of Christianity at that time, was the doctrine of damnation. He was, of course, very sensitive to the fact that in Christianity the peasant girl and Pascal, as Christians, shared the same sentiments; he was sensitive as a socialist, eager for human solidarity, to the Christian communion. But this communion was bound up with the exclusion of those who were cast out; this was the *non possumus:* "I will therefore attack the Christian faith. What seems to us its strangest aspect and, dare I say the word, what is most odious to us, what is barbarous, what we shall never accept is this: that strange combination of life and death which is called damnation."[30] We know that throughout his life Péguy was obsessed with damnation. This obsession was closely linked with a complementary obsession, with the city and communion. If, at that time, he preferred the socialist city to the Christian communion, it was because the socialist city, according to his idea of it, did not exclude, did not damn anyone. It is difficult to be sure whether Péguy, once he had returned to Catholicism, was ever reconciled to this dogma and ever accepted it.

It is just as difficult to know what movement of thought and feeling brought Péguy back to Catholicism, to declare himself publicly a Catholic. What we have said about his criticism of the modern world on the one hand, about his fascination with Pascal on the other, offers us nevertheless a guiding thread. Modern ideologies seemed to him to be unaware of and to be helping to destroy the conditions of human action, the distinctive characteristic of man, that is liberty. For the free act of necessity entails a wager: "one is constantly brought back to the various forms of *wager* the moment one tries to look more deeply into the problems of work and action and in general, at the problems of life."[31] But the Pascalian analysis of the act of faith seemed to him to be identical with the mechanism of the free act. Or, more generally, humanity as implied by Christianity is also that which is revealed in the precise observation of human nature. Summing up what used to be called *les moeurs divines,* he wrote "[m]an must choose in all freedom. There must therefore in the last analysis be a total risk; . . . one must always come back to this form of wager."[32] And he continues to follow Pascal in affirming vehemently that Christianity does not need proofs: "It is so that man could balance himself on the knife edge, could balance on the knife edge of liberty, that Christianity has never had, has never required proofs. If by ill-chance Christianity were to be *proved* . . . liberty would fall."[33] Pascal wrote: "It is in lacking proof that they [the Christians] show their good sense." Christianity seemed to Péguy to be a sort of infinitely prolonged echo of human liberty; and when Pascal had written: "Christianity has put the infinite everywhere," Péguy continued as follows addressing Christianity: "You have eternalized, infinitized everything. You have carried the scale of values to the infinite."[34] For the former, as for the latter, Christianity had extended the gravity of free action to the infinite. If we accept that the infinite gravity of free action presupposed and in one sense exacted a real risk of damnation, we must admit that Péguy, once he was reconciled to Catholicism, ended by accepting this dogma. Be that as it may, it is certain that for the mature Péguy as for Pascal, Christianity "knew man."

This reason for becoming a Christian might not perhaps have been enough were it not for the additional reason: Christianity is a communion—that is to say, a city. Péguy always declared that between the socialism of his youth and the Catholicism of his maturity there was no break, only a deepening from one to the other. The church seemed to him more and more to be the city par excellence, centered around the relation between grace and liberty, in which all human sentiments were carried to the infinite. To be a Christian, Péguy was never tired of repeating, was not to hold particular opinions or to have particular virtues; it was to be a citizen of a given city. Since he considered the church essentially from this angle, it was only natural that he should confront directly the theological-political problem of the relation between the church and the earthly city, between the spiritual and the temporal. The contradictions in Péguy's position when dealing with this thorny problem go a long way to explain the extravagance and the unfairness of some of his political judgments.

The Theological-Political Problem

First of all, and here Péguy separated himself explicitly from "a certain trend in Pascal," he refused to despise the world, nature. On the contrary, he admired Pierre Corneille, who, especially in *Polyeucte,* "never spurned the world in order to praise himself."[35] Condemning the world in order to elevate oneself was not only a particular tendency of Pascal, it was the typical and immemorial error of the "devout party," the clerical party. One of the major reasons, it seemed to Péguy, for the dechristianization of the world lay in the refusal of the clergy to respect and to take seriously the profane world, the specifically human world. This was not a simple political error, a false political approach, but a religious fault, a sin against the creation, so to speak.[36] Every fully achieved human action, in particular every initiative (whether it be a state, an economic enterprise, or simply a family) prolongs the divine creation in a human way: "It is in one sense and literally man himself who participates in the creation not only from the passive aspect, but from the . . . active aspect."[37]

The pivot, both evident and mysterious, on which human history turns is the articulation of the temporal and the spiritual, of the city of men and the city of God, the fact that the spiritual "needs" temporality, that grace "needs" nature and liberty. According to a formula which Péguy continually changes and expands in a thousand forms: "The eternal is in the dwelling place of the temporal." From this sprang his meditations, so penetrating and so beautiful both in his prose works and in his poetry, on the foundations of Christianity; on that conspiracy of pagan culture (Greece and Rome) with the Jewish revelation to prepare the "cradle" of Christianity. "It is assuredly one of the greatest mysteries in the world, and perhaps the greatest—this disquieting, this mysterious place left to the temporal in the total mechanism and thus in the government, in the destiny of the spiritual."[38]

This is where Péguy's thought runs the risk of losing its thread. Of course, he knew that the spiritual was not the temporal; but his desire to reestablish the dignity of the temporal against the devout party and also against the modern ideologies which depreciated that dignity in another way and for different reasons, his tendency to see the paradoxical proximity and affinity between the operations of grace and those of nature, led him to look for the fulfillment of his desire and of his vision in a community which would reunite within itself pagan holiness and the Christian holiness, the city of nature and the city of grace. This community sometimes took the form of what he called "Christendom," sometimes of what he called "France." Even if he maintained explicitly the difference between the two notions, there is no doubt that he visualized Christendom (or France) as a body at once civic and mystic in which the Christian virtues tended to become confused with the natural virtues of the "race"; in his worst moments Péguy used the idea of race (the "French" race) to encompass and subsume what he ordinarily differentiated: nature and grace. This explains some absurd sentences in which he suggested that a "French" saint and a "French" sinner would form a community from which a "German" saint would by his essence be excluded. Péguy did not go so far as to say that a German saint was an impossibility, a contradiction in terms, but it must be said that he came close to it. People of good judgment, be they agnostic, atheist, or Christian, are repelled by this sort of extravagance and for the same reasons: all reject the confusion between the temporal and the spiritual, between politics and religion, a confusion which might give birth to the worst political storms. They are right. However, the rejection of Péguy's excesses should not lead one to misunderstand a fundamental aspect of the theological-political problem, or even of the political problem, which Péguy perceived so accurately and with deadly intensity: there is a specific sacredness of the political order as such, of the civic community. The great pagan achievements, the Greek city-states and Rome, are witness to this. Modern man tends to misunderstand this reality because he is the heir and the product of two great influences which seem to be contradictory but which on this issue come together: man is the heir of Christianity, which has tended to transfer all the sacredness from the terrestrial city to the divine city, to the Church, and he is the heir and the product of the laicization or the secularization of Christianity which has tended to abolish the sacred as such, with the result that modern man wants to consider politics only as the prosaic organization of interests and the pacific coexistence of opinions. This situation lasted until the moment when man's nature, weary of being deprived of civic sacredness, rebelled and abandoned itself to the perverse sacredness of modern totalitarianisms.

Some works seem to belong more particularly to the nation which gave birth to them. The foreigner who approaches them sees them more often as a curious monument than as the exponents of thoughts of interest to the whole of humanity. Nevertheless, when these writings are profound, the national specificity is but one means of access to the universal. The fiercely French character of Charles Péguy's personality and of his writings should not conceal from us the fact that his thought is important for all who are concerned with the destinies of Europe.

Notes

1. From the name of Émile Combes who, as president of the Council of Ministers in 1902–1905, put through an aggressively anticlerical policy (closure of church schools, organized campaign against Catholics).

2. For long librarian of the École Normale Supérieure, Herr converted generations of its pupils to socialism. He also exerted considerable although secret political influence, especially through his hold over Jaurès.

3. All references are taken from the prose works of Péguy, Paris: Gallimard, Collection *La Pléiade,* in two volumes, called here I and II.

4. II, 536.

5. II, 508.

6. II, 509.

7. II, 520.

8. II, 520.

9. II, 37.
10. II, 37.
11. II, 313.
12. II, 314.
13. II, 315.
14. II, 417–18.
15. II, 1160.
16. The idea of a "new encyclopedia," which would be "socialist," was very much in the air at the time.
17. II, 324.
18. II, 325.
19. II, 680. (Present author's italics.)
20. II, 683.
21. II, 683–84.
22. II, 686.
23. II, 700.
24. II, 729.
25. II, 211.
26. II, 218.
27. II, 1536.
28. II, 1327.
29. I, 191.
30. I, 192.
31. I, 775.
32. II, 418.
33. II, 482.
34. II, 487.
35. II, 1445.
36. II, 357–58.
37. II, 346.
38. II, 1220.

Christianity and Democracy: Some Remarks on the Political History of Religion, or, on the Religious History of Modern Politics

Pierre Manent

1993

Whoever compares the relations that obtain today between democracy and Christianity, particularly the Catholic Church, with what they were during the greater part of their common history, has the feeling that each one of the two protagonists has ceased to resemble itself, that it has become wholly other than it was. Democracy consents to the presence in its bosom of a numerous mass of believers. With the exception of a very small number of "rationalists" without an audience, it no longer plans "to destroy the infamous thing" (i.e., Christianity); and the famous proclamation of René Viviani today sounds like an amusing curiosity from the Belle Epoque: "Together, and with a magnificent gesture, we have extinguished in heaven stars which will never again be relit."

The change accomplished, or suffered, by the Catholic Church, however, is even more striking. The Cardinal Archbishop of Paris, and the Holy Father himself, ask Christians to discover in their religion the true, although long-hidden source, of the most precious good that is at the heart of modern democracy: the rights of man. The Catholic Church today celebrates the sacred character of religious liberty, of the liberty of conscience that it formerly denounced with thunderous indignation. In the encyclical *Mirari vos* (15 August 1832) directed against Lamennais, Gregory XVI speaks of this

The article originally appeared in the 1993 collection *L'individu, le citoyen, le croyant* (Publication des Facultés universitaires Saint-Louis) and in English in *Crisis* in two parts (January 1995 and February 1995). It is republished with permission.

97

very fecund cause of the evils that today so deplorably afflict the Church,
to wit indifferentism, the vicious opinion which, by the perversity of the
wicked, gains credit everywhere and according to which the salvation of
the soul can be obtained by whatsoever profession of faith, provided that
morals conform to the rule of the just and the honorable . . . and from
this poisoned source of indifferentism has come the false and absurd
opinion, or rather delirium, according to which the liberty of conscience
of each ought to be affirmed and defended.

As late as the beginning of this century, Saint Pius X, in the encyclical
Vehementer nos (11 February 1906) addressed to the people and clergy
of France, condemned the separation of the church and state as a "supreme injustice" done to God, and also as contrary to natural right and
to the law of nations, contrary to the fidelity due to oaths, contrary finally to the divine constitution and the liberty of the church.

What happened? How are we to understand so complete a change of
appreciation on the part of the supreme heads of an institution that loves
to underscore the centuries-old, even millenary, immutability of its
thoughts and words? Must one follow the historians who, in order to
explain past conflicts, are prone to invoke an enormous "misunderstanding," bound to "historical circumstances," follow them into the still
doubtful combat in which the parties are drawn irresistibly beyond the
natural and reasonable limits of their opinions? Before concluding in
such an irenic manner, one at least must determine the intellectual content of the debate, that is, the motives advanced by the church when it
condemned the principal propositions of modern politics. If the church
initially, and for so long, declared itself against democracy, it is because
it had the sentiment, or rather the conviction, that the modern democratic movement was directed fundamentally against itself, that is, against
the true religion and thus against the true God. It is impossible even to
enter into the great subject of the relations between democracy and the
church if we do not first clarify this central fact.

The Modern Movement, or the
Emancipation of the Will

The movement of the Enlightenment, the vector of modern politics, had
for its goal, and result, the establishment of the lay, liberal state, "without opinion,"—particularly without religious opinion—of what was called
"the neutral and agnostic state." The dominant Catholic opinion was that
this agnosticism of the state was in fact state agnosticism and that this
state agnosticism was in fact a state atheism. In this judgment the Roman magisterium itself joined the Catholic writers of the so-called "re-

actionary" school such as Joseph de Maistre and Louis de Bonald who were so influential at the beginning of the nineteenth century.

What is true in the Catholic affirmation that the liberal state is not neutral, or "agnostic," but rather atheist? It is the fact that the liberal state, in its first project, or primary purpose, wants to institutionalize the sovereignty of the human will. Recognizing only free and equal individuals, it has no legitimacy except that founded on their will: the institutions of this state have for their raison d'être the manifesting of this will through suffrage, then the putting of this will into action by a representative government.

Such a project certainly does not affirm, with "the foolish" of Scripture, that "there is no God." Not only does it say nothing about God, but it says nothing, or very little, about the world and even about man. However, by positing that the political body has for its only rule or law the will of the individuals who compose it, it deprives the law of God of all political authority or validity, whether the latter is conceived as explicitly revealed or solely inscribed in the nature of man. It refuses all authority to that which has by definition, naturally or supernaturally, the highest authority. The man of the Enlightenment implies, or presupposes, that there is no God or that He is unconcerned with men, since he rejects, or at most considers as "private," as optional, obedience to the law of God.

One might add, if there is a God, the human will cannot be "autonomous," or "sovereign"; to affirm this "autonomy" or "sovereignty" is to deny the existence of God.

Certainly, the atheism of presupposition or of implication is not exactly the atheism of affirmation, or atheism simply. Few men truly know what they think and what they want, and many will be liable to affirm simultaneously the divine law and human sovereignty; as was often said at the time of the Second Vatican Council, many will believe "in God and in man." But one does not judge a political and spiritual situation according to the idea of it that the least enlightened members of the community make for themselves. Moreover, the intention, and to speak truly, the antireligious passion, of the great men who in the seventeenth and eighteenth centuries elaborated these new doctrines, was clearly enough avowed. The church therefore judged in its wisdom, let us say from 1791 to 1907, from the Brief *Quod aliquantum* condemning the Civil Constitution of the Clergy to the encyclical *Pascendi* reproving modernism, that the modern political and intellectual movement *willed* the eradication of the true religion.

Keeping in view the motives behind the original conflict, we foresee also the motives behind the later reconciliation. After all, this insurrection, this revolt of the human will—to continue to speak the language of the church of the nineteenth century—by the effect of its progress and its triumph, is going to transform itself into institutions, habits, sentiments—into "human things" where human nature and the divine law necessarily will find, in some form, their place. After all, if God exists, the human nature created by Him, that even without the support of the secular arm retains awareness of the exigencies of His law, will inhabit and humanize, that is, Christianize, the state created by the sovereign or human will in its revolt. Whatever the successes of the "Revolution," the moment of some "restoration" always comes. Even if we admit that the modern will essentially revolted against God, God is necessarily stronger than it, and this means that the nature of man is stronger than the human will. Hence, at the end of some generations, the satanic pride of the Enlightenment, duly humbled by reality, gives way to the firm resolution to organize a rational society full of solicitude for human needs and where the church can live, speak, and exercise its influence: our society. The church, which has concern for men, cannot curse such a society.

Things did happen in this manner to a certain extent, but only to a certain extent. The will of the Enlightenment, humiliated by democratic reality, by bourgeois prose, revolted against the bourgeois democratic society that it took to be a humiliation. The revolutionary spirit, the spirit of sovereignty, revolted in the form of socialism and communism against its first incarnation. The church, to be sure, explicitly condemned these revolts, at least in the case of communism. They acted on it, however, in two contrary senses. These demonic revolts encouraged it to reconcile itself with the very democracy that the revolutionaries wanted once again to overturn, and with which it henceforth shared responsibility for the things that are. But they also confirmed its hostility to modern democracy, which appeared to engender endlessly ever more radical revolts against the church. It is in this way, precisely as a fatal sequence, that the encyclical *Quanta cura* (8 December 1864) condemned as a single ideological and political series: naturalism (we would say: liberalism), socialism, communism.

The historical landscape would be clear if we did not have to take account of a third possibility. Certain quarters of Catholic opinion agreed with socialism and communism in their hostility to democracy, which as Catholics they had learned to detest. And while some reconciled with democracy in order to confront the communist threat, others were favorable to communism out of hatred for democracy. This last reaction was particularly observable during the twenty years that followed the Second Vatican Council, which, moreover, quite curiously did not renew the condemnation of communism. In this manner were realized all the possible theological-political dispositions or arrangements subsequent to the French Revolution.

Perhaps one will grant such a summary presentation a certain plausibility. But, it will be said, it is too dependent not only on the point of view of the church but also, less excusably, on the most immoderate of Catholic rhetoric. What is this "demonic" will to institutionalize the sovereignty of the human will, to substitute the latter for the law of God or for the finalities, aptitudes, and necessities of the nature of man? Is not this a way of speaking that is perhaps acceptable in the heat of a bitter conflict of vast import, but incapable of establishing an historical explanation? I believe, on the contrary, that we have here the guiding thread of the correct explanation; if not that, we have at least an exact description.

Three massive facts must here be taken into consideration. First, the history of modern philosophy, from Machiavelli to Nietzsche, appears as oriented to and animated by the elaboration of the concept of will. Next, the intellectual center of modern democracy is constituted by the notion of the rational will, elaborated, at the center of this history, by Rousseau, Kant, and Hegel. Finally, the first and decisive affirmations of the will, of man as will, were conceived and formulated in an explicitly polemical relation with the ecclesiastical institution and the Catholic understanding of the world—to which one can add, as culmination and superfluous proof, that Nietzsche at the end of this spiritual history, joined the unlimited affirmation of the human will to the unlimited polemic against Christianity. It is difficult to find in human history a closer representative linkage.

Let us look first at the third point. The modern project to establish political legitimacy on the will of the human individual has been led to its completion. It has been transformed into the institutions, mores, and sentiments of our democracy. This reality satisfies us, and we no longer perceive the extraordinary audacity of the original project of establishing the human world on the narrow point of the human will. A fact, however, must help us experience the astonishment indispensable for understanding. This invention was neither necessary nor even probable. The *proof* is that one can describe very well the human world, particularly political existence, that one can conceive and institutionalize very well political liberty, without having recourse at all to the notion of the free individual endowed with a sovereign will.

Aristotle's *Politics* gives a description and analysis of political life that in a certain way is exhaustive—in any case more complete and subtle than any subsequent description or analysis. The bringing to light of the elements of the city, the critical and impartial analysis of the claims of the different parties, the exploration of the problem of justice, of the relations between liberty, nature, and law: the phenomenology of political life is presented without either prejudice or lacuna. Whoever wants to orient himself in the political world, for the sake of either action or understanding, finds in Aristotle's *Politics* a complete teaching. It is therefore the case that only a historical *accident* could have obliged us to dismiss Aristotle and given us a reason to invent the notion of the sovereign will.

According to Aristotle, every human association has for its end a certain good; and every human action is done in view of a certain good. Therefore, when Aristotle studies the elements that constitute the city, he only encounters groups and "goods," each group defining itself by the type of good it seeks and can attain, and on which it ordinarily bases its claims for power. At no time does the individual with his will appear: Aristotle does not even have a word to name him (more exactly, the sovereign individual will). The landscape is reversed with the founders of modern politics. Henceforth only one element enters into the composition of the legitimate city, the one for which Aristotle did not even have a word, the sovereign individual. Next to the *Politics,* the book of the ancient city, let us put the *Social Contract,* the book of modern democracy. Not only does Rousseau say very different things from those that Aristotle says, not only does he contradict him frequently, but quite strikingly the tone, the movement, the very principle of the thought are wholly different: something has happened that places thought under an unprecedented law of attraction, or repulsion.

The Aristotelian analysis of human action and association had been received and formally ratified by the Catholic Church. In the eyes of the latter, however, a new community has appeared, among those of which the human world is constituted: the church itself—*vera perfectaque respublica,* or *societas,* the perfect republic, or society, because its object, its raison d'être, its end, even its Author, is the perfect Being, the Sovereign Good, God Himself. Henceforth a supernatural community, the church, was added to the natural communities. Its dignity necessarily was incomparably superior to theirs, as eternal salvation and eternity are incomparably more important than temporal well-being and time. Assuredly, this posed some problems.

Aristotle had envisaged the case of a man, or a group, whose virtue was incomparably superior to that of the rest of the political body. He concluded that one must either give him total power or ostracize him. And medieval Europe, in its relation to the church, oscillated between these two positions. In accord with the first line of reasoning, the "plenitude of power"—not only spiritual but also temporal—was granted to the church, and it claimed it for itself. In accord with the second, the church was excluded completely from temporal power. The human world was constituted as though it was closed upon itself and self-sufficient, under the sole power of the emperor. This is what Dante and Marsilius of Padua wanted. In this way Aristotle was of no help in resolving the new theological-political problem: certainly it cannot be said that one is in a position to resolve a problem when the principle of the solution can engender two strictly contradictory solutions with equal plausibility or legitimacy; when the premises, that is, imply two contradictory conclusions. An accident that Aristotle had not foreseen, and could not have foreseen, obliged Western man to renounce Aristotle's philosophy.

To have a chance of finding a solution, it was necessary to make oneself independent both of nature and of the accident that is not natural—what Marsilius of Padua calls "this cause [that] neither Aristotle nor any other philosopher of his time or before him could have observed," this "miraculous effect produced a long time after Aristotle's time by the Supreme Cause beyond the possibilities of inferior nature and of the habitual action of the causes found in things." It was necessary to sever oneself from the complexity of groups and goods, both natural and supernatural, to decompose human sociability, both natural and supernatural, and then finally to reconstruct the political body from the element that survives at the end of this effort of abstraction: the free individual. The new political body, neither natural like the city nor supernatural like the church, is created by human will in order to effect what it wants.

The movement of modernity is structured by the stages of the will's emancipation. However, even as philosophy properly speaking pursued the radicalization of this notion, one can see throughout the nineteenth century in the order of action and of political theory, beginning from a certain date, a contrary movement, or a countermovement. The French Revolution is the moment when the movement of Enlightenment (we can also say "liberalism") experienced fright at the results of its action. It became fearful especially before the notion of the sovereignty, or the will, of the people. The latter had become a terrible reality as a result of the action of the French Revolutionary Convention. According to the quite striking formulation of Benjamin Constant: "There are weights too heavy for the hands of men." While as a consequence of the aggressively antireligious action of the Revolution the Catholic Church in the nineteenth century was going to clarify and harden its opposition to the political movement of modernity; a part of that movement, the part properly liberal, was willing to join with, if not always the church, at least

Christianity, or with "religion" in general. It is at the moment of, and as the result of, the French Revolution—and with reference to the problem of the will—that the partisan arrangements with which we have lived so long were determined.

On the right, the conservatives, or reactionaries, reacting expressly to the Revolution, reject the will; they see in the exercise of it and in the affirmation of its free exercise the source of all disorder. Man is only worthy in his position as heir or inheritor. It is by inheritance, or in the attitude of the heir, that man receives the most precious goods of which he is capable. Such is Edmund Burke's conviction, determined from the first moment of the revolutionary tempest. With some, reaction goes so far that they are led to maintain two extreme and perfectly contradictory positions, precisely on the problem of the will. Joseph de Maistre affirms on the one hand that nothing of what man expressly has willed can be good, that good can only come to him from what he has not willed. Simultaneously, he posits the necessary existence of a sovereign will to hold together society—and, one can assume, to repress the efforts of revolutionary wills—in short, a sovereign will that has the task of repressing the rebellious human will. On the left, on the side of the revolutionaries, later the socialists and the communists, they continued to affirm the human will. They even promised themselves "next time" not to let it be captured by "Thermidor."

It is in the center that the intellectual situation is the most complex and interesting: as I just noted, the liberals are caught between their doctrinal heritage and their new fear in the face of the revolutionary event, which their doctrines had perhaps caused or in any case had accompanied and facilitated. It is then that religion finds again, or rather finds, since it had never before truly appeared in this light, its specifically modern political and moral credibility. What had been its defect becomes its merit. It is now praised for the very reason it was formerly and even recently criticized: it is something *above* the human will. Evoking the Convention's attack on the church, Constant writes, with gratitude and approval: "The smallest saint, in the most obscure hamlet, resisted successfully against the entire national authority drawn in battle against him." Quite a remarkable affirmation on the part of this anticleric who, by birth, education, and conviction belongs to the eighteenth century, and whose Huguenot ancestors—like the soldiers of the revolutionary army in 1793—used hammers to flatten saints' images on the facade of churches, even those found "in the most obscure hamlet." However, it is to Alexis de Tocqueville that we must turn for the most precise analysis of the difficulties and contradictions of the new political and religious situation.

Democracy and Religion According to Tocqueville

Tocqueville, like most liberals of the nineteenth century, has the feeling that there was something artificial and violent, artificially violent, if it can be put that way, in the hostility that the eighteenth century exhibited toward Christianity and the church. It is necessary to return to a more "natural" situation: "It is by a kind of intellectual aberration, and assisted by a sort of moral violence exercised on their own nature, that men distance themselves from religious beliefs: an invincible penchant leads them back to them. Unbelief is an accident: faith alone is the permanent state of mankind." Tocqueville does not concern himself to justify such considerable propositions, but their political import is clear. If religion has its anchor or support in nature, it can do without the support of political institutions. Therefore, the dismantlement of the old regime, and even the separation of church and state, contrary to what most French Catholics think, are not at all contrary to the interests of religion. Better yet—and here we have one of the principal assertions of his argument and of post–revolutionary liberalism in general—it is by being separated from the political order that religion can best exert its political beneficence: "Religion which, among the Americans, never mixes itself directly in the government of society, must therefore be considered as the first of their political institutions; for, if it does not give them the taste for liberty, it singularly facilitates for them its use."

How does religion so singularly facilitate the use of liberty? The answer lies with the relationship that religion has with the will.

Modern democracy—this theme is the guiding line of my exposition—is founded on the emancipation of the will. This emancipation, leading to the idea of a total liberty of man to decide his destiny, has two opposite but equally disastrous consequences. The first is fear before this unlimited liberty. Under the empire of this fear, the modern individual is tempted to renounce this liberty, this sovereignty of the will that modern democracy proposes to him, and presents to him as legitimate and even as sacred. "There are weights too heavy for the hands of men." Not only does he recoil before this new liberty, but he even risks abandoning his former liberties:

> When there no longer exists any authority in religious matters, as well as political affairs, men soon are quite frightened at the sight of this independence without any limits. The perpetual agitation of all things renders them anxious and exhausts them. Since everything is in motion in the intellectual order, they desire that at least in the material order everything should be firm and stable. And, no longer able to accept their former beliefs, they give themselves a master.

Paradoxically, the emancipation of the will in this way can move men to consent more easily to despotism, because of the intellectual and moral uncertainty in which they are obliged to live.

But it has another consequence that is basically its opposite and that is perhaps more natural. Instead of giving rise to fear, it can give men the desire to exercise this will in all its new amplitude. Democratic man spontaneously has the feeling that the human will, in the form of the will of the people, has the right to will everything and anything; it willingly approves that "impious maxim" that "in the interest of society all is permitted." Thus, modern democracy gives rise to a new passivity and a new activism. These two contrary consequences of the new liberty together and equally foment a new despotism.

Now religion, by determining and fixing the moral order, by putting order in the soul, renders less pressing the democratic desire for "material" order, all the while, to be sure, rejecting the impiety that "all is permitted." "At the same time that the law allows the American people to do everything, religion stops it from conceiving of everything and forbids it from trying to do everything." Simultaneously tempering the new activism and the new passivity, religion helps democratic man to keep his balance. The coin, however, has another side.

In the United States, religion is separated from the state, from the political order; but it has a power of influence and opinion in society. It exhibits, therefore, the disadvantages inseparable from all power of opinion, in particular that of hampering liberty. Tocqueville goes so far as to write, "The Inquisition never was able to inhibit the circulation in Spain, in large number, of books contrary to religion. The rule of the majority does even better in the United States: it has taken away even the thought of publishing such books." Even in the United States religion does not escape from the fatality of power: it no longer has political power, no longer is a state religion, but it has become a "social" power, a "social religion," if one may put it that way. And it appears from Tocqueville's acknowledgment that "liberty" has not gained in the process.

We find ourselves, then, before a strange contradiction. Tocqueville seems to be suggesting that religion in the United States singularly facilitates the use of liberty by singularly diminishing the quantity of liberty. This, in fact, is his thought, but we must immediately state it more exactly: Religion in the United States singularly facilitates the use of political liberty by singularly diminishing the extent of intellectual liberty. So put, there is no contradiction. We understand easily, in fact, that the dangers of political liberty are decisively limited when—contrary to what happens, alas, in Europe—citizens do not entertain "revolutionary ideas" concerning man and the world but rather are content with ideas transmitted by the religious tradition for the essentials of their moral life.

In truth, however, this social power of religion is more a social power than a religious power. The shocking comparison with the Spain of the Inquisition runs the risk of leading us into an error: there is no question here of religious fanaticism. Americans themselves basically share Tocqueville's analysis; the latter only reproduces for us the awareness that Americans have of themselves. Religion is a part of their social habits: it is in this light that they are attached to it. It is a matter then of conformism and not fanaticism. Tocqueville writes:

> It is also in this light [that of utility] that the inhabitants of the United States themselves consider religious beliefs. I do not know if all Americans believe their religion, for who can fathom the depths of hearts? But I am sure that they consider it necessary for the maintenance of republican institutions. This opinion is held, not by a class of citizens or a party, but by the entire nation; it is found among all ranks.

To be sure, we are left with a great difficulty. How can religion be truly useful if it is viewed by the faithful from the point of view of utility? Certainly the utilitarian conception of religion is as old as politics, but it assumes at Rome, according to Machiavelli, for example, the class difference between an unbelieving patriciate and believing, even superstitious, plebs. But is it possible for this difference to pass into the interior of the soul of each citizen, so that each American should be simultaneously the unbelieving patrician and the sincere plebeian? This is what Tocqueville assumes. This, obviously, is inconceivable, unless the American citizen allows what he truly believes and what he truly thinks to fall into a propitious penumbra. Such a social and religious situation presupposes as one of its necessary conditions a general absence of intellectual rigor.

Tocqueville, we recall, claimed that religious belief is inscribed in the nature of man, that therefore it did not need the support of the state, and that contrary to what French Catholics and even the church itself thought, a separation of church and state is both desirable and possible. But what happens to this fundamental assertion if it appears that men thought to believe "naturally" in fact believe "socially"? The religion of Americans is founded in principle on the rigorous—because natural—separation of faith and politics; however, it appears, in fact, as the most political of religions. The separation of religion and the state produces a confusion of religion and society. If political liberty benefits as a result, religion loses in sincerity, and intellectual life loses in clarity and honesty. One sees that the very reasons Tocqueville advances to justify and promote the *rapprochement* between the old religion and modern democracy also provide motives for the refusal, so long maintained, by the Roman Catholic Church to lend itself to this reconciliation.

The most important lesson we can and must draw from this examination of the Tocquevillian analysis is to bid farewell definitively to the opinion, advanced and refuted by Tocqueville, that there is a "natural," hence apolitical, state of religion. Now we are in a position to envisage the political history of Christianity in an impartial fashion, as a succession of theological-political arrangements, of solutions to the theological-political problem, no one of which can claim to close that history, on the ground that it would be, finally, "conformed to the nature of things" or "conformed to reason." The solutions are linked not because history is increasingly more rational but because each solution always ends by revealing itself to be as unsatisfactory as the one that it succeeded. I would like to try to sketch the history of these solutions.

A Brief Political History of Religion

Let us begin by considering the first theological-political solution, the medieval one. The church is the true republic, the perfect society, the association par excellence in which man finds his ultimate end. All other associations have, so to speak, an ontologically inferior rank. They are therefore logically and "naturally" subordinated to the perfect association which in the person of its head holds the plenitude of authority or power *(plenitudo potestatis)*. This plenitude of power can be conceived as being direct or indirect in character. The direct plenitude is hardly practicable, and, moreover, it is contrary to the divine commandment that enjoins the disciples of Christ to leave to Caesar the things that are Caesar's. Creation in itself is good, human nature is capable of tolerably organizing the earthly city by the means of reason alone, as the pagan politics and philosophy of Greece and Rome evidence. One can envisage seriously only an indirect authority that leaves a subordinate but very large place for autonomous politics for the empire. From this, however, is unleashed a permanent division and uncertainty since two loyalties necessarily share the heart of each Christian. Moreover, one of the two great protagonists, the empire, does not succeed in fulfilling its idea with even a minimum of plausibility. Another solution must be found.

The second solution is that of the absolute national monarchy. Each king wants to be, and acts as if he were, "emperor in his kingdom." A plurality of perfect republics emerge, the national monarchies, whose members, first of all their heads, have religious opinions: they are either Catholic or Protestant. The perfect Christian republic, the seamless cloth, which, to be sure, never had existed as such but whose notion had had such a power over the minds of men, henceforth was dismembered. Earlier, one had in an inchoate way Christendom; in its place now there are Christian state religions.

The new historical compromise is the following: religion remains a command, but this command is essentially administered by the temporal sovereign: *cujus regio eius religio.* That which motivates the adoption of this system, however, is also what renders it intrinsically untenable, because contradictory. A lay or profane human will declares ex officio and obliges his subjects to recognize that the state religion is superior to every human will. In the case of absolutism the prince simultaneously is superior and inferior to the church that he enthrones. This introduces certain uncomfortable paradoxes such as was already the case with Queen Elizabeth I of England who, although head of the Anglican Church, is doubly incapable—both as a layperson and female—of distributing the sacraments (i.e., of performing the acts that constitute the life of the church). This specific form of the difficulty, or contradiction, characterizes in each case the national history.

The national monarchy was intended to overcome the medieval duality of the priesthood and the emperor, "to reunite the two heads of the eagle," to bring it about that Christian subjects ceased "to see double." On the contrary, the identity of the body politic was disturbed at the same time as the identity of the theological-political head, the prince, was ever more divided: ever more absolute, and thus "more superior" to the church, but in order to be more Christian. This escalation obviously could not continue indefinitely.

The most interesting case in this context is undoubtedly Louis XIV; the revocation of the Edict of Nantes simultaneously reveals the sublimity and the precariousness of his position. Certainly the monarch's faith was its first cause, but the revocation was more a monarchical than a Catholic act. The monarch who is now proclaimed as the new Constantine or Theodosus has been for some years close to schism with the papacy. In addition, Innocent XI will let it be known that the Revocation pleases him little. This episode contributed to the contrary movement of the English Glorious Revolution; it rendered complete and definitive the opposition of enlightened European opinion to the system of absolutism. The sovereign of the age of absolutism proved his sovereignty by giving religious commands. By more and more subordinating religion to himself, he increasingly weakened the rationale and vigor of his sovereignty. Another solution then must be sought.

One can distinguish three ways of leaving absolutism. The English solution is entirely unique. It is a simultaneously caricatural and weakened absolutism, which doubtlessly is why it is called "liberal." At the time of the Glorious Revolution and the subsequent Act of Settlement, the English aristocracy imposed on the king and the people a state religion, or rather, perhaps, a national religion. This religion guaranteed that England would not return to Catholicism and that it also would not espouse too ardent a version of Protestantism. The force of the state was put behind the weakest religion. I say the weakest religion because, of all the versions of Christianity that divided and still divide Europe, the only one that strictly speaking is "unbelievable" is Anglicanism, unless one admits—according to the epigram of Joseph de Maistre—that God became man for the English exclusively. Clearly this version left dissatisfied what remained of the Catholics, as well as the fervent Protestants. The latter readily had recourse to the American solution.

The English Protestants, dissatisfied with the state religion since the beginning of the 1620s, had acquired the habit of emigrating far from the Old World and of founding in the New World self-governing communities that were homogenous in matters of religion, the townships of Puritan New England. Puritanism is characterized by a certain confusion of religion and politics. Tocqueville observes, "Puritanism was not only a religious doctrine; it merged on several points with the most complete democratic and republican theories." While absolutism tended, without being able to succeed, toward the exclusive affirmation of political command, while religious commands became the material, the occasion, or the pretext, Puritanism, fleeing absolutism, recognized as legitimate only religious commands. In Protestantism, however, the entire community was alone empowered to make these commands observed. This arrangement is remarkably ambiguous. If, in American Puritanism, religion regulates all the details of social and even personal life, it does so in a special way. This religious power or authority is exercised "democratically" by all the members of the body on each one, and by each one on all. Thus, one can describe this power, not as that of religion over society but as that which society exercises over itself by means of religion. This equivocation and indetermination contains the subsequent history of America.

Each day there are occasions when society governs itself, when democracy is at work for reasons other than the putting into practice of religious commands. Americans progressively experience that their. society is securing its hold on itself, that it acts on and by itself. It remains sincerely religious, but religious commands, which at the beginning constituted the entirety of life, occupy a more and more restrained place. No one wants to abandon them, and they still are held to be respectable and useful. But the center of gravity of social life is henceforth elsewhere: democracy, understood as the working of society upon itself, becomes self-sufficient. At this point, religion can be completely separated from politics—the situation observed and appreciated by Tocqueville and on which I commented earlier.

Now, what happens in continental Europe during this same period? Absolutism, because of the contradiction I underlined, exasperates and hampers the search for an absolute sovereignty of the political order over the religious. It was this search that gave to the movement of continental Enlightenment its political wedge. After the expulsion of the Jesuits—which was heavy with political significance—this movement will culminate in the Civil Constitution of the Clergy. With the latter, a theological-political cycle is closed. The nation is born; it takes upon itself the attributes of the church; thus it is the *vera perfectaque respublica* found at last. To be sure, the nation-form did not put an end to political-religious conflicts. On the contrary, it stirred up new ones, the first, and greatest, as a result of the Civil Constitution of the Clergy. Let us think also of Kulturkampf in Bismarckian Germany, of Combism and the expulsion of the religious congregations from France. But beyond its properly political power the nation exercises such a spiritual power that it succeeds in being—much more so than the national monarchies—both empire and church. It is the nation, even when anticlerical, that more than the Most Christian King "reunites the two heads of the eagle."

In August 1914, French Catholics, including Jesuits, rushed forward to die with joy for the France whose republican regime a few years before had wickedly persecuted them. The nation inspired throughout Europe sacrifices that no king and no church had ever obtained.

From the nineteenth century onward, moreover, in each country historians and philosophers saw in the construction and development of nations, particularly of their own nation, the meaning or sense of European history. In this way *the* theological-political problem no longer appeared except as enveloped in a national context. It was more of a French or German problem than a universal problem, *the* theological-political problem. The nation truly was the human association par excellence, the sole true *respublica*. But there were several nations in Europe, and August 1914 marks the beginning of the end of the nation. The wars of the twentieth century have worn away the charm of the sacredness of the nation. And in Europe today, the nation, which triumphed over the church as a perfect republic, is now in the process of taking a back seat in turn.

We are, therefore, at the end of a cycle. The situation seems rather satisfactory in western Europe; at least it is peaceful. The protagonists are weak and tired. The church has been completely domesticated by the nation; the nation, for its part, is exhausted. Its effacement is inscribed in the dual development whose irresistibility is underscored by authoritative voices: on the one hand, the massive immigration of non-Christian populations; on the other, the construction of a so-called supranational Europe. The instrument and the framework for the solution to the West's theological-political problem, this nation-form that for so long appeared as the ultimate political and spiritual horizon, no longer owns the future. Because of this, one can conjecture that there will be a resurrection of the theological-political problem in an unprecedented form. To be sure, the legitimacy of democracy is self-evident today throughout Europe, and the "privatization" of religion, largely accomplished, has suppressed almost all occasions of conflict. However, since the context for the exercise of democracy (i.e., the nation) is on its way out, the problem of the definition of a new framework will swiftly become a problem of the first order. Democracy—understood as the autonomy of individuals and groups—hardly suffices, in fact, to define the public space. Religion is necessarily interested in the increasingly urgent problem of the "self-definition" of Europe.

On the other hand, at the end of this cycle, uncertainty also attaches to religion. The quite visible diminution of religious practice should not lead us to the dogmatic conclusion that this tendency is destined to continue indefinitely. Bossuet perfectly formulated one of the two reasons for our uncertainty on this point: "Religious sentiments are the last thing to be effaced in man, and the last that man consults." Whatever the future holds, we can at least try to analyze more precisely the present situation.

The Present Situation

What defines the church as an agent in the human world, as a "spiritual body," is that it bears a specific, proper thought or doctrine: it says *something* about man. It thereby, as Tocqueville noted, limits the arbitrariness of the democratic will, of democratic sovereignty, by reminding the latter that man cannot do whatever he wills. At the same time, the church's thought or doctrine contains commands, which is its nature, indeed its duty to want to have respected. The church necessarily tends, therefore, to usurp the role of the solitary instance of legitimate command in democracy, the government.

It is said that this problem has been resolved precisely by the separation of church and state, the sole viable solution to the theological-political problem. In reality, however, it is when one considers the question of government, or of command, that one sees how much separation—far from being a stable situation that leaves the two protagonists intact—is an endless process that implies the growing and indefinite domestication of the church.

The political, juridical, and moral foundation of separation is that religion is a *private matter.* Now this idea—polemically decisive in the process of the disestablishment of the church—is much less consistent than is generally thought. It claims to say that I have the right to observe or not to observe Easter, as I have the right to end my meal with cheese or dessert: *Privatsache.* The decisive question is avoided: Does or does not the church have the right to command me? The liberal, and seemingly reasonable response, will be yes, if you have consented beforehand to its command; no, if not. So be it—but then the question arises, How are the seeking out and obtaining of this consent organized and institutionalized? One cannot speak of consent as if it were a given existing by itself and simply available or not. It only appears by means of an institution that manifests it, and sometimes produces it. How can the church make individuals agree with its commands? What facilities does it have, what obstacles does it encounter, when obtaining it? After all, an elected democratic government, founded in principle on consent, requires the obedience even of those who did not vote for it, even if they hate it as Voltaire hated the church. Does the church have the right to avail itself of consent of this sort? In short, the separation of church and state, of the private and the public, is founded on an essential inequality of consents, which gives a decisive advantage to the public institution over the private one. The inequality of the consents demanded or required translates into the essential superiority of the state over the church in the regime of separation.

In this extremely disadvantageous situation, the church, the religious institution, basically has the choice of two ways of proceeding. It can accept literally the "regime of separation," and give the appearance of believing in the *Privatsache.* Down this path, it then seeks to govern men as much as it can within the context of the limits permitted it by the regime of separation. This is pretty much what the Catholic Church attempted to do in France between the "rally" to the Republic and the Second Vatican Council. However, to govern is to govern. To govern in civil society is *not so* different from governing in the state. Because the reality of governing undermines the constitutive convention of the regime of separation, the church's conduct is very difficult. It is difficult practically, because the state is necessarily hostile, or at least not terribly sympathetic. It is difficult morally, because the church must now play a role that is structurally hypocritical. It can only fully play its role in civil society by exercising "governing energy," which gives it a quasi- or parapolitical role—in truth, a political role—a role that it must necessarily deny. I am tempted to say that it is only when it accepts it grudgingly that the church can play well the exclusively private role conceded to it under the regime of separation. This situation is so uncomfortable, and exposed to so many inconveniences, that the church embraces with relief the second way of proceeding, the one followed for the most part by the postconciliar church. It no longer presents itself as the most necessary and most salutary *government,* doing its best in a political situation contrary to the good of souls. It becomes simply the *critic* of all governments, including that which was for centuries the government of the church. It becomes the collective "beautiful soul," presenting itself to men as "the bearer of ideals and values." An "ideal," or "value," in contrast to a law, cannot be commanded but is left solely to the free initiative and "creativity" of each individual—because man is the "creator of values." The church escapes from the discomfort of its political situation by substantially transforming the character of its message. For the past generation, the churches propose "Christian values," which, unlike the old Decalogue and also unlike democratic law, are impossible either to obey or to disobey. The church repeats, in a more emphatic way, what democracy says about itself. Under the rubric of "values," it is hopeless to make "the gospel message" listened to, or at least heard, except by engaging in humanitarian and egalitarian overbidding. Assuming, along with Tocqueville, that democracy needs a brake or restraint to facilitate the good use of liberty, religion, once arriving at the truly "ideal" state, certainly cannot provide it. It simply accompanies democracy as much in its reasonable as in its foolish conduct.

After this long survey, must we therefore conclude that the first, strongly negative reactions of the church confronted by democracy were basically well founded? Must we say that after two centuries of an often confused and conflicted history, democracy as the institutionalization of human sovereignty seems to have completely subjected the Christian churches, and even the long resistant Catholic church? This conclusion would be rash. As I indicated while considering the destiny of the nation, the foundation of modern democracy—human sovereignty—is not the immediate author of the framework or written code by which it exercises itself. It cannot be so. Whether it busies itself within the framework of the city, the kingdom, the empire, or even the whole

Earth, it does not immediately make decisions by itself: determination is not contained in the principles of democracy.

The political momentum, primarily territorial, of democracy is essentially indeterminate. It depends on historical inheritance, on the action of great men without a mandate, and on simple chance. The actualization of human sovereignty simultaneously manifests human impotence and ignorance, the disproportion between wills democratically registered and the sum of wills. Democracy appears, then, as a partial and contingent agent, quite brilliantly illuminated, but severed from the fabric of all humanity. For the latter includes the dead, the living, and those yet to be born. This complete humanity, without a possible political expression but out of which democracy necessarily operates—where can it be found? In which ledgers does it write itself? That of nature? But it is precisely modern humanity that desires to be the sovereign over nature, creator of its own nature. By affirming its indeterminate sovereignty over itself, democratic humanity basically declares that it wills itself, without knowing itself.

Yesterday's church denounced, and with indignation, the impiety of this will. Today's church, or its most astute representatives, makes known with a benevolence tinged with irony the import of this lack of self-knowledge.

Thus, the political submission of the church to democracy is, perhaps, finally, a fortunate one. The church willy-nilly conformed itself to all of democracy's demands. Democracy no longer, in good faith, has any essential reproach to make against the church. From now on it can hear the question the church poses, the question that it alone poses, the question *Quid sit homo*—What is man? But democracy neither wants to nor can respond to this question in any manner or form. On democracy's side of the scale, we are left with political sovereignty and dialectical impotence. On the church's side, we are left with political submission and dialectical advantage. The relation unleashed by the Enlightenment is today reversed. No one knows what will happen when democracy and the church become aware of this reversal.

Translated by Daniel J. Mahoney and Paul Seaton

Part Four

Understanding Totalitarianism

In "Totalitarianism and the Problem of Political Representation," Pierre Manent offers a distinctive contribution to the necessary and noble task of thinking about the totalitarian phenomenon. And in his essay on Aurel Kolnai, he highlights the distinctive achievement of the too little known Hungarian-born philosopher in analyzing "the utopian mind."

One of the original features of these essays is Manent's use of Marx's "On the Jewish Question" to analyze the liberal democratic state's ambiguity vis-à-vis democratic society and "the moral contents of life" it officially authorizes and protects. Without in the least sympathizing with revolutionary illusions, Manent draws on Marx in understanding the distinctive character of liberal representative politics and the discontent these politics necessarily engender in many segments of society.

This discontent needs the illumination of analyses such as Kolnai's. Genuinely human consciousness is structured around reflection on the relationship between the "is" and the "ought." The improper articulation of this relationship in the utopian project is a sobering reminder of the essential place of conscience in human thought and points to the need for responsible political action rooted in a recognition of the permanent limits that frame human thought and action.

Totalitarianism and the Problem of Political Representation

Pierre Manent

1984

It is a commonplace to note that one of the sources of the totalitarian project is found in the idea that it is possible for man to model society in accordance with his wishes, once he occupies the seat of power and possesses an exact social science and employs adequate means for this task.

It is the case that well before the totalitarian development, modern "artificialism" assumed that it is possible for man *truly to divide himself*, to be within society and at the same time completely outside it, on the Archimedean point from which he will remake the imperfect world. This is an idea or notion whose singularity is not generally gaged. Certainly there are those who insist upon the hubris inseparable from such a perspective and on the systematic use of violence that is its inevitable consequence. But it is quite rare that someone asks the most straightforward and most pressing question that one must confront when one considers an idea: is it even *thinkable*? It is possible *to will* what one cannot think or what is impossible for man to conceive. The imagination can always persuade man that he thinks or knows what, in fact, he only wills.

Thomas Hobbes was the first to formulate the artificialist idea, with the clarity that characterizes him. In his view, man can be considered under the twin aspects of *matter* and *artificer*. These two words are extraordinarily expressive; the first signifies pure passivity, and the second sovereign "constructivist" activity. Man is so sovereign that, in this context, Hobbes goes so far as to invoke the divine *fiat*. Thus, man can

This article originally appeared in French in *Commentaire* (number 26, Summer 1984) and appears here with permission.

have the same relation to himself that God has toward nothingness, or at least toward the "unformed and empty earth" of which Genesis speaks.

Artificialism and Political Representation

The political being of man resides at two poles. On one side there is society, constituted by individuals and the element in which they live, and on the other there is the seat of power. We are dealing with the same man, however. How can the necessary unity of these two poles be conceived? It can be conceived by means of the notion of *representation*.[1] We find here a second presupposition of totalitarianism, tied to the first. It has often been noticed that one of the most effective techniques of totalitarian ideology is an immoderate use of the notion of representation. In totalitarian ideologies, the Führer represents the German people, the First Secretary of the Communist Party represents the politburo, which represents the central committee, which represents the party, which represents the proletariat, which represents the people, which finally represents humanity itself.

It is clear that the device of representation is a matrix or a form that can be filled with very different contents. Let us look at some of the possibilities:

By a change in the definition of the representative. The representative can be Hobbes's absolute sovereign, as in the history of the absolute monarchs of "the golden age of Kings." Or his natural individuality can be abolished and the distinction between *matter* and *artificer* will remain strictly within the interior of the contracting individual, who then can be considered under two relations, as both legislator and as subject. We then have the "general will" and "direct democracy" of Rousseau's *Social Contract.* Clearly in this case the representative as such disappears, although artificialism remains intact. It is even rendered more rigorous and pure. But it is even more difficult to conceive than it was in Hobbes's case, and this very difficulty will give rise to Immanuel Kant's project. One can also imagine a legislative body that exercises the people's sovereignty without nullifying it. This is an inexact category, to be sure, but all modern representative democracies fit into this category.

By a change in the definition of the represented. Instead of being an "abstract" individual, the original represented can be defined as a worker or class of workers, or it can be defined as a German or as the German people. In these last two cases the contract, the free act of contracting, (i.e., the election of the representative), is preempted by the nature of the represented. What defines the represented in the contractualist theories is that he is a free individual who has free will. What defines the represented in totalitarian doctrines is a characteristic trait that does not depend on his will but that belongs to his nature or his birth (as in the case of Nazism) or to his social condition (as in the case of communism). In this last case, because the represented is not considered *sub specie voluntatis*, representation requires the self-designation of the representative.

We see that the form or matrix of representation leads itself to very different, even politically contradictory, contents. Naturally one will object that some of these representations are fictitious and deceptive, and others authentic, and that the distinction I am working with between the form and the content of representation is untenable. I freely admit that there are deceptive or illegitimate political representations and others that are authentic or legitimate. My claim is only that if there have been so many illegitimate political representations, it is not only because of the blindness or perversity of men but above all because of the intrinsic indetermination of modern representation.

I have mentioned the names of Hobbes and Rousseau, who are generally considered to be the founders of the representative idea and of the modern democratic view, respectively. One might think, therefore, that they both had something to do with the advent of representative democracy. However, both categorically rejected the idea of the representation of the will, an indispensable condition for the very idea of representative democracy. For both, the will belongs to the individual and cannot be separated somehow from him in order to bestow it on another. There is an irresistible power and continuity to the representative idea, however. Within this idea, even before the advent of totalitarian representation, there is the possibility of radical disagreement over the answers to be given to questions as fundamental as the following: Who is represented? How is he represented? By whom is he represented? and even: Is it possible for him to be represented? The delirious totalitarian identifications have as their condition of possibility this indetermination in the modern idea of representation.

Another condition of possibility of totalitarianism belongs to a paradox that follows this indeterminacy: the greater the value and the dignity of the represented are affirmed, the more the value and dignity of the representative are, too. And the more the dignity of the representative is augmented, the more that of the represented is necessarily diminished. The logic of representation is self-destructive or self-immolatory. For a long time it has been noted that the specific perversity of the modern idea of representation is located here. It is a perversity in virtue of which the will of the sovereign people comes to subjugate the people. It is important to consider under what modest and innocent auspices this terrible apparatus began to take shape.

We have seen that Hobbes is the founder of modern artificialism. We then noted that the original *artificer* was the powerless individual in the state of nature—in his position as a member of civil society, as we would say today. It was he who created the absolute power of Leviathan. Why? To protect *himself*. The Leviathan is the instrument of this poor devil threatened at each moment by another poor devil, his neighbor. Two things strike us: this instrument, like all instruments, has a use, a raison d'être, a purpose: it is the security of the individual or civil peace. It is a very modest purpose, that of the extreme liberal or the "night watchman" state. Yet, in order to attain this modest goal, the instrument necessarily must be *unlimited*. What a paradox this notion of an unlimited or *infinite instrument* is! What a radical novelty in the human world! Did not Saint Thomas, following Aristotle, teach that an unlimited instrument, a *martellus infinitus*, is a contradiction in terms?

As soon as power is conceived as an instrument fabricated by the members of society for their service, it logically becomes infinite or unlimited. What does this mean? Simply that the members of society do not have the right to oppose what it does or wills. This is so for a simple reason. If they had this right, the representative would not truly be *their* representative.

The radical separation of power and society, the instrumentalization and infinite extension of this power, the representation of society by a power so defined—we see here the "common matrix" of democracy and totalitarianism. The formulation is undoubtedly vague. It aims to signify the affinity of certain cardinal notions, but it also means to exclude the notion that democracy and totalitarianism are two species of a same genus or that democracy leads to totalitarianism as the cloud bears the storm. I also said "radical separation of power and society." I must now emphasize this point.

The State and Civil Society

It is a commonplace that totalitarianism is defined as the absorption of civil society by the state. As a consequence, the antitotalitarian act par excellence is to assure the independence of civil society vis-à-vis the state. I do not deny the descriptive accuracy of this characterization of totalitarianism, but this definition risks overlooking something essential. In order for the totalitarian state to absorb civil society, the distinction between the two must first of all have been recognized and established, if not in the society in question, at least in an existing society with which the first has relations, if only by means of knowledge. And the society subsequent to the absorption (such as the totalitarian regime) is radically different from the society anterior to the distinction (whether one calls it the "old regime" or "feudalism"). In order for the state to be able to embrace society to the point of suffocating it, it must first of all have been emancipated from society; and in order to be so drawn out or liberated, it is necessary that its meaning has been essentially changed from what it was under the old regime. The only way to separate rigorously the state or the central power from society was precisely to consider it as a *representative instrument* of that society. From the moment it is seen in this way, the possibility of totalitarian oppression is created.

One must not let oneself be intimidated by the good favor that the idea of civil society enjoys today. This favor, in fact, encourages too many confusions. The civil society that we know and the representative state mutually belong to one another. Intellectually, they were conceived together, in relation to one another. Marx says it quite well in "On the Jewish Question": *"The formation of the political State*, and the dissolution of civil society into independent individuals . . . are accomplished by *one and the same act."*[2] Historically, it was the power of the state that created our civil society by destroying the intrasocial or "intermediate" powers of the old regime. The generative principle of our civil society and of the state that is correlative to it is that no power has the right to be exercised in the interior of civil society since all legitimate power is representative and the locus of representation is the central state. This principle can only admit the single qualification that the supreme Representative can tolerate representatives of a lower rank or order. All the powers that nonetheless are exercised in society—the power of knowledge or of competence (doctors or professors, e.g.), the power of religious institutions, that of the business entrepreneur—are exercised despite the generative and legitimating principle of the society, because the powers I just mentioned are not founded on representation. The sole power—besides the power of the state and the local representative powers—whose exercise is not contrary to the representative principle is that of labor unions, or at least unions representing their members who have no power in the society.[3]

I would like to consider with some care what the separation of the political authority and civil society, by means of representation, means for civil society. In other words, what is the meaning of the transition from the old regime to bourgeois society?

1. The "material and spiritual elements" (Marx) of the society are the same in the bourgeois society as they were in the old regime: property, family, religion, knowledge, and so forth. In some fashion they are the same in every society.

2. These elements are stripped of the immediate *political inscription* they had in the old regime. Under it, they were politically inscribed in the social landscape by the power that exerted itself inside of each of them. As others have said, the society of the old regime was a "society of bodies," a corporate society. They now slide into the so-called "private" sphere. Religion no longer exerts a power over consciences. It becomes instead a free activity, the free expression of the individual conscience that is guaranteed by law. The economy is no longer organized in guilds. Every individual has the right, guaranteed by law, to engage in industrial or commercial activity, and so forth.

3. The "material and spiritual elements" are conserved in the new society. But after having passed through the medium of the new individualistic civil society (or through the medium of "human rights"), they are, however, modified, sometimes radically so. For example, the disappearance of the semi or parapolitical role of the father of the family overturns previous intrafamilial relations.

What is the relation of the representative state to these material and spiritual elements of social life? Does it represent these elements? The answer is no. How could it? It represents individuals, independently of what they are and do, abstracted from their family, their profession, their religion. Must we say that the state is indifferent to these elements? In principle, that indifference is its official raison d'être. For example, the liberal, secular state allows everyone to pray to God as they see fit, but it is strictly external to religion. Is this official attitude its real attitude? Can we think that in the social world two essential elements, like the state and religion, or the state and the economy, can be really indifferent or external to one another, without a defining relationship? That is not possible because the social world is a *plenum*, and our social nature abhors a vacuum. What is this relationship, then?

1. The material and spiritual contents of life are *presupposed* (*vorausgesetzt*—the term is used frequently by Marx) by the liberal representative state. In order for there to be religious freedom, there has to be religion, to have economic liberty, there must be an economy. Presupposition (*Voraussetzung*, as Marx says) is the weakest form of affirmation; to be presupposed is the poorest form of existence.

2. We have said the liberal state does not represent the contents of life; it represents individuals who possess economic and religious *rights*. Man is defined as the being who has rights. The state represents all of these rights. If man is defined as the being who has rights, the fact that he has rights is more important and stronger than the material on which he exercises these rights (such as the economy, religion, etc.). Consequently, the purely instrumental state is in fact quite superior in authority and legitimacy to the contents of life that, in the official version of its purpose, it modestly limits itself to guaranteeing. All the activities in civil society are *authorized*, but the contents of these activities in principle lack authority. They are only a particular application, and specification of the rights of man, and no power is legitimately asserted in their midst. The only thing that can have genuine authority in this society is the state, the institution that authorizes activities and guarantees that human rights are effectively respected.

3. The consignment of these social activities, of the contents of life, to the *private* sphere necessarily leads to their disqualification, to their *diminutio capitis*. Of course, officially, in current discourse, and in what I will call the primary awareness of social actors, the "private" is extremely valorized, since the political authority—the representative state—is held to be exclusively at its service. In reality, however, only what is directly inscribed in its political institutions is effectively and durably valorized in a society. In a slow and gentle manner, civilized and imperceptible, liberal authorization and representation tend to cast the social activity of men into the limbo of mere facticity without any authority. How can we not appreciate that the relegation to the private sphere is in some sense a disqualification? The state says, in short: That does not interest me, that is your business, it is only your concern. That is, until the moment when the state changes its mind. Then this matter is too important to be left to the private sphere, and the state must assume responsibility for it. If socialization or nationalization thus accompanies liberal privatization as its shadow, it is because no human activity in society can be solely private. From the moment when liberal authorization casts social activities into the purportedly tutelary shadow of the rights of the individual, the exigence (inseparable from the human condition) of public inscription and acknowledgment of these

human activities returns in an ever more imperious form. Nationalization attempts to fill the void created in the public space by the privatization of human activities, a privatization that is contrary to the eternal nature of the human world. Of course, nationalization only succeeds in enlarging this void.

The public space of our societies is established by representation, by the acknowledged and maintained distance between the state and society. The state that takes direct responsibility for social activities cannot guarantee their public inscription; on the contrary, it abolishes what remained of public space in the society. The state transforms itself into a sort of enormous private person, only controlled by the constraints of the global market and the international system.

Is it not a great paradox to say that liberal authorization puts in danger the very thing it authorizes? Nonetheless, it is true that one must beware of authorizations. For example, it is not the same thing to authorize an individual to follow the religion of his choice and to authorize the religion that he chooses or can choose. Each domain of human life has its conditions and its laws, which can be imperiled precisely by the authorization given to all to do what they want in this domain. One is reminded of an extremely striking passage in de Maistre, in which he says that one does not really tolerate the Catholic religion except when one allows it to exist in conformity with its dogmas, its maxims and its discipline. And naturally Joseph de Maistre makes it clear that one does not truly tolerate the Catholic religion when one tolerates alongside it other religions it would not tolerate if it had the opportunity to be itself. On this particular but exemplary point, de Maistre perceives very intelligently the fundamental difficulty affecting liberal authorization.

The Ambivalence of the Democratic Process

As we have seen, it is the authority of the contents of life that is radically undermined in the representative framework. However, this nullification is only a nullification in principle. As long as there are men there will be religion, families, art and so forth, these elements therefore will continue to exercise an authority, but one that is more and more feeble as the democratic or representative process develops. This movement of the attenuation of the contents of life is very slow. In fact, in the initial phases of the process, these elements—or certain of them— will appear to acquire an additional authority. In this first period, which covers a good part of the nineteenth century, the state, whose authority was immensely augmented in principle, in fact was circumscribed within the limits in which it had found itself in the old regime. On the other hand, the elements of life conserved something of the political inscription they enjoyed under the old regime, while now they apparently were reenforced by the authorization and the liberty with which the new order favored them. The nineteenth century therefore is the golden age of the "capitalized": the Family, Religion, Art and so on,—of what we call, following Marx, "bourgeois ideology." But this ideology is quite contradictory. It lives simultaneously on what it denies (the political inscription of the old regime) and on what denies it: the destruction of the contents of life by the rights of man. But even with its hypocrisy and its "values," it often allowed Europeans to adapt themselves gradually to their new role as "individuals."

I have already emphasized that there is an essential indeterminacy in modern representation. But this indetermination can go in either a totalitarian or liberal direction. In order for it to take the liberal route, it is necessary and sufficient for the social authorities who have enough intelligence and time to adapt institutions to the representative principle. The ways in which these authorities acquitted themselves of this task is the history of the progress of democracy in each country. The democratic process is so much more controllable and the representative indeterminacy goes so much more easily in the right direction, to the extent that the particular body politic is the one to initiate the process. In this case the process occurs under the direction of the social authorities, and the dialectic between social authority (which expresses the authority of the contents of life) and democratic authorization ("the rights of man and citizen") remains controlled in its modes (but not in the basic direction of its irresistible movement) by the former. The process can be controlled because at each stage the following stage is unknown. It is not known in what it consists, and it is not even believed to be possible. At each stage, prudent men—I have in mind the conservative liberals, or the liberal conservatives—believe that the democratic process has come to its end and the new order is established. It goes on this way, indefinitely. This situation is most prominently that of England. England has almost completely escaped totalitarianism because its social authorities have always had control (sometimes only by a hair, as at the time of the first Reform Bill in 1832) of the process. But a price was paid for this blindness to the radicality of the democratic phenomenon and even to its significance (the letters between John Stuart Mill and Alexis de Tocqueville show this wonderfully well). One is left with the not always self-conscious bourgeois ideology that we call "Victorianism."

When a body politic is behind the process (and all body politics other than that initiator, England, therefore, are tardy), the problem becomes very difficult to resolve, and totalitarian, or at least para- or pretotalitarian phenomena appear. Why? As a consequence of a movement of *double negation.*

The Spectacle of Democratization

The spectacle of an advanced society and its success proves to the "foot-dragging" society that the institutions that appear to it to be indispensable to life and to social cohesion are not so. From the eighteenth century on, England proved to the French that a society can exist and prosper without an independent church, without a king who really governs, without an exclusive nobility. English institutions, already a mixture of social authority and modern representation, stigmatized the French institutions, which remained characterized by political inscription. To the French observer, English social cohesion appeared to arise solely from the interchange of the free activities of individuals, individuals who appeared disconnected from institutions. The hypothesis of modern representation appeared to be realized in England. There, contractual and thus nonpolitical relations seemed to suffice for social coherence. Civil society is self-sufficient, or at least it only needs a purely exterior and instrumental state, which limits itself to guaranteeing the rights of individuals. The liberty or sovereignty of the individual does not have to be instituted because it is identical to the spontaneity of his nature.

Simultaneously, this disconnected individual of the new order shows up in a completely different light that contradicts the previous impression. The observer, in fact, notes that the contents of life that no longer are politically inscribed in the social landscape continue in reality to beset the free citizen: in fact, the latter is harried by that from which he just freed himself. For example, the representative state in principle is "atheistic" since religion in this regime no longer has power, yet nonetheless many citizens call themselves Christians, sometimes rather emphatically. Or the observer also may note this: democratic institutions make the have-nots the legislator for the haves. This means that the state, in the political order as such, abolishes private property, or at least does not acknowledge it, since "a *property qualification* is the last *political* form in which private property is recognized."[4] And yet citizens cherish property, and the state itself, in a contradictory assertion, does not hesitate to affirm that its principal role is to protect property. Thus, on one hand, the liberal representative state proves to the observer that it is possible for man to rise above these contents of life, since the man whose sovereignty he institutionalizes is, in principle, without a religion, without property, and without family. But at the same time this same man vehemently affirms the "value" of these contents of life, thus renouncing his sovereignty as inscribed in the state. He never fails to proclaim his submission to the contents of life, above which, however, he has elevated himself by instituting the representative state. The external observer of an advanced society is quite aware of the paradox that formed the point of departure of this essay. Once the representative apparatus is set up, man finds himself simultaneously in two contradictory situations: installed in the seat of power, he is the sovereign over property, religion, and family (and in virtue of modern representation all citizens in some way occupy the seat of power); but as a member of civil society he proclaims the sublimity of religion and the sacred character of property and the family.

The observer thus concludes that the human sovereignty of which the state is but an abstract and partial expression is, invisibly, wholly present in civil society. But this implicit and invisible sovereignty is not able to manifest itself, because it is hampered by the existing society and by the contents of life that beset the latter. It will be necessary and sufficient therefore to cancel civil society in order for human sovereignty to become one with the spontaneous dynamism of the individuals of civil society.

We may state the point differently. Since the state is the intermediary that expresses man's sovereignty over his own life, this sovereignty must be fully realized by suppressing the intermediary. Human emancipation cannot be fully achieved except by the negation of political emancipation, which is "abstract, limited, partial" (Marx). The separation of society and the state must be ended.

My purpose is not to connect totalitarianism immediately to Marx's thought. It is, rather, to connect totalitarianism and Marx's thought to a certain situation of political consciousness: that of the man who, while belonging to a regressive society, observes the strange metabolism between society and state that constitutes the inner life of a democratic regime or liberal society.

The Totalitarian Moment

The difference between an advanced society and "backward" ones leads, for the reasons I have stated, to the notion of the self-sufficiency of civil society. His position leads the observer to adhere strictly to bourgeois ideology on this point, and even to trump it: the free association of individuals suffices for social cohesion, the political authority is superfluous or harmful. On the other hand, belonging to a society in which the contents of life still have a political inscription, he is particularly sensitive to the implicit negation of these contents by liberal authorization. He perceives quite vividly that the privatization of the contents of life is a disqualification. He sees it much more clearly than the citizen of the advanced society—even the one sharing his political "opinions"—because the latter lived through the adaptation of the contents of life to the new regime, for example, the transformation of religion into a "value" from the social power it had been. The French socialists of the nineteenth century will be passably interested, in their own way, in religion. Ultimately the transformation of religion into a "value" is as much of a negation of religion as the Marxist definition of it as alienation. But it served the valuable purpose of permitting the transition between the two societies. One must be thankful for the bourgeois ideology in that it made livable an unthinkable social situation. But if this society was not thinkable for the observer, it is because in it he lives a thoroughly false life. He experiences together, therefore, two contradictory sentiments: he trumps the bourgeois idea of the self-sufficiency of the apolitical civil society, and he fundamentally disdains the existing bourgeois society in which men lead such a false life. Human sovereignty is wholly present in the *essence* of this society, while all its *appearances* (i.e., all the realities), are false. All the appearances (i.e., the realities) of civil society must be abolished to have its essence emerge. As soon as civil society no longer has the means to put itself forth as independent of the state, its sovereignty will be intact. The absorption of civil society by the state is only the appearance of a transformation that in its essence is the absorption of the state by civil society. The state is the *ratio cognoscendi* of human sovereignty, civil society its *ratio essendi*.

But how is one to ensure the fusion of the two? As we have seen, the state and civil society mutually belong to one another and reciprocally condition each other. The representative state always presupposes society. A third term then must intervene, strictly external to the state as well as to society: the party. The party does not represent society, nor is it a repetition of the state. Instead it expresses and activates the union of the two.

When totalitarianism is defined as the absorption of civil society by and in the state, the third term or factor (in some sense the most important) is forgotten. Exercising "real" power, the party is confounded with the state or the state's role. Covering society with the tight-knit fabric of its "cells," it is coextensive with society. The party assures the "unbreakable" unity of society and the state because it is confounded with one and the other. However, while simultaneously mixing with both it remains strictly external to them: being confounded with the state, it is rigorously distinct from society; confounded with society, it is rigorously distinct from the state.

To exist as the party, it must maintain the "place" of society as well as the "place" of the state. It needs society in order to deprive it of its autonomy; it needs a state in order to deprive it of its power. It is by suppressing the essential consistency of each of the two while preserving their "place" that it expresses their unity. In a certain sense, the totalitarian party *realizes* the condition of awareness of the person I have called the observer.

I do not wish to suggest by this that it "applies" the conclusions of that observer, those of Marx, for example; as scholars of Marx have sufficiently underlined, Marx himself hardly knew what concrete political steps could put his vision into action. Where could the instrument for an action based on this vision have come from? The instrument charged to transform this vision into action could only come from the very matrix that is the source of this vision.

The Importance of the Jacobin Episode

It is necessary to take into account the French Revolution. It is the Revolution, moreover, that, more than any other thing contributed to fix Marx's vision on an essential point: the contradiction between the representative state and the contents of life it presupposes and is supposed to represent. It is during the unfolding of the Revolution that he sees this point shine forth. Numerous passages from "On the Jewish Question" make the point; I will only cite one:

> Certainly, in periods when the political state as such comes violently to birth in civil society, and when men strive to liberate themselves through political emancipation, the State can, and must, proceed to *abolish and destroy religion* but only in the same way as it proceeds to abolish private property, by declaring a maximum, by confiscation, or by progressive taxation, or in the same way as it proceeds to abolish life, by the *guillotine*. At those times when the State is most aware of itself, political life seeks to stifle its own prerequisites—civil society and its elements— and to establish itself as the genuine and harmonious species-life of man. But it can only achieve this end by setting itself in *violent* contradiction with its own conditions of existence, by declaring a *permanent* revolution. Thus the political drama ends necessarily with the restoration of religion, of private property, of all the elements of civil society, just as war ends with the conclusion of peace.[5]

What Marx here describes with a truly extraordinary intensity of expression is what we would call an aborted totalitarianism, or the checkmate of a totalitarian enterprise. I do not claim here to propose an interpretation of the French Revolution or of the years 1793–1794 (the zenith of the French Revolutionary Terror) in its relation to totalitarianism. But the preceding analysis obliges me to make a few remarks.

What characterizes the French Revolution is that the totalitarian or paratotalitarian element, the Jacobin club, was born about the same time as the representative authority. It did not truly act except on and through the intermediation of the Convention, which remained the central locus of the drama. And Thermidor, at the same time that it was the victory of civil society, was the victory of the representative authority over its totalitarian double. It was the Convention itself, or a part of the Convention, that conducted the "totalitarian" enterprise. But when the "totalitarian" enterprise is conducted by the representative instrument, which thus seeks to realize the coincidence of the representative and the represented, this can only lead it to (what Marx calls) "a violent contradiction with *its own* conditions of existence" (my emphasis). The representative authority involved in this action cannot be ignorant for very long that it is annihilating society, its raison d'être. Revolutionary action could only be led from a place truly exterior to the couplet of representative state and civil society.

But if Thermidor saved France, the failure of political Jacobinism furnished a political matrix that promoted the condition of awareness I attempted to describe. The Convention recognized the impossibility or unthinkability of what it had attempted to realize. But killing Maximilien Robespierre was necessarily a political deed, marked by all the concrete characteristics of a real deed: deliberations, alliances, secrets, decisions, violence. The struggle between the politics of the impossible or unthinkable and the real city, or the conditions of possibility of every city, showed itself to contemporaries and was crystallized in their memories as a struggle between equally real and thus equally possible political procedures in which one happened to triumph. The checkmate of the politics of the impossible thus inscribed it in European consciousness as a political possibility.

On top of the idea of the coincidence between representative and represented, which the Convention found impossible, was superimposed the image of a possible political action, one that would not be vulnerable to a new Thermidor. Henceforth, professional revolutionaries largely cut off from the real condition of men will circulate throughout Europe. They will be chased by governments and ignored by peoples, but this small band—Gracchus Babeuf's companions, the adherents of the revolutionary idea—will be naturally obsessed with the condition of consciousness I have described. They will spend their lives looking for political circumstances that will allow for the realization of the action that Robespierre's fall on the Ninth of Thermidor [27 July 1794] left incomplete.

The French Revolution caused the contradictions of modern representation to manifest themselves with such a dramatic intensity that from then on, above the real history of nations, above the slow work of democratic representation, an emblematic history was being wrought: men whose clarity and firmness had to them something of ancient characteristics led mankind to the threshold of the land promised—and denied— by the idea of modern representation. A moment of indecision on Robespierre's part, or the rain that fell that day, prevented the impossible or the unthinkable from becoming real.

Translated by Daniel J. Mahoney and Paul Seaton

Notes

1. It is absolutely important to be clear that, in Hobbes, the distinction between representative and represented is not equivalent to the distinction between *artificer* and *matter*. Individuals in the state of nature create, by their contract, the absolute sovereign, whose sovereignty in turn gives existence and constancy to the political body. They are the *authors* of the actions of their representative, in such a way that ultimately—and this is most important to note—the *same* individuals are both *matter* and *artificer*. Representation is what allows them to be both at the same time.

2. Karl Marx, "On the Jewish Question" in *The Marx-Engels Reader,* ed. Robert C. Tucker (New York: Norton, 1978), 45–46.

3. In a democratic country, when circumstances give an opportunity to a totalitarian enterprise, civil society is vulnerable because this totalitarian enterprise can direct against the intrasocial powers the democratic ideology itself, without needing to invoke its own ideology. More precisely, it can involve the representative principle in a purely instrumental fashion. Contrary to conventional wisdom, the representative idea intrinsically weakens the legitimacy of civil society and puts its independence in danger.

4. Marx, "On the Jewish Question," 33.

5. Marx, "On the Jewish Question," 36.

Aurel Kolnai: A Political Philosopher Confronts the Scourge of Our Epoch

Pierre Manent

1995

As early as the middle of the eighteenth century, it was possible for Adam Ferguson to write that we had entered "the age of separations."[1] Ferguson's is one of the first and most striking formulations of an idea that has become a commonplace to us and conveys as much satisfaction as disquiet—satisfaction at the advance of knowledge which makes possible the division of labor, especially intellectual labor; disquiet at the impossibility of a synoptic grasp of the scattered elements of human learning. There are many separations. If there is any that arouses more disquiet than satisfaction, it is the long-standing division between political and moral philosophy.

A political philosopher—or a *political scientist,* as we now have to call him—who describes shrewdly the workings of the body politic, or issues judicious suggestions for the improvements of these workings, will habitually do this without concerning himself with the question of the kind of human being who inhabits or will inhabit it. Such a theorist is anxious not to let a value judgment escape him, lest it spoil the scientific nature of his work. The moral philosopher, on the other hand, examines minutely the perplexities of the moral agent, but normally without attending to the fact that these perplexities may be intimately bound up with the political regime in which the moral action unfolds. His fear is of obscuring or sullying the specificity and the purity of his field of enquiry.

Among the reasons for this remarkable divorce between moral and political philosophy, there is one we should mention immediately. Over

---

This essay originally appeared as the introduction to Aurel Kolnai, *The Utopian Mind and Other Papers* (London: Athlone, 1995) and is republished with permission.

the last two centuries, at points widely separated on the political spectrum and on the basis of divergent and even contradictory analyses of the nature of modern society, there has emerged a single conception of political action. This conception rests on the assumption that as soon as a certain rational arrangement of our institutions has been achieved, the whole human problem will be essentially solved—or that whatever remains problematical in human affairs will not affect the essential and definitive validity of the political structure. The happy contemplation of a certain institutional automatism, the servo-mechanism that is supposed to guide the body politic on its way to being what it ought to be, excludes all fundamental questioning about the motives of man in society or about the ambiguities and tensions that characterize the relation between man and citizen. This idea of an ultimately infallible "political mechanism" may be given a liberal or a socialist content, and it can prompt initiatives with very different practical consequences. But it retains one single essential characteristic—that of being *utopian.*

Aurel Kolnai is one of the philosophers of the twentieth century who have given most attention to the growing power of the utopian mind, the spirit which both expresses and aggravates the loss of meaning in human action—our loss of any relation to values. Kolnai belongs also among thinkers who have given the most attention to the "ideologizing" of modern politics. From the moment when the conviction grows—however justifiably within certain limits—that man can and ought to change society by making it conform to his ideal, there looms the risk that, paradoxically, the content of the ideal will become less and less desirable as its form—its *ideal* character—is embraced with increasing zeal. There is the risk that in the name of utopia the legitimate search for social improvement will be perverted into an exercise in destruction. Thus, the seductive power of utopia is owed not so much to its value-content—the social, moral, and philosophical ideas which give it an intelligible outline, or the passions and aspirations that first attract its zealots and enthusiasts—as to its promise of a certain formal perfection, which will infallibly and definitively reconcile *reality* and *value,* reconcile the *is* and the *ought.* Kolnai's study of modern society and politics convinced him that the utopian mind is an object sui generis, quite distinct from the political stances or sociological ideas that it will engage as its ministers. The utopian mind deserves philosophical study on its own.

At this point two caveats suggest themselves. The first caveat is this. It may well be true that the utopian mind works more spontaneously in the social and political ideas of the left; yet, as Kolnai himself remarks, the utopian mind has no analytically necessary connection with ideas of the left. For the same leftist sociological ideas (the idea which sees the emancipation of the working class as a central requirement of modern society, for instance) are just as susceptible of commonsense presentation (reformist, moderate) as of utopian. In the second place, we must note the existence of what could be called "rightist" utopias. There are the moderate utopias of the moderate right. Economic liberalism, for instance, according to which market mechanisms can by themselves solve the problems of social man, has an incontestably utopian stamp. But there are also the extreme utopias of the extreme right. These come in two kinds: (1) reactionary utopias, common on the Continent until quite recent times, which see a glorified ancien régime as the natural order of human society or as the order required by Christianity; (2) subversive utopias, like Nazism, which attract those whom they attract by a particularly murderous vision of racial purity. In short, if Aurel Kolnai's approach in this book may be called conservative—in a sense we shall have to clarify—it would be a grievous error to see in his critical analysis of the utopian mind a conservative attack on, let us say, socialism or democracy.

The second caveat to be entered here concerns the impression of excessive generality created by the idea of the utopian mind. The idea of utopia is much more determinate than the idea of "modernity," for example. Yet the idea of modernity has long had the freedom of the philosophers' city, if only by virtue of the flamboyant criticism that was directed at the modern world and modern ideas by such writers as Friedrich Nietzsche and Martin Heidegger. The idea of the utopian mind is still less imprecise than the idea of political rationalism, the target of Michael Oakeshott's sharp—if not mortal—barbs.[2] Above all, we should not charge the analyst with the abstraction that is apparent in the *object* of his study. It is not in Kolnai but in Marx that one comes across ideas as abstract, emphatic, and vague as that of the "reconciliation of man with man and with nature." The extreme generality of the idea of the utopian mind is not something with which one might justly reproach Kolnai. Excessive generality is the reproach that Kolnai himself wants to make against utopian thinking.

It appears that what first drove Kolnai to his study of the spins of utopia was his dissatisfaction with the usual criticism of utopias: that they are "unrealizable," "too beautiful" ever to exist in this world. Such criticism is obviously true in one sense. The state of complete human satisfaction envisaged by utopia is indeed unrealizable. But such criticism is superficial, because it leaves out what is special about utopia. It is precisely its unrealizable character, or the particular nature of its unrealizability, that provides the motive power for attempts to realize utopia and is responsible for the peculiarly destructive effects of these attempts.

Utopia is not unrealizable in the way that a barefoot ascent of Everest is unrealizable. It is impossible in empirical fact for the human body to harden itself to the point where it could surmount those icy slopes barefoot, but no essential contradiction of human nature, or of the laws of gravitation, is to be found here. Kolnai emphasizes that what singles out the utopian project is precisely its being unrealizable a priori—that is, its being *contradictory* or *unthinkable*. The reproach one can and ought to make against the political utopian is not that of wanting to realize what is not realizable but that of wanting to realize—or at least claiming to want to realize and acting as if he truly wanted to realize—what is not even thinkable, what neither he nor anyone else can completely think out without contradiction. The man who gives himself unrealizable but thinkable objectives, such as climbing Everest barefoot or conquering the world, incurs ridicule, or, like Alexander the Great, he commands the admiration that we will accord to one who fails nobly because he has undertaken too much. One who gives himself objectives which are unrealizable *because* they are unthinkable destroys or corrupts, both in himself and in those he seduces or subdues, the natural relationship between ideas, motives, and values, on the one hand, and human action, on the other. What he attacks is the internal constitution of the human world.

In Kolnai's eyes this "unthinkable" or "contradictory" character of the utopian project is immediately apparent from its claim that the new order of humanity must be attained by the conscious and deliberate actions of an enlightened group that is in full command of the direction in which they are headed, fully aware of each stage on the way, *even as* the new order itself nevertheless represents perfect spontaneity or total freedom. On the one hand there is the artificial, the self-conscious, the preconceived; on the other, there is the natural, the spontaneous, the unforeseen. These will mingle, support, or hinder each other yet be inextricably entangled in ordinary society; in the utopian project they are at the same time violently divorced and totally confounded. During the phase of "constructing" the new order, they will be violently divorced. But then it seems they will be totally confounded in the new order that is realized. The distinction between two phases—of before and after the institution of the new order—does not remove the contradiction. For even during the phase of construction, the utopian group or sect *simultaneously* desires sovereign mastery over nature or history *and* docile servitude under it.

This contradiction is especially characteristic of totalitarian utopias.

In the Bolshevik project, for example, the organization and action of the party are kept rigorously apart from civil society and even apart from the working class that they are thought to represent. Yet at the same time, this organization and action are identical with the irresistible spontaneity of the historical movement for which society provides the location and the instrument. (That is the basis of their legitimacy.) The emphasis differs in the project of National Socialism. Here, deliberate political action is the servant not so much of history—though Nazism did itself claim to be borne along by the wave of history—as of nature, the nature which precedes and transcends every human project, a purely biological or animal nature, lacking all specific human characteristics. The superhuman is claimed and constructed in the name of the subhuman. Though it uses the language and the disguise of a distorted "biological science," it represents the same, familiar utopian contradiction. In every case the totalitarian project simultaneously affirms the absolute sovereignty of man—his triumph over necessity through his own efforts and his ushering in of the reign of liberty, or else his creation of the superman—and his absolute enslavement, either to historical necessity or to blood and race.

Kolnai's analysis, of which I have here been able to give merely the bare bones, has the considerable merit of defining clearly the concept of totalitarianism. This idea once attracted considerable attention, largely as a result of Hannah Arendt's work,[3] but today it has fallen somewhat out of favor, at least in Anglo-Saxon countries. But whatever totalitarian regimes may have in common with dictatorships and despotisms, their specific characteristic—the one that most markedly affects their functioning and their impact on the societies enslaved by them—is their utopian logic. It is in this utopian kernel that the explanation is to be found of the strange yet absolutely central role of terror in these regimes. The totalitarian organization or party must not only show that it is still the only victor in the political struggle, the one and only sovereign; it must also make people understand and feel that a new reality has replaced yesterday's shabby and corrupted world. Yet, according to the theory, this new reality will be realized only when the totalitarian organization has withered away and the new man has been left to his spontaneity. To get over this contradiction, the regime compels society— that is, the old society now overturned through its violence—to *say* that it *is* the new reality, the new world transported with happiness; it compels it to acclaim its total subjection as a complete liberation. Thus, it is the office of terror both to affirm and to deny the distance between the surreal world of utopia and the real world.[4]

The reason why there is such a temptation to consider totalitarianism as simply an extreme version of ordinary or perpetual despotism is, as we have just seen, precisely the element of unthinkability that resides in its specific project or proper essence. How, then, can the unthinkable be thought? The analyst or interpreter must force himself, let us say, to think objectively somehow what cannot be thought subjectively. If he wants to render the temptation harmless, he must show how this subjectively unthinkable, contradictory end is nonetheless objectively possible. The better he can show how the utopian project helps man to escape from his condition, the more he is obliged to show how such an aberration is possible, how it has its origins and the conditions of its possibility in the shared human situation.

On this point, Kolnai establishes, with a great wealth of psychological analyses, the continuity of the utopian mind, even in the extreme form of totalitarianism, with mental attitudes that are commonly encountered among ordinary people and in ordinary society. He carefully distinguishes the different varieties and gradations of perfectionism and of what could be called the utopian mind in its moderate form. This is responsible for what Kolnai calls departmental utopias, which relate to a limited sphere of human life. Above all he shows how the utopian mind is born of a perversion—something which, if not natural, is at least intelligible—of our relation to values. It is natural to desire the incarnation, or realization, of positive values. In this sense, for every significant theme of human action and for every value, it is natural to desire a coincidence between the *is* and the *ought*. But in ordinary, nonutopian life, everyone is aware, despite this desire, not only of his own inadequacies and of human inadequacy in general, but also of the tension between different positive values (not to speak of the ambiguity and indetermination of every one of them), of the way in which urgency can shift value-priority, of the weight of necessity and the role of contingency. Departmental utopianism, then, selects a *single* value and claims that its realization will lead infallibly to the realization of all other values, or at least the main ones. For example, it is supposed that morality will bring prosperity, health, and happiness. But extreme or totalitarian utopianism—that is, utopianism par excellence—allows itself to become obsessed with, or infatuated by, the evident desirability not just of a particular value, or even all of them together, but of the coincidence of the *is* and *ought* as such. It will experience a burning desire for resolute action—so that this coincidence may be effectively guaranteed. By a subtle but decisive displacement, the idea of "evidence" is transported from the intellectual to the volitional sphere. Since it is far from evident to the intellect what would count as such a coincidence of *is* and *ought*, the will takes its place and conceives the desire for that which it cannot conceive—while making the intellect believe that it conceives it. But then, in reaction, there is an inevitable rebound, and the feeling of contingency and freedom emigrates from the volitional to the intellectual sphere. Cut off by the will's decision from all authentic contact with the real world, the intellect feels an intoxicating license to justify and motivate whatever actions the utopian will dictates. Thus, the respective places in the human economy of theory and practice, intellect and will, are interchanged.

To see these diagnoses of utopianism as metaphysical subtleties would be a great mistake. As Kolnai deploys them, they make a powerful contribution to our understanding of certain particularly strange features of totalitarian action. Take Bolshevism. This is characterized by an astonishing formal rigidity of ideological framework, coupled with an almost incredible arbitrariness in the ideas that form the immediate accompaniment of action. (Thus, simultaneously, the party is always right: yet, between one day and the next, such and such a hero of the revolution becomes an inveterate enemy of the people.) The rigidity of the ideological framework certifies the absolute legitimacy of the totalitarian organization and the self-evident desirability of its action. Since the will is thus guaranteed and strengthened in its self-evidence, revolutionary action enjoys absolute freedom in its choice of means and measures, and in their justification. And, whereas the ideology affirms that "socialism is achieved," action—that is to say, terror—is justified by the claim that many individuals, even within the party, even among the companions of the supreme leader, are busy day and night in the work of reestablishing capitalism. Thus, the ideas that constitute or go to formulate the utopian project are not there to create a bond between the agent and values, to guide his action or inform his will; on the contrary, their function is to liberate the will from all rules, from any mental content whatsoever, and to protect the agents of utopia from all spontaneous and personal contact with values.

For all its intrinsic aberrancy and the destructiveness of its practical implications, this inversion of the roles of theory and practice has been, if not directly caused, then made possible at least by an intellectual development which seems quite innocent and even salutary—it is one with which we are, in any case, perfectly familiar—namely, the virtual disappearance of "practical reason" from the political thought of the last three centuries. It is a commonplace that political philosophy has traditionally been conceived, largely under Aristotle's influence, as a practical science. But now it has tended to become pure theory. (The almost complete substitution of the idea of political theory or science for that of political philosophy is the linguistic expression of this noteworthy fact.) The social or political scientist tends to regard the body politic as a "system" or "structure" whose functioning he endeavors to describe, while so far as possible ignoring the motives or ends that lead men to act in this structure or system. That is to say, he refuses to take account, as philosophy once did, of what links him, the observer or thinker, to the object of his study. He refuses to take account of what makes both of these human. For the most part he is content to rely on what is a virtual tautology—that men act in accordance with what he calls their interest. Since "interest" is defined here as what the agent himself thinks it is, the political scientist's assumption amounts to this—that men act as they desire to act, or desire to act as they act.

The rationale of a development such as this seems to me to be the following. An Aristotelian analysis of human conduct in terms of motives or ends—in terms, that is, of *our* motives or our ends—seemed to lead almost inevitably to a *ranking* of these motives and ends, and the subsequent elaboration of a dogmatic philosophy of human nature or human good. This conception of human nature and human good leads to the conception and promotion of a political regime "in conformity with the nature" of man. But this in its turn seems to endanger the liberal idea of a political power which is neutral between various conceptions of human life or between various worldviews. It is clear that the transformation of political philosophy and its practical knowledge into a political science that is *value-free* is closely bound up with the development of liberal and representative political regimes. Thus, in so far as it rests on the dwindling of ideas of practical reason and the hypertrophy of theory or science, the utopian or totalitarian temptation is bound up with an intellectual development that is inseparable from the progress of our civilization. How, then, can we triumph over this temptation without reintroducing a dogmatic idea of human nature which would conflict with our liberalism, besides being heavy with the threat of reactionary utopia? It is as an answer to this question that Aurel Kolnai's conservatism is so important.

We are not obliged in ordinary life, or in the political arena, to act in the light of any clearly defined image of human nature—any thick concept of human nature. To do so would involve us once again in those arguments I have just mentioned over the definition of the "highest good," from which our fathers escaped with such difficulty when they conceived of a state which would confine itself to guaranteeing the external conditions of free action and abandon any pretension to tell us what our good is. We are born in and act in a world already structured by institutions, models, achievements, traditions—by traditions, moreover, which do not force us to be "traditionalists," precisely because we have the good fortune to be heirs to the tradition of rationally criticizing traditions. We do not have to construct an alternative world, an alternative society, as the utopian mind supposes—a construction for which we should find ourselves forced to borrow features of the world and society that we already have. (Separated from other features that complete and correct them, these would lose their value and even their meaning.) Rather, our task is quite different. It is to explore our world phenomenologically and thence to derive our concepts and motives. Any legitimate reason for transforming the world will arise from the world as it reveals itself to this kind of inquiry. I have just alluded to the phenomenological outlook. Although Kolnai hardly mentions phenomenology in this work, he was a student of Edmund Husserl, and his fundamental inspiration certainly came from that quarter. It is perfectly possible to "bracket" the ultimate categories once beloved by metaphysics and their claim to capture all that there is of nature or history. A scrupulous description of the framework of thought through which we express our humanity is enough, if not to guide all our actions, at least to provide a sound orientation for our thinking and living.

In order to define this "phenomenological conservatism" more clearly, it is well worth comparing it with the conceptions of two writers to whom Kolnai thought himself closely allied: Karl Popper and Michael Oakeshott. Like Popper, he believes that reforming activity presupposes a fixed—hence traditional—framework without which the reform cannot even be thought or appraised. In order to assess what changes, we must have something which does not change.[5] Like Oakeshott, he holds that the human world is structured by "idioms of conduct" and that human life, as Europe has come to savor it, finds its mainspring and its happiness in an attentive fidelity to the immanent meaning—and thus, for the most part, to the traditional procedures—of each of these idioms, whether culinary, scientific, or political.[6] But, in fact, Kolnai also sets himself firmly apart from these two authors. He thinks that Popper's conservatism is too exclusively epistemological, too much concentrated in the value of a traditional frame of reference for the progress of knowledge and the appraisal of reforms: that Popper is not sensible enough of the *intrinsic* merits, both moral and vital, of a conservative attitude. In the last analysis, Popper puts too much faith in the reformatory ideas of the age. As for Oakeshott, Kolnai thinks he goes too far in his criticism of "rationalism" and puts reason itself in jeopardy; that he exaggerates the virtues of "immanence," of "habitual" and "unreflective" absorption in a traditional "idiom of conduct"; that he failed to see both the necessity and the possibility of the mind's acknowledgment of objective rules, formulable in universal terms, such as moral laws; and even of its striving, within certain limits, to define something resembling a human nature, albeit in sketchy and tentative fashion. If Popper's political philosophy is tainted with "progressivism," Oakeshott's is tainted with "obscurantism," with the conviction that it is possible to be a conservative and nothing else.[7]

A second and fundamental objection Kolnai makes against Oakeshott's moral philosophy is that it gives no place to *conscience,* through which a human being is able to bring his conduct into living contact with the universal rules of morality; nor to that splitness, that interior dialogue, by which one is reminded of the irreducible distance between what one does and what one ought to do, what one is and what one ought to be. This is one of the main objections Kolnai makes to the utopian mind, too. According to Oakeshott's extreme conservatism, morality consists in spontaneous conformity to the moral idiom of our civilization and to the habits it has developed—or ought to have developed—if it had not been in part overlaid by reflexive and abstract conceptions of morality. But the utopian mind empties conscience even more radically. In its contemplation of a future state of humanity in which reality and value, *is* and *ought,* coincide, it contemplates a human condition in which conscience will have no function and no meaning. The man of the future, man par excellence, is a being without conscience. It follows that what is given to us as conscience in our present state is, in the utopian's eyes, merely social man's dissatisfaction with our actual and provisional condition, a dissatisfaction which will naturally come to an end when utopia is realized.

Thus, whereas Kolnai judges Oakeshott to display a kind of aestheticizing extremism in his striving to be a conservative and nothing else, the distinctive mark of Kolnai's own conservatism could be said to be its giving so large a place to conscience, understood as the capacity and the duty of every person to judge situations, actions, and human beings (himself included) not only in the light of the idioms of conduct implicit in our civilization but also in the light of explicit and universal rules. Certainly conscience as such is not conservative. On the contrary, since it judges—wisely or unwisely—in the name of a moral absolute, it can easily become the principle of a revolutionary attitude if it is left to run on its own. That is why, in practice, totalitarian undertakings find so ready a support among sincerely conscientious people who are indignant at the misery of the poor, say, or at national humiliation—moving them to place their moral energy in the service of a conception which destroys the very idea of conscience. But this is the point. It is because there is a natural and necessary tension between the conscientious and the conservative attitudes that the prudent man has to learn how to combine them, to learn that the relative weight of each depends on circumstances and on the agent's ability to compose and harmonize, judiciously and even stylishly, the various legitimate themes of free conduct. A conscience with a lively sensitivity to universal moral demands but also well aware of political constraints, of ambiguities and conflicts of values and the uncertainties attending action; a conscience which, when it is at odds with the world, does not hurry to condemn the world but takes time to weigh the adversary's reasons; in short, a conscience informed and armed with a conservative political philosophy; here, says Kolnai, is the rock on which the totalitarian temptation, and the more general utopian temptation, will founder.

Kolnai's criticism of the utopian mind is pertinent and convincing, and his phenomenology of the social world contains a wealth of suggestions. Nevertheless, it seems to me that there is an important question that he largely ignores: what is it that has brought about the devastating spread of the utopian spirit in modern times, especially the twentieth century? As I have already pointed out, one can only admire Kolnai's demonstration of how the utopian illusion rests so naturally on the human relation to values and to the desirable, yet goes on to falsify and pervert it. But is this psychological genealogy enough? The real theme of Kolnai's investigation is not so much the utopian mind as such, which is always possible and present to some degree in every age. It is the modern, extreme form of the utopian mind: namely, totalitarianism. Kolnai does show that there is a legitimate place for a study of the social, political, and spiritual circumstances which have favored the development of totalitarianism, and among these it would seem that he accorded central importance to the mechanisms of mass society. But he does not enquire more deeply into them.

Certainly the utopian mind displays more than enough striking and clearly defined characteristics for it to be treated as a kind of essence. The fruitfulness of Kolnai's analysis amply justifies singling out this mentality for study. Not only that—there is even a danger of blurring the sharp outline of totalitarianism by concentrating on an enumeration, however erudite and discerning, of the circumstances which have favored its development. But between the uniqueness and solidity of the essence on the one hand, and the multiplicity of circumstances to which the analyst seems free to refer or not as he sees fit on the other, there seems to be too great a hiatus. Something is still wanting in the analysis. I am led to think that the missing link we are looking for, between the essence and the circumstances, can be found only in the study of ideas. Is the utopian mind an ever-present possibility for the human relation to values as it is actualized under particular circumstances? Perhaps this is so, but if these circumstances are to set in motion such a radically new historical phenomenon, with the consequence that this natural possibility should be realized and stabilized in an essence as prodigiously effective as that of totalitarianism, then the explanation has to lie in the working of some intellectual system that can make what is in fact unthinkable apparently thinkable, or present a contradictory project of the will as a positive scientific theory. From time to time Kolnai does recall the theories that seem to him to be particularly suggestive of the contradictions of the utopian mind, especially the theory of Rousseau. But it seems to me that Kolnai is insufficiently attentive to the actual workings of intellectual mechanisms and systems of ideas—not only in what makes all sorts of totalitarian projects possible but also in the development of modern politics more generally.

In my discussion of the dwindling of practical reason and the enlargement of the theoretical point of view, I have already pointed to what seems to me to be one of the intellectual preconditions for the existence of the totalitarian attitude. To this as it were negative condition, I should like to add a positive one.

Let us remember that Kolnai sees the central contradiction of the utopian project in the fact that man is given two strictly contradictory roles. The utopian wants man to be responsible for a radically new social world yet thinks of him as the passive product of the society which precedes him. He is thus at the same time the omnipotent master of society or history and its raw material or docile creation. He is both sovereign maker or sovereign artificer and mere matter. How can one avoid thinking here of Thomas Hobbes who, in his *Leviathan,* presents us with social man in precisely this double role, described in these very terms? Certainly Hobbesian absolutism has hardly anything in common with modern totalitarianism. But I would like to suggest that certain fundamental categories of the modern politics whose framework Hobbes did so much to determine—especially the categories of "sovereignty," "representation," and the "artificial" body politic—are pregnant with the possibility of the development or dialectic whose study might shed a strong light on the genesis of totalitarianism. In this way—thanks to our making room for this third term, which is the workings of a system of ideas—might one not articulate more completely and adequately the study of particular historical circumstances with the general phenomenology of the human world?

This is only a suggestion. Whether or not there is the need that I suppose there to be, this does not in the least impair the essential validity and importance of Kolnai's study of these matters. After all, we have plenty of judicious historians of modern political philosophy. Only very rarely do we come across thinkers like Kolnai, with the nerve to link political reflection with a phenomenology of the human world, to meet a historical emergency with their gaze fastened on the invariants of the human condition, with the nerve and the capacity to assume the role of a political philosopher.

Translated by Francis Dunlop and David Wiggins

Notes

1. See Adam Ferguson, *An Essay in the History of Civil Society* (1767), volume 4, 1.

2. See Michael Oakeshott, *Rationalism in Politics and Other Essays* (London: Methuen, 1962).

3. See Hannah Arendt, *The Origins of Totalitarianism* (New York: Harcourt Brace, 1951. Rev. ed., New York: Meridian, 1958).

4. On these points, Kolnai's analyses are very close, though he could not have known them, to those developed by Alain Besançon in his great work *Les origines intellectuelles du léninisme* (Paris: Calmann-Lévy, 1977), English translation, *The Rise of the Gulag* (New York: Continuum, 1981).

5. See Karl Popper, *The Poverty of Historicism* (London: Routledge & Kegan Paul, 1957); see also "Towards a Rational Theory of Tradition," in *Rationalist Annals* (London, 1948).

6. See Michael Oakeshott, *On Human Conduct* (Oxford: Oxford University Press, 1975); see also *Rationalism in Politics*.

7. Kolnai wrote a noteworthy review of *Rationalism in Politics*: see *Philosophy* 40 (1965), 263–64.

Part Five

Democratic Individualism

Much of Pierre Manent's work centers around an analysis of democratic individualism and its effects on the moral contents of life. Many welcome such individualism as a liberation from the tyranny of tradition and imposed obligations whereas others lament it as a solvent of authoritative and humanizing communities and forms of association. But the indisputable fact is that modern democracy is based on a principle of individual consent that dissolves traditional sources of authority and weakens human ties that had hitherto been understood to be natural. In the two essays "On Modern Individualism" and "Recovering Human Attachments: An Introduction to Allan Bloom's *Love and Friendship*," Manent explores the effects of democratic individualism on the capacity of human beings to "put reasons and actions in common." His essays are in no way a lament for lost community but rather a reflection on the enduring tension between the modern principle of consent and the natural human desire to recognize a public order, a realm of shared endeavors, greater than that of the isolated or disconnected individual.

Following Alexis de Tocqueville, Manent recognizes that the reconnection of human beings in modern societies depends on statesmanship or political art. But the reconnection of "disassociated" men in democratic times is *not solely* the work of political art. This task has natural supports, summed up by Bloom in the Platonic term, *eros.* Manent retraces Bloom's diagnosis of our erotic maladies and his prescriptions for a recovery of human ties given in his last book, *Love and Friendship.*

On Modern Individualism

Pierre Manent

1995

On the last page of the final chapter of *Democracy in America,* where Alexis de Tocqueville puts forth what he calls the "general survey" of his subject, he sums up the comparison that he has just made between the new democracy and the old order: "They are like two distinct orders of human beings." In fact, this is indeed the feeling that both partisans and adversaries of the modern democratic and individualist movement have had, and still have today: a new type of humanity has left the old type behind and gone its own way, extending the gap between the two ever wider. In a certain sense, this shared impression is more important than the other points on which the two schools of thought disagree, for it suggests that there has been something like a radical change in the human situation.

Both schools of thought, moreover, are correct. As opponents of democracy have warned, the growth of the democratic tendency has acted as a solvent of community and "belonging." To the degree that other communities and forms of "belonging" appear under democratic conditions, they do so on the basis of individual consent, which is the founding principle of the new regime. At the same time, defenders of democracy are also correct when they point out that this dissolution also constitutes a liberation, since henceforth no one need accept an obligation to which he does not consent. The hopes of the latter have perhaps been disappointed, while the fears of the former have not been definitively confirmed (a circumstance that certain "reactionaries" may view as a source more of disappointment than of relief). But the effectual

This essay, which originally appeared in the summer 1995 issue of *Commentaire,* was translated from the French by Philip J. Costopoulos and appeared in the January 1996 issue of *The Journal of Democracy.* It is republished with permission.

truth of this liberation that is also a dissolution—or this dissolution that is also a liberation—remains. The fact of emancipation is there.

The communities to which people belong in the democratic world no longer command them. In the domestic sphere, the law has abolished the power of the head of the family, and mothers and fathers (now co-equal as parents) demand less and less obedience from their offspring, whom they tend more and more to see as likenesses and coequals of themselves. In the national sphere, even a government that is legitimately (that is to say, democratically) elected dares not order citizen-soldiers to die for their country: if a state undertakes military operations that involve some risk, it entrusts them to a professional (sometimes "all-volunteer") military. In the Catholic Church, the Roman magisterium, even while maintaining intact the place of "ultimate ends" in its authoritative teaching documents, has since the end of the Second Vatican Council ceased, in its ordinary pastoral ministry, to insist upon the urgency of salvation and the imperious necessity of obeying the church's commandments in order to obtain it. Officials of its hierarchy even meet in congress with representatives of other religions. Finally, the past itself, understood as the community of those who are dead, has lost all authority to command, whether it be in the moral, social, political, or religious sphere, and is no more than a collection of "memorable places" thrown open to historical tourism.

Searching for the State of Nature

These facts are well known. Some might say that they are difficult to interpret—too massive, as it were, to say much to us about how people really live under democracy. Fair enough. Let us then consider the domain in which modern humanity records its intimate life—indeed, where it ever more completely records its ever more intimate life. I am speaking, of course, of literature. Certainly it would be futile to try to summarize the thrust of all modern literature in a single formula, nor am I trying to elaborate some pet "theory of literature." Yet in the final analysis, it seems to me that from Marcel Proust and Louis-Ferdinand Céline to the "theater of the absurd" and the *nouveau roman,* modern literature has sought to unmask the falsity of all human relationships, the illusory character of love, and the ludicrousness or fraudulence of language. The upshot is an exploration of what it means to become an individual. Modern literature pursues this enterprise with a doggedness and a fervor that alone explain, far more than mere "fashion," the obsessive preoccupations of the avant-garde and the literary innovations that characterize it.

A will to knowledge is at work here, elaborating a kind of negative anthropology that is supported not by faith but by distrust—by an explicit lack of faith in any and all human attachments. In its intensity and radical character, this movement opposes and seeks to displace the two great authorities that previously nourished literature: the Greek and Roman classics on the one hand, and the Christian Bible on the other. No more the heroic quest, no more the voyage along the path to wisdom, no more the pilgrimage of the soul toward God, but only and precisely a "journey to the end of night," where one at last discovers what it is to be a pure individual, outside of social bonds and even outside of language.

I will now do what I just said would be pointless, and attempt to encapsulate this tendency in a phrase. This movement is an attempt to return by means of literature—through literary investigation and literary instruments—from society to what philosophers used to call the *state of nature,* meaning that state where only individuals exist, and exist only in their individuality. Civilization keeps perfecting itself as democratic nations entwine the globe in a network that grows ever larger and ever more densely studded with technological, juridical, and political devices designed to ensure that all peoples can live together (or at any rate, to ensure that peoples prevented from living together by geography and history can at least "communicate"). Yet at the same time, the life of the mind in these nations is dominated by the effort, in the realm of literature and perhaps in that of art more generally, to undo or "deconstruct" all human relationships. This double movement, of artificial construction and deconstruction, contains nothing contradictory, for each of its two moments obeys the same principle: there are no natural links binding people to one another; people are therefore the authors of their own links, the artists of their own connections. This is why, despite the communications superhighways that girdle our planet, literature speaks stubbornly of the impossibility of saying anything. Behind the devices and artifices of an ever more technologically sophisticated civilization—behind what Rousseau in the eighteenth century was already calling "the vast machinery of happiness and pleasure"—lurks the abyss of human unconnectedness. New York is more than ever the capital of the world: beneath shimmering skyscrapers, yuppies with portable phones that enable their owners to talk to distant parts of the world within seconds share the streets with homeless drifters who stumble about in worn-out shoes, babbling harmlessly to themselves in private languages that no one else can understand.

This democratic predicament, this experience of the liberating dissolution of bonds, contains a mission for each individual, for each is "condemned to be free." This, recognizable under quite different rhetorical guises, is the specific pathos of modern individualism. Just as for Sören Kierkegaard to be a Christian is to become a Christian, so for the self-aware modern to be an individual is to become an individual—and to become one to an ever-greater degree than before.

Assuredly, the development of modern individualism has not been a triumphal march, no matter how victorious liberalism might seem today. Modern individualism has aroused against itself some exceedingly resolute foes, especially in our own century. The two great revolutionary projects of the twentieth century raged against it, after all. I will say just a word about them.

The revolutionary critique and project of the extreme left constituted an attempt to recover human community (the "species being" of man, in Marx's words) by leading the process of the bourgeoisie's dissolution to its end and "expropriating the expropriators." Experience would show, however, that where there is no longer any private property, there is no longer any common or social property, and no more public realm. As Aristotle long ago pointed out in his criticism of Platonic "communism," when the unity of the city is pushed beyond a certain point, the city itself is destroyed in the process.

The revolutionary critique and project of the extreme right rejected the very idea of civilization. The extreme right claimed to see through to the nothingness that lurked behind civilization's brilliant facade in order to prepare the way for a sovereign decision, a prodigious (which is to say monstrous) effort of will that would create the unity of the chosen political group. This group would then hurl itself outward, devastating a shattered world. The justification, or rather philosophical accompaniment, of all this was the notion, borrowed from communist ideology, that violence, whether open or hidden, had been lurking there all along, subsisting in the absence of authentic human relationships. Though I would not attempt to "deduce" the reasons for the most unfathomable event of this century, the Holocaust, I would suggest that the Jews' status as the targets and designated victims of the Nazi project had something to do with the situation of the Jews and Judaism after the modern emancipation, in whose wake Jews found themselves neither a religion, a territorial nation, a race, nor any other fixed social or political entity. Jewishness, then, represented a kind of pure human tie— the human relationship as such, if you will—in the form of a particular people.

However one gauges the significance of this last point, it is clear that beneath the appearances that each tried to project of building a new kind of community, communism and Nazism were actually unprecedentedly virulent promoters of what I call the absence of the natural human bond, which is the premise of modern individualism and something that the artifice of civilization both employs and overcomes.

Must we then admit that, schooled by the frightful experience of our century, we can do nothing but accept with docility and resolution the task that we find contained in our situation as individuals? Are we effectively "doomed to freedom," powerless to achieve the critical distance needed to judge our own situation? I do not believe that. Certainly, we are and wish to be individuals. That means, however, that we are and wish to be *human* individuals. But insofar as we are human, what do we have in common? This is a question—simple, prosaic, maybe even a bit dull—that modern politics never gets around to asking. (Socialist politics does an even poorer job than its liberal counterpart here, for liberal politics at least assumes that we all have our status as individuals in common.) As human individuals, what is proper to each of us and what is common to all of us? The doctrines on which our political regime is based never confront this question because they presuppose that the individual is the only source of all legitimacy and that anything which is added to the individual, meaning in the first place the body politic or the state, is only a more or less regrettable necessity, and not something that has any real human *meaning*. Yet the political order—including the liberal regime that is so familiar to us—constitutes in fact *a certain method of holding things in common*.

Searching for What Is Common

What is to be held in common? To answer this question would require a long excursion into political philosophy, but I can offer an example that may prove suggestive. Instituting a political order, prior to consulting the will of any individual, requires first the staking out of a common territory. A common territory is the barest requirement of a political community, to be sure, but it is also in a sense the most necessary. This can be seen if we examine the ongoing process of "the construction of Europe." From year to year, the territory that is considered "Europe" gets bigger, and looks as if it will keep on expanding indefinitely. What is this body politic, this "political Europe" that people talk about, when it cannot even clear the minimum hurdle of fixing a common territory? But if political Europe is not in the making, what is all that activity going on at European Union headquarters in Brussels and at the European Parliament in Strasbourg, where something is surely being accomplished? They are just advancing civilization, first of all by multiplying the organs of communication.

West Europeans often feel that their indifference toward territorial questions is vindicated by the outbreak of savage territorial disputes in Eastern Europe, particularly in the former Yugoslavia. Actually, the lesson is the reverse. The hypersensitive territoriality of Eastern Europe's ethnic cleansers is the inverted image, and in part the effect, of our own lack of territorial consciousness. If we refuse to accept first of all political responsibilities, the definition of a common territory, and if in consequence we fail to rethink the fatal idea of an indefinite expansion of Europe, what we are pleased to call the political construction of Europe will in fact be its dissolution.

Of course, this substitution of civilization for the political is not a simple aberration or weakness. One could even cite some rather good reasons for it. If the political order consists in holding certain things in common, in organizing the "common good," so to speak, then we cannot ignore the reality that what unites people most intensely is also what divides them most intensely. In particular, the higher the plane on which the common realm is pitched, the more it will tend to divide rather than unite. The loftiest type of truth, religious truth, was the most active principle of unity and community before becoming the most corrosive principle of separation. That is why it was finally necessary to subtract religious truth from the common domain: to make it no longer a subject of public commandments, but rather what the Germans call a *Privatsache* (a personal matter). At that point, the nation became the highest common entity, the new basis of human association in Europe. The rub, however, was that there were a number of nations; before long, they were waging dreadful wars against one another. A lot of reasonable and well intentioned people have taken the view that it is time for Europe to renounce this political form, and for Europeans to learn to live together within the realm of civilization alone. Most of those who talk about "Europe" today are thinking along these lines, and "Europe" is now only a high-sounding but abstract frame for that democratic individualism which I have taken as a point of departure for my reflections here. But while I readily admit that one can renounce the nation as a political form, I do not believe that people can live long within civilization alone without some sense of political belonging (which is necessarily exclusive), and thus without some definition of what is held in common.

Someone might point out that I have been neglecting a particularly precious possibility, the possibility that human relationships might be affirmed as such, for their own value and on their own terms, so that no one has to establish what is common, a work that is always arduous and which threatens to lead to untameable conflicts. It might be said that we can affirm a principle of action that is at once individualistic and communitarian by beginning with the observation that what is held in common is humanity itself, the fact of being human, and then allowing this fact to work with its own fertile indeterminacy. This is a tempting option, for it allows us to get around the difficulty of thinking hard about what should be held in common. On this view, one might say: Only one thing is needful, that people respect one another's humanity. Immanuel Kant has already given this approach its most rigorous formulation, in every sense of the term. The Kantian subject says, "What I ought to respect in the other is the respect that he has (or, inasmuch as he is rational, that he ought to have) for the moral law." But the modern individual hardly loves the law; in fact, he detests it, and it is hard to see how this hatred that he bears for the law can be combined with respect for the law. Kant's rigorous understanding of respect for others, then, becomes displaced by a sentimental version that grounds itself in compassion. Our humanism is humanitarianism. Unfortunately, when pity is asked to do the work of a political principle, it rather quickly encounters severe limits. Let me emphasize what they are.

As Jean-Jacques Rousseau, who was its first great promoter, noticed early on, pity (understood as compassion for physical suffering or misery) scarcely distinguishes between men and beasts. This helps to explain why in the West today the defense of "animal rights" is becoming increasingly vehement. For this same reason, pity can never be the sufficient principle of any properly human community.

Pity as such is an emotion or a passion; it is highly dependent on images, and hence is vulnerable to the manipulation of images.

Pity is selfish; the condition for its possibility is that I myself am not suffering, and that I am aware of that exemption. Pity makes me feel the pleasure of not suffering.

Pity is indeterminate; any suffering can arouse it, and it contains within itself no principle of evaluation or comparison. The whiner who suffers loudly and visibly elicits our tears, while we pass indifferently by the brave man who "keeps a stiff upper lip" and refuses to reveal his pain. One might retort that the urgency of the need to act is a rather evident principle, but in fact this is evidently not the case, for one has so many urgencies from which to choose. Moreover, pity does not necessarily bring with it the idea of action designed to put an end to the pathetic situation that aroused it in the first place. If I come across a torturer tormenting a victim, I can kill the torturer; interpose myself "peacefully" between the torturer and his victim; make a token gesture of interposition (precisely to testify to the pity that I feel); ask myself whether the victim does not share some of the blame for his own predicament; remind myself that a half-century ago the grandparents of the victim were the torturers and the grandparents of the torturer were the victims; and so on. Pity's chief limitation can be summed up briefly: it does nothing to get us out of the state of nature. It is a feeling that might possibly arise between two human individuals considered in the abstract, outside of any given political order, but so are cruelty and indifference. There is no immediate evidence of being human, no immediate experience of "the other," that dispenses us from the necessity (which is also an obligation) of building a political order, and therefore of asking ourselves about what is to be held in common. This in turn means posing in all its fullness the political question—that is to say, the question of justice.

Yet is there not a specific type of relationship—one that constitutes a very characteristic form of justice among us—by means of which our society harmoniously combines individual liberty and social obligations? I am referring, of course, to the institution of contracts. Through the contracts that he makes with his fellows, each individual is the author of his every obligation. At the same time, he sets limits to his own whimsy and self-indulgence, since *pacta sunt servanda* ("contracts must be honored"). In actuality, in both its effectiveness and its meaning, the contract is indeterminate, or at least underdetermined. Every contract depends on a context. In its most stripped-down (but often most decisive) definition, the context means the correlation of forces, the relative strength of the parties involved. The socialist tradition has always stressed the degree to which the labor contract between worker and employer is an unequal social and economic relationship masquerading under the guise of a free agreement between two legally equal individuals. Vital as this instrument of human association might be, the contract also leaves unanswered the question of what is common. Returning to our example of the worker and the employer, we ask, what is common? Is it the business enterprise? The social class? The market? If one were to consider carefully another type of contract, the contract of marriage, where that which is the most private, one's body, becomes in a way common property, one would be led to still more interesting reflections.

Contractual justice is necessary, but not sufficient. We certainly cannot excuse ourselves from broaching the question of what we ought to hold in common. Yet this in turn brings us up against an ambiguity, one that I will discuss by way of a conclusion. What is common, what may be the common denominator, is what every individual possesses and what all the others also possess: for example, a body. All individuals have bodies, so the body is a common denominator—but an individual's body is in no way held in common, and is even that which is "most one's own." The distinction becomes decisively important when we consider human rights, which, contrary to what some of their more spirited defenders believe or hope, are concerned with the common denominator rather than what is held in common. That which is "common" about the common denominator does not lead us beyond the scope of mere individualism, for it *defines* that scope. By contrast, what is common in the strong, full, and almost sacred sense of that term is something whose embrace or appropriation transforms the individual by taking him beyond himself. Can we observe, discover, or in some way acknowledge that there is something—it would be precisely the "public thing" (the commonweal or *res publica*)—greater than ourselves? And can we hope that this public thing will make us greater than ourselves? Only with these two other questions in mind can we take the full measure of the magnitude and the gravity of the question: What is to be held in common?

Recovering Human Attachments: An Introduction to Allan Bloom's *Love and Friendship*

Pierre Manent

1996

Allan Bloom's great inquiry has its origin in the very simple observation that our societies are the least erotic of all. Of course, appearances can be deceiving. But the very fact that we are so eager to tell all, to show all, and to look at everything—and to do so without blushing— proves that we flee Eros rather than see it as it is. One cannot simply see eros as it is, because it is impossible to find a neutral place between desire and law, or shame, where we could objectively contemplate the phenomenon. What we really do is cast over it a net of abstractions—the "facts" and "rights" of "sex" for which the female magazines enthusiastically provide the weekly tally. This gives us a fictitious mastery and allows us to derive our greatest and completely uncarnal pleasure: our feeling of superiority over all preceding worlds because our science and our "realism about life" have triumphed over the prejudices that once dominated.

Each epoch is captive to its conventions. Ours would not be worse in this regard, except for its pretense to have done away with all conventions. Each epoch therefore must win for itself the truth of human experience against its most cherished prejudices. It is not because everyone in principle is a citizen that there no longer are reasons to ask oneself about citizenship, its meaning, and finally its decline. The for-

Pierre Manent was the French translator of Allan Bloom's last, posthumously published book *Love and Friendship* (New York: Simon & Schuster, 1993), published in French as *L'Amour et L'Amitié* (Paris: Éditions de Fallois, 1996). This essay originally appeared in French as part of a symposium on Bloom's life and work in the journal *Commentaire* (Number 76, Winter 1996–1997). It appears here with permission.

tunate liberty left to each to believe or not to believe in God takes nothing away from the necessity for each to pose anew the question *quid sit deus*. Allan Bloom thinks that this effort to discover authentic experience is today most necessary in the domain of private attachments, in the realm of love and friendship, because it is at once the most natural and the most threatened. Why is it particularly threatened? It is not only because the illusion of objectivity of which I have spoken has perhaps penetrated it more deeply than it has affected the political or religious domains. It is also because the only vocation that contemporary man recognizes is that of being an individual. Modern man aims to become ever more the author and artist of all his ties—to be always more unobliged or disconnected.

There is much to be said in favor of this emancipation. It is freedom and deliverance. Whether the tie is political or religious or concerns love or friendship, it risks being tyrannical and mutilating—and it is almost always so to some degree. At the same time, these bonds are born of experiences that give form and content to life and that everyone recognizes, once they let down their guard, as the most precious part of life. In short, human desire is inseparably desire for connection *and* for freedom. A fine discovery, the skeptics will mutter. Of course not, but it still is a matter of importance to discover the variety of human connections as well as of liberty, with the conflicts and the complementarities they involve. Today we satisfy ourselves with saying, above all, do what you want—nature then will somehow not fail to make you happy. As the Duke of Wellington once said to a passerby who had mistaken him for someone else, if you believe that you will believe anything!

Understanding Rousseau

How, then, are we to recover the rich complexity of our connections? Where are we to begin? And how are we to avoid arbitrariness? Bloom naturally starts from the last great interpretation of love—he starts from romanticism as elaborated by Jean-Jacques Rousseau and his successors. But one might object that we are not romantics. This objection is true. But we are disillusioned or sobered romantics who commit ourselves to "realism." To orient ourselves in this great subject, we must first recover the meaning of romanticism by understanding Rousseau. Bloom's superiority lies in the fact that he most profoundly grasped that Rousseau not only is a writer and philosopher of the first rank but that he also is the last great reformer of the West (Friedrich Nietzsche is, in this respect, only a distant second). As a philosopher, Rousseau above all wants to understand, but as a reformer, as someone who wants to change men's objects of esteem, he formulates a philanthropic project. To be sure, his project depends on the understanding, even if it is not completely adequate to it. Rousseau begins with and always returns to the claim that man, by nature, loves only himself and can only love himself. At the same time, he cannot lead a truly human life unless he loves other men as he loves himself, and unless he loves something greater than himself as he loves himself. He must therefore construct a second nature in which paradoxically he will love only himself while loving someone other than himself. This second nature can be the city, of which the *Social Contract* provides the design. However, the development of great states, the expansion of commerce, and Christianity's influence all contribute powerful obstacles to the realization of this admirable form of human association. For Rousseau, it is thus more judicious, and finally more satisfying, to construct this second nature around the human couple. This is because one can find support for this project in the first nature whose power remains intact, since it is inscribed in the natural difference between man and woman. No one, in any language, wrote about this difference with as much exactitude of observation as Rousseau does in book five of *Émile*. Book five is a kind of précis of thoughtfulness about life. This ordinarily escapes us because we believe that on this subject everything that can be said is equally plausible and indefensible, and we thus read *Émile* with the superior smile of the sobered Romantics that we, in fact, are.

The "Effectual Truth" of Romanticism

If Rousseau's construction is so beautiful and so true, why do we smile at it? Why have we ceased being romantics? According to Bloom, Rousseau's construction remains too much just that, a construction and a project. The project is to weave the entire human bond around the aforementioned difference, to have the entire human world turn around the pair of lovers, soon to be faithful spouses, to make the possibility of a noble and happy life coincide with the possibility of a happy couple. Intellectually speaking, this entails an oversimplification of human life. It leads in practice to burdening the couple with a superhuman responsibility and subjecting them to excessive pressure—a pressure that weighs with greater cruelty on the most vulnerable link, the woman as spouse and mother. The romantic project aims at condensing all of life's possibilities into the perfectly complementary human couple. But as Bloom shows by studying what the Rousseauian vision becomes in the great romantic novels of the nineteenth century (from Mme. de Renal to Emma Bovary and Anna Karenina), the adulterous wife is the "effectual truth" of romanticism. If the romantic vision is defective, if Rousseau despite his prodigious understanding of the relation between the sexes nonetheless simplified the problem of human connections, what should we do and where should we turn if we do not wish to be merely post-romantics who orient ourselves exclusively in terms of the vision we reject? Otherwise, we condemn ourselves to a perpetual irony about our own passions—the irony about which Benjamin Constant spoke so well, because it caused him so much suffering.

A Mirror of Nature

The limitations of Rousseau's vision are included in his project, the most disinterested and most humane of projects, but still finally a project. As soon as one wants to transform the world, one gives up to some extent the comprehension of it. One is obliged to focus on a part of the whole, toward which we direct our intervention; one is obliged to forget the whole where alone one can find the truth. To make of the couple a whole, Rousseau almost had to forget the larger whole that is the city, and the even more vast whole which is the whole of everything. But where are we to look for the true image of the whole? Who will succeed where Rousseau failed? Where can one contemplate the infinite variety of all the bonds that can connect man to a friend, the city, the world and the gods? Bloom convincingly suggests that Shakespeare is this pure mirror of nature. Bloom's first book, in fact, was called *Shakespeare's Politics*.[1] In *Love and Friendship* he discovers in Shakespeare the full display of the human phenomenon and how love, the city, and divinity are joined and articulated; pagan eros and Christian sanctity, the interplay of love and law, and of war and love. I cannot here retrace his tour through Shakespeare or his profound reflections on comedy and tragedy. I will emphasize one point. Bloom reminds us that Shakespeare not only portrayed unforgettable pairs of lovers (he even speaks with a sort of trembling admiration about Antony and Cleopatra); less famous but equally and perhaps more interesting are his pairs of friends. Bloom focuses the spotlight on the pair formed by Hal and Falstaff, the young prince who will inherit the throne of England and the obscene barfly. What connects such different human beings when there is not an initial bodily attraction? What connected Michel de Montaigne and Étienne de la Boétie? Allan Bloom quite impressively helps us to discern the strange bond whose expression is not an embrace but conversation, whose element is not feeling but reason, whose purpose is not to engender beings of flesh but to discover in common the truth about man. This is a bond whose meaning we have lost, even if we frequently use the word *friendship*.

On this point, no matter how lucid and disillusioned we may think we are, we are the most sentimental of men, simply because we do not think that reason is something real that can truly unite us. We only see in it an instrument or a "rationalization" of our needs, desires, and "values." By heeding Jane Austen's irony, by seeing what Shakespearean characters as different as Prospero, Falstaff, and Ulysses have in common, by recovering the meaning and substance of Montaigne's essay on friendship, Bloom alerts us to the incandescent secret of this way of life which is the life of reason, the life dedicated to understanding life. It has its mysteriously faithful reflection in a book many have read but few have understood, because in general those who think they love thought are closed off to the counsel and premonitions of the body, and those who have the opposite dispositions are in general too distracted to think things through to the end. I am speaking, of course, about Plato's *Symposium*. It is the last stage of Bloom's investigation, where he erects for us "the ladder of love." It is left for each reader to ascend its rungs. He will understand why "the love of wisdom" (philosophy) is literally, and nonmetaphorically, the most erotic of the soul's dispositions, the one that leads toward its highest possibility and that consequently is capable of forming the strongest human tie because it is the most genuine one.

We are not condemned to remain disillusioned or sober romantics, sterilely oscillating in politics, as well as in love and friendship, between a deliberately constructed illusion and an ironically anticipated deception. A mysterious but luminous energy circulates among the different levels of human life and the variety of human connections, and it does not circulate in vain. In the end, eros, because there really is an "end," is one with the desire for understanding and self-knowledge, and this desire, too, is not in vain. I would summarize the humanity and the severity—and hence, the gravity—of this book as follows: life is worthy of being loved because it is capable of being understood.

Translated by Daniel J. Mahoney and Paul Seaton

Note

1. See Allan Bloom (with Harry V. Jaffa), *Shakespeare's Politics* (New York: Basic Books, 1964).

Part Six

Thinking and Acting Politically

Politics, Manent frequently affirms, is a distinctive sort of reality, and it requires appropriate kinds of thinking to be properly comprehended. As a partisan of the dignity of the political, he appreciates men whose greatness lay in their capacity to think politically, that is, to grasp political reality, especially modern political reality, in its distinctiveness and complexity. Having learned from masters such as Raymond Aron and having studied the thought and action of the greatest French statesman of the twentieth century, Charles de Gaulle, Manent carries on, in his own way and idiom, their thoughtful analyses of the contemporary European scene and the prospects for viable political life today.

Manent's chief theoretical insight is that democracy's intrinsic "indetermination" of territory and population, as well as its principle of legitimacy, individual consent, require extrademocratic factors to give it determination or "flesh." Theoretical democracy, however, denies all intrinsic legitimacy to nondemocratic principles and factors. Paraphrasing Montesquieu, Manent counsels democracy to temper itself: "Today, the true friends of liberty are inclined to think, if not always to dare to say: 'Who would say it! Liberty itself has need of limits.'"

Raymond Aron and the Analysis of Modern Society

Pierre Manent

1998

When Raymond Aron died in November 1983, the left-wing newspaper *Libération* announced: "France has lost its prof." This designation was even more significant coming as it did from a newspaper born in the events and spirit of May 1968, one that represented all that Aron had fought in the last part of his life. It is true that from November 1940 (when he began to write in London for the review *La France Libre*) to the time of his death at the age of 78 (he was still writing weekly columns for *L'Express*) Aron was France's professor, in at least two ways. He was so as a journalist, regularly producing informed and judicious commentary on the domestic and foreign economic and political developments of the country; but he also was a professor in the proper sense, holding positions at the most prestigious institutions of higher learning. The book that the American reader has before him is a direct product of Aron's courses at the Sorbonne.

Whoever has not had the pleasure of taking Aron's courses or seminars does not know the extent to which academic discourse can be marked by clarity, gravity, and nobility. The writer of these lines is one of those who were initially attracted to Aron's teaching by the charm of his voice.

Among the books that stemmed from Aron's university teaching, *Main Currents in Sociological Thought* seems to me to be the most capacious and profound. The title, in French (*Les étapes de la pensée sociologique;*

This essay originally appeared as the foreword to Raymond Aron, *Main Currents in Sociological Thought*, volume 1: *Montesquieu, Comte, Marx, Tocqueville, and the Sociologists and the Revolution of 1848* (New Brunswick: Transaction, 1998). It is republished with permission.

The Stages of Sociological Thought) as well as in English, only gives a faint idea of its content. The book is, in fact, a very rich reflection on modern society and on the condition of modern man.

Modern man's life is governed by two great ideas. In the domain of action it is governed by the idea of freedom, and in the domain of knowledge by the idea of science. Aron's life and thought are situated between two extremes; on the one hand, that of a science of history and of society which attempts to abolish freedom (this was Marxism's destiny) and, on the other, a "creative" freedom which would reveal the hollowness of all so-called "objective truth." Friedrich Nietzsche and his innumerable epigones occupy this second pole. It is fair to say that Aron's entire life and work were a battle against these two extremes.

The two volumes of *Main Currents* move between two authors with whom the problem of the relationship between science and freedom comes to the forefront. They formulate projects for establishing the greatest possible room for each of these goods. I am referring to Montesquieu and Max Weber (volume 1 of *Main Currents* opens with an interpretation of Montesquieu and volume 2 culminates in a treatment of the thought of Max Weber). The first, in the middle of the eighteenth century, was simultaneously the theoretician of modern liberty—which is founded on the progress of commerce and on the separation of powers—and of a new social science which aimed to coordinate the various "things which govern men" (*The Spirit of the Laws*, 19, 4). This science would receive the name of "sociology" in the nineteenth century. The second figure, in the years leading up to the First World War, wanted to preserve both the principle of causality, which is the condition of all rational knowledge, and the sense of free and significant human action. This led him to conceive a sociology that aimed to do justice to the "subjective" viewpoint of the agent and to a politics that struggled against the impersonal bureaucratization of the world.

The authors treated in the two volumes of *Main Currents* are mainly German or French. In any case, they belong to continental Europe. This does not merely convey the biographical fact that Raymond Aron was a French writer whose formation was largely German, and who fought Marxism with weapons borrowed in part from Max Weber. More profoundly, it signifies that the development of modern society and modern freedom was much more problematic in continental Europe than in the Anglo-American world. However, the difficulties that the great continental countries experienced in institutionalizing modern freedom led, as a consequence and compensation, to a very profound inquiry into the specific nature of modern society. As Raymond Aron reconstructs it, this investigation led continental thinkers to propose three main responses to the riddle of modern society. In Karl Marx's view, modern society is defined by capitalism, that is, private property in the means of production. In Auguste Comte's view, modern society is defined by industry, that is, the application of science to the transformation of nature; and, finally, Alexis de Tocqueville argues that it is defined by democracy, that is, equality of conditions producing their effects in all of life's domains, and first of all in the political realm. To be sure, these different answers are not necessarily incompatible. One can very reasonably maintain that modern society is all three. And Aron, who was unaffected by any inclination to systematization, was disposed to discover various aspects of the social world with the assistance of these different authors. However, he was not inclined to submit to a supposedly "empirical" eclecticism. This empiricism, in fact, makes it impossible to account adequately for a decisive feature of modern experience, the disconcerting feeling of being carried away by an irresistible current to a finally "universal" humanity. This sentiment is equally present in the otherwise divergent reflections of Marx, Tocqueville, and Comte. But what *is* it that carries us along? To use Tocqueville's evocative expression, what is the *generative principle* of modern society?

Someone might suggest that since Aron raised these questions history has ended or at least has settled down. For example, has not the fall of communism discredited the Marxist interpretation of history and economics? This is certainly the case concerning the Leninist interpretation of Marxism. But it is not because the world is more capitalist than ever that the definition of modern society as essentially capitalist is false. And in any case, supposing that Marx is legitimately discredited, Comte and Tocqueville remain our contemporaries. Who can deny that democratic individualism, on the one hand, and the application of science to the transformation of nature, including human nature, on the other, constitute the two determinative features of our "global" world?

Anyone who seeks to understand modern society therefore will do well to study these great authors by taking Raymond Aron as his guide. One might argue that the dangers presented by the extremism of Marx and Nietzsche have disappeared in the West (although their thought remains potent enough to bring some discredit to the prosaic liberty of modern democratic society). But the question of the best balance between science and freedom is still with us, and the road from Montesquieu to Weber, and back, must always be retraced.

De Gaulle as Hero

Pierre Manent

1992

Hostis habet muros; ruit alto a culmine Troia . . .
Sacra suosque tibi commendat Troia penates.

(Aeneid, II, 290, 293)

Je n'appelle plus Rome un enclos de murailles
Que ses proscriptions combient de funerailles;
Ces murs dont le destin fut autrefois si beau
N'en vent que la prison, ou plutôt le tombeau;
Mais pour revivre ailleurs dans sa première force,
Avec les faux Romains elle a fait plein divorce,
Et comme autour de moi j'ai tous ses vrais appuis,
Rome n'est plus dans Rome, elle est toute ou je suis.

(Sertorius, III, 929–36)

What is a hero? Do heroes exist? Why should we praise them, if there are any? I feel too unheroic to decide these most intimidating questions. But, if in the vacancy of my soul, or at least of my mind, I leave out of account what realists call reality; if I conjure up far-flung possibilities; if I dream of unheard of achievements: no modern man since Napoleon seems to tally exactly with the poetic convention of heroism more than Charles de Gaulle. Indeed, if hero there be, de Gaulle is a hero.

I say a hero; I do not say a great man. Although de Gaulle was a great man, or at any rate, a great statesman in the second part of his career, when he single-handedly founded the Fifth Republic, the first generally accepted republic in French post-revolutionary history. Between 1940 and 1944, he could not be a statesman just because the state, the legitimate state, was missing.

In May to June 1940, France suffered what one is tempted to call an

---

This essay originally appeared in the fall 1992 issue of *Perspectives on Political Science* and is republished with permission.

epic defeat; within a few days, what once had been generally believed to be the strongest army in the world had just been outmaneuvered, outflanked, outwitted, outgunned, indeed, routed and broken to pieces by the German army, which in the first days proceeded too rapidly to stoop to take prisoners. This military disaster was immediately followed, perhaps preceded, at any rate accompanied by a political panic. Within a few weeks, the French government had fled to the Loire, then to Bordeaux. In this unsafe haven, Paul Reynaud, président du Conseil, resigned out of perplexity and was succeeded by Marshal Pétain who knew at least what he wanted: the armistice. Less than one month later, Philippe Pétain received full executive and legislative powers from the National Assembly, which thus immolated itself and the Third Republic. Not only the French nation had suffered a humiliating defeat at the hands of the hereditary enemy; the republican regime had disintegrated under the shock as well. Even before the signing of the armistice on 22 June, de Gaulle, then defense undersecretary, had flown to London whence, on 18 June, he issued his *Appel,* calling the French people to resistance.

The Question of the Armistice

De Gaulle's refusal of the armistice was the decision from which the whole Gaullist epic sprang. Our understanding and appreciation of de Gaulle's conduct during the Second World War hinges on our understanding and appreciation of this refusal.

De Gaulle considered the armistice the capital fault of Pétain's government. He knew that, at the time, the battle on French soil was lost. Some sort of truce or even capitulation was necessarily in order. The government could have legitimately instructed the commanders in the field to sign such a "local" truce or capitulation. But at the same time it would have had to repair to Algiers "carrying along the treasure of French sovereignty which had never been surrendered for 14 centuries" (*Memoirs* 3:249). To this end—saving the French sovereignty—the government still had the means: the broad expanse of the empire, the undamaged fleet, the largely intact air force troops who were serving in Africa or the Middle East or who could even be salvaged from France. In de Gaulle's eyes, the actions for which the Vichy regime is most often blamed—the "collaboration" with the German army and even with the Nazi regime, the handing over of refugees and Jews to the Gestapo—irresistibly followed from this first abdication of sovereignty.

This question of the armistice is a most difficult question of moral and political casuistry. Strikingly, and to de Gaulle's ire, the armistice was not laid to Petain's charge at his trial. Raymond Aron, in his *Mem-*

oirs, wrote thus: "I inclined to believe [the armistice] inevitable. At any rate, those who had signed or accepted it did not appear to me to stand dishonored thereby." What shall we say?

First, we must bear in mind that if we concede the legitimacy of the armistice, we concede thereby the legitimacy of Vichy, which was brought into being for the purpose of signing the armistice. If we concede the legitimacy of Vichy, we concede the legitimacy of Vichy's policy, because this policy, in its main line, follows from the armistice (and from, you will pardon me to call, the spirit of the armistice). It was all a question of saving what could be saved: of transacting, maneuvering, and compromising in order to shield the French people, as much as humanly possible, from the consequences of their defeat. If you adopt this tack, Vichy's case will not fare badly. As a matter of fact, and on the whole, the French—including the French Jews—were in some measure protected by the existence of Vichy. As a matter of principle, and even of justice, it is difficult—as soon as you have accepted its coming into being—not to find excuses for a regime that was looking only for excuses. Circumstances and necessity, once they have been accepted as the principle of a regime, speak potently in advocacy of whatever the regime has done.

Raymond Aron was undoubtedly right to note that not all the early partisans of Vichy were morally objectionable men; there would have been many objectionable men in France at the time! De Gaulle, by the way, conceded as much, however reluctantly, in his *Memoirs.* However, it is not a question of the moral quality of one or the other. It is a question of the moral content of a political position or decision. In de Gaulle's eyes, the armistice was radically objectionable because it meant the forsaking of a sovereignty that had never been forsaken by a French government, which was not forsaken by any other European government. The forsaking of sovereignty was the gravest act that could be done by a political actor in his or her political character.

Some may object that this high-sounding sovereignty is just highfalutin discourse, because France, by any measure, was no longer sovereign in June 1940 and could not by any means—fair or foul at the disposition of Frenchmen—be made sovereign anew. I will not enter the debate about the practicability of the translation of the French sovereignty to Algiers, nor will I go deeply into the meaning, or meanings, of this most pregnant word "sovereignty." But I will venture a remark about the relationship between defeat and the political will.

What does it mean to acknowledge defeat? Is it to admit: we have been defeated in the field? Gaullists and Vichyists agreed on this score. The question, then, is: but do you accept and consent to the defeat that you acknowledge? This is the issue. It is tempting to describe the partisans of Vichy as perhaps ungenerous but hard-nosed realists, and the Gaullists as gallant but starry-eyed paladins. Nothing could be more erroneous.

The broader question is: which elements of reality do you consider? Or, in which frame of space and time, in which "whole" do you live and do you purport to act? If the nation, the body politic, has lasted for fourteen centuries, and if the natural and noble desire is to see it last indefinitely, you could not properly consent to a defeat that means the forced obliteration of its independent life.

There is an auspicious disproportion between a great body politic and any defeat, however stunning: a disproportion of substance, a disproportion of weight. A tiny body politic—for instance, a small tribe—can be quite shaken out of legitimate existence by a stunning military defeat; not so a great body politic. Only the obstinate will not to accept what one is forced to acknowledge answers the moral nobility of political life. Conversely, it may be that those who accept defeat end by not acknowledging it; the partisans of Vichy, as already noted, claimed that its mission was to shield the French people, as much as humanly possible, from the consequences of defeat. Old Pétain, the imposing and moving ghost of a wasted victory, meant and was meant to stand between the French and reality. It is this strain of complacent flight from reality that, more than its crimes, gave Vichy its unbearable character: a would-be Father of the Nation, hectoring admirals, unbelievable and unbelieving sermonizers. Because it ceased to battle, Vichy did not and could not acknowledge that the war was going on.

Since the former armistice (November 1918), or at least since the occupation of the Ruhr (1923), France had stopped acting like an independent body politic. Following clumsily the clumsy lead of Britain, France had stumbled from circumstance to circumstance until it stumbled into war and defeat. In June 1940, it was preparing to follow slavishly the perverse lead of Nazi Germany. This Gordian knot of maneuvers, velleities, bungling, and disaster had to be cut. The situation of France cried for a liberating act of will.

The *Appel du 18 juin* was precisely this liberating act of will. It was liberating, first, because it was just that: an act of will. By it, a single man, without high title or command, who was soon to be outlawed and sentenced to death, said that political and moral man can rise above the circumstances, however dire. This act of pure moral will also conveyed more political understanding than could be found in the political and military establishment remaining in distraught France. In France's worst hour, de Gaulle's two-minute pronouncement delineated with astonishing sweep and sharpness the map of the circumstances, the nature of the whole, and the character of the war in which the disaster had oc- curred. Here was a protracted war, of which the field was the world itself and in which, accordingly, the French defeat was a local and re- versible episode. In this founding and pregnant proclamation, de Gaulle gave time and space, that is, faith and reason to the French cornered and blinded into despair.

De Gaulle and the Third Republic

Can we discern, in the early career of Charles de Gaulle, intimations of this stunning strength and breadth of will by which a junior general called French commissioned officers and soldiers to come over to London and place themselves under his command to carry on the fighting and to keep France in the war?

De Gaulle's first career did not seem to announce what he would become; between the wars, he was chiefly a military reformer and lob- byist, with a zest for writing. As a lobbyist, he was tireless, obstinate, unprejudiced, and shrewd, although many grew weary of his singleness of purpose or were ruffled by what they construed as his arrogance.

As a military reformer, he displayed an outstanding lucidity of which good judges as different as the German generals and Sir Winston Churchill bore testimony. I am no military expert but there was a major bone of contention: Were tanks to be used only as ancillary to the in- fantry, as the French High Command—routinely following the Great War precedent—maintained to the bitter end, or was it necessary to devise and build a new military instrument welding the infantry and the tanks into a new organic whole: *la division blindée* or *cuirassée,* the armored division, *die Panzerdivision?* With the new advantage the new technol- ogy gave to the offensive attitude and conduct, de Gaulle saw more than a tactical matter. Here was a new instrument of war for a new kind of war and a new world. On 26 January 1940, while France dozed away the phoney war, de Gaulle made a last effort and sent a *memorandum* to eighty principal figures in the government and the army. In this, his last dutiful pleading, he warned:

> The French people ought not to be allowed to fall into the delusion that the present immobility answers the character of the current war. Quite the contrary. The motor confers to the modern means of destruction such a power, such a speed, such a range that the present conflict will be distinguished by moves, surprises, irruptions, chases, the amplitude and the rapidity of which will outstrip infinitely those of the most lightning-

like events of the past. . . . Let us not deceive ourselves! The conflict which has just begun could well be the most extended, the most intricate, the most violent among all those which have brought desolation to mankind. The political, economic, social and moral crisis from which it flows is so deep and it exhibits such a character of ubiquity that it will fatally result in a complete upsetting of the situation of the nations and of the structure of the States. Now, the invisible harmony of things offers a military instrument exactly adequate to the huge dimensions of this revolution. It is high time that France draws her conclusions.

Undoubtedly, de Gaulle belonged to the tiny band—among decent people—who understood what was going on.

As a military reformer, de Gaulle received more rebukes than attention, and more attention than success. Nevertheless, it was an acknowledgment of sorts when, the debacle already set in, he was given command of the fourth *division cuirassée,* which did not exactly exist; he had to bring it into existence and action. He carried out this thankless mission dutifully and honorably. Of more interest to us in retrospect are the names of those who gave serious attention to de Gaulle's military doctrine: Leon Blum and Paul Reynaud. In Blum's case, apart from the sympathy that seems to have arisen between these two very different men, Blum's interest remained mainly platonic; as a convinced socialist, he could not really believe that military questions mattered, nor that military debates were much more than bourgeois tricks or, at least, delusions. Paul Reynaud was the most clear sighted and streetwise—if you allow me the word—among the French politicians. De Gaulle soon convinced him, and a teamwork evolved from their accord. Reynaud brought the colonel's vision and sense of urgency into the Chamber: to no avail. And this teamwork would have remained fruitless except for one decisive move: on 6 June, with disaster already upon them, Reynaud called de Gaulle to the government as defense undersecretary. Owing to this position, the *général de brigade à titre temporaire* was enabled, and entrusted, to establish relations with the English government and its new head, Winston Churchill. But for this, de Gaulle would have remained an interesting figure known only to the specialists of military history.

I think it both just and illuminating to draw attention to the handful of hazards and acts of will that, in a great trial of history, put a handful of men in a position to master evil broken loose. It is also a dramatic picture to contemplate how poor brave Reynaud, sent for in March 1940 as a first recourse, called in de Gaulle, who was still in a subordinate position, a few months later. Reynaud dared not follow his advice and repair to Algiers; but finally, at the very last minute, de Gaulle was in a position to act by himself. In addition, Reynaud did not cave in to discouragement or defeatist pressure before letting de Gaulle go to London with 100,000 francs from secret funds. A few days before, on the Loire River, while the last government of the Third Republic was taking a brief respite in its flight toward Bordeaux, a strong, good, and intelligent man, Georges Mandel, comforted de Gaulle, who was on the brink of resignation, and persuaded him to carry on.

Contemplating this hour of trial, I observe de Gaulle's frightening solitude while nearly the whole French military and political establishment was consenting to defeat. However, I notice also how a few generous men gave de Gaulle a helping hand and sent him to Churchill, who in his turn gave the critical welcome. These generous few were also discerning men; they recognized de Gaulle's capacities and the goodness and relevance of his political perspective. Their attitude suffices to establish the fact that the general's first decisive steps were no arbitrary freak. Or, could we say that, some way or other, these men divined de Gaulle's mission?

De Gaulle's Mission

The word "mission" is appropriate to use because de Gaulle's course of action was radically different from anything prescribed by law: be it the French political law or constitution or, for instance, the English common law, or what is called the law of nations. We could say that de Gaulle subordinated everything—including every political law or custom—to a paramount law: the law of *honor* as he saw it. The legitimacy of his action lay in its motive: honor.

Honor, particularly military honor, has no recognized place in modern moral life despite, or because of, the amplitude and destructiveness of modern wars. Indeed, as a self-sufficient motive, honor has long ceased to exist. A course of action is praised, or at least authorized, when it can claim as its motives the protection of life and limb, the relief of man's estate, the bettering of the human condition, the realization of social justice, the self-government or even self-aggrandizement of a human association, or the accomplishment of some ideological goal. De Gaulle disclaimed every modern motive, or, at any rate, he did not resort to any. He stepped into the French, and soon the world scene, impelled and authorized by no other power than himself—not as a self-appointed guide beckoning toward a dazzling future, but as a man who happened to be solely and wholly dedicated to military, political or national, and personal honor.

After, and through the *Appel,* de Gaulle retained and claimed no other legitimacy than this motive of honor. He could claim it because, at the crucial test, precisely by means of his *Appel,* he was saving the French honor, and because he knew in his bones that he had the will and the capacity to uphold it until the world was forced to acknowledge that France had regained her honor with her rank.

De Gaulle's singular character lies in this point: he simply and inflexibly pronounced himself, and made others admit, that he was the trustee of French honor, and, consequently, of French sovereignty and destiny. He was designated this trustee not through any democratic or otherwise representative delegation, but by the sole power of his own will and dedication. There was nothing antidemocratic in his attitude; it was indeed a trusteeship; as soon as circumstances permitted, de Gaulle would hand over his power and responsibility to the free suffrage of the French people. The extraordinary pride with which he set himself not only above the whole French military and political hierarchy but also above the democratic convention or legitimacy itself is succeeded, in fact accompanied, by an extraordinary humility by which he made himself the democratic servant of the people. In this more than human blending of pride and humility lay de Gaulle's heroism.

In his political and moral being, de Gaulle owed nothing to democratic convention, legitimacy, or custom. In his political action, he never turned against democracy; indeed, he twice decisively helped to reinstate or consolidate it. Is not this weaving together of magnanimity and moderation distinctive of the truly great man?

It is undoubtedly true that the intrinsic nobility of a human motive is no proof of the wisdom of the action it inspires. The energy of national honor may generate more heat than light. A great part of de Gaulle's analytical and rhetorical skill went accordingly to demonstrate that the rebirth of France was not only the natural desire of every decent Frenchman, but, also, the rational desire of every good European and friend of the Free World. But the French renaissance had its conditions, its military, political, and moral conditions. Nearly the whole of de Gaulle's policy was to have these understood or at any rate accepted by the French resistance and by the great powers traditionally allied to her, principally Great Britain and the United States of America.

De Gaulle's Policy

The debacle of May–June 1940 placed the relations of France and the two great Anglo-Saxon powers on an awkward footing. France and Britain were immediately alienated from one another; each felt betrayed or at least abandoned by the other. The English reproached the French for the armistice that left England alone and terribly exposed to the mighty

German army. The French reproached the English for the slenderness and conduct of their expeditionary force; they reproached them for Dunkirk, for holding back their air force during the battle for France; they reproached them for. . . . Defeated people have many complaints. In America, Franklin Roosevelt and his advisers were stunned by the French collapse; henceforth, they considered the French, all the French, with distrust. The French, therefore, reminded their American friends of Washington's policy after the Great War and confessed that they felt themselves deserted a long time ago. It is no surprise in this context that the relations between de Gaulle and Winston Churchill and Roosevelt were so often thorny. It is no use blaming one or the other two. Churchill and Roosevelt had good reasons to suspect de Gaulle and vice versa. However, we can try to set de Gaulle's policy in its true light.

His policy was founded upon a kind of fiction; the armistice was null and void; France had never quit fighting; and the Vichy government had not a speck of political or moral legitimacy. Of course, these propositions did not tally with reality. They had to be made true and real by de Gaulle's action, which was meant to bring France or, at any rate as many French forces as possible, into the war again, and to have their participation accepted and acknowledged by the Allied Powers, so that, in the end, France could be counted with the United States, Great Britain, and the Soviet Union as the victors over Adolf Hitler.

Everything came about accordingly. However, the final success of de Gaulle's strategy was so unlikely at the outset that, if it was acknowledged as an extraordinary feat by some, it was considered by others as a meretricious parade—a lie made "true" not by the transformation of reality, but by its nearly unanimous parrot-like repeating. This charge that has been raised, for instance, by Hannah Arendt, needs examining.

Again, the broader question is the question of the frame of reference. In which frame of space and time, in which whole, do you purport to act, or do you look at your actions and those of others? As de Gaulle repeatedly underlined, the relevant frame of reference was not limited to two disastrous months of the year 1940, not even to the few years preceding them. It encompassed the "Thirty Years War" in the course of which Germany twice made her bid to European and worldwide domination. In addition, it must be admitted that between 1914 and 1918, France bore the brunt of German assaults; this matchless contribution to the victory of the West left it with a large credit account. In spite of that, soon after the war, Britain and the United States turned their back on France, who was feeling in its bones that, because it had been bled white, it would be unable to withstand alone, or with too grudging a support, the next German onslaught. This feeling, or rather, knowledge of abandonment goes far to explain the inconsistencies of French military and diplomatic policy between the wars.

Moreover, how can the English speak so glibly of a French "desertion" in May–June 1940, when the German thrust found them without an army? If it is true that they took a brave stand this same year under the inspiration of Churchill—a stand that de Gaulle praises again and again—it can be added that Germany did not try an all-out effort against the British Isles. It may be easier to resist defeat when you have not been thoroughly attacked.

As for the United States, it had so inconsiderately abandoned Europe after the Great War; it had so blindly underpinned the German recovery; and its diplomacy now remained so tied to an unrealistic and immoral Vichy option, that one may be pardoned—or so I imagine the general felt on bad days—if, after two disasters at Sedan and two recoveries on the Marne, one does not feel inclined to bear with the self-righteousness and bullying of friendly America.

It seems, indeed, that at times Roosevelt and his advisers would have been content to let France and the French live in a kind of neutrality occasionally improved by on-the-spot bargains with such Vichy proconsuls as happened to be in the empire (as exemplified by the Darlan-Eisenhower agreement or understanding at Algiers). This line of policy, if it had been consistently pursued, or if de Gaulle had not been there to prevent its implementation, would have landed us all in disaster. However, the frame of reference ought to encompass not only the right quantity of past—if I may say so—but also the right quantity of future: It ought to take into account what will come after victory has been won. De Gaulle warned that if the French people did not feel that France was among the victors; if they felt that after being vanquished and ill treated by the Germans that they were spurned and condemned by the Allied Powers to which, at the bottom of their heart, they remained faithful, they risked turning toward the Communists. (By the way, I must confess that I never cease to be amazed that French rightists cannot bring themselves to understand what good fortune it has been for France and for themselves or their like in 1944 that the man embodying the *Resistance* and the *Liberation* in the eyes of the French and the world should be a conservative and Roman Catholic general.)

In a weighty letter to Franklin Delano Roosevelt (26 October 1942), de Gaulle wrote: "Victory ought to reconcile France with her friends: it would be impossible if she had not a share in it." The great American president did not answer.

One cannot charge de Gaulle with ignoring, or making his partisans ignore, reality. Already, in the *Appel* he showed a very exact understanding of the nature and the conditions of the war that was just beginning. He stressed that France was not alone, that the British Empire carried on the fighting; he suggested neatly that the "huge industry" of the United States would soon contribute "to vanquish the enemy by means of a superior mechanical force." De Gaulle knew how grateful France was destined to be toward Great Britain and the United States, but he regretted that the Anglo-Saxon powers, obnubilated by the debacle, were so prone to forget how far the war stretched back into the past and how much they, consequently, owed France. De Gaulle's conduct during the war was not founded upon a "lie," not even a lie meant to come true later with the event. It was, in the whirlwind of the present, a reminder and an anticipation of justice.

There is no doubt that the general made himself "unbearable" to the English and the Americans. He conceded as much himself in his *Memoirs* without swagger and without regret; he ought not, because he could not be other than "unbearable." He was the scrupulous and intransigent trustee of all the marks of French sovereignty because these marks were all that remained of France's treasure and what would soon give France's living soul the means of animating her recovering body. His intransigency necessarily flowed from his, and France's, powerlessness. (By the way, a European observer should be forgiven if he remarks that an apparent lack of moderation in the pursuit of sovereignty is not necessarily a vice; that the conclusion of the war would have been more friendly to liberty in the East of Europe if Churchill had not at the outset decided to follow dutifully Roosevelt's lead; and that he is a bit upset when he sees the great Churchill announcing to the world, with the emotion of a bride, that he has had the privilege of sharing the president's confidence and intimacy during a few inebriating days. Some Gaullist stiff-necked "arrogance" would have been good for European liberty.)

The Difficulty of Being Just

Many intelligent and good people in France dislike or even hate Charles de Gaulle. Most of them are markedly on the right of the political map. This phenomenon needs at least a tentative explanation.

Once more, we must go back to the debacle and the armistice and to the choking grief it meant for so many French. Despair is like sin. It gives rise to two sets of sentiment; it prompts the heart in two directions: one may desire, or at least accept consolation or healing; or one may reject it and prefer to go on despairing or sinning. I would readily suggest that Gaullists are lovers of France who welcome consolation and that anti-Gaullists are lovers of France who spurn consolation.

Nobody, in Europe or in the world, had deserved to be defeated, enslaved, tormented, or killed by Hitler. France, despite all its faults, did not deserve to be humiliated, ill treated, and corrupted by this curse. De Gaulle was the healer and comforter of France. Those good French people who dismiss all thought of being healed or comforted are more stiff-necked than de Gaulle ever was.

I do not pretend to convince you. Perhaps you noticed that the language one spontaneously adopts when speaking of de Gaulle is not the language appropriate to nearly any other statesman, however great. How do we account for this irresistible appearance of words and thoughts coming from the realm of epic or religion? The more sober hypothesis seems, to me, to be that Charles de Gaulle is indeed a hero.

Note

1. The Polish, Belgian, Dutch, and so forth, *legal* governments flew to London, as de Gaulle did.

Democracy without Nations?

Pierre Manent

1996

If we try to characterize the contemporary political world, our first observation will no doubt be the victory of democracy, with 1945 and 1989 marking the dates of the collapse (in quite different ways) of the two most terrible enemies that democracy faced in our century. This does not mean that democracy is everywhere peacefully established nor that where it *is* established it may not encounter considerable difficulties. It means, rather, that the democratic principle of legitimacy no longer has a politically credible rival anywhere in the world. Even the upheavals associated with "Islamic fundamentalism" do not, in my view, undermine the general validity of this appraisal. Be that as it may, I will consider here only the Western world.

The democratic principle of legitimacy is the principle of *consent*: a law or obligation is not legitimate, nor am I bound to obey it or fulfill it, unless I previously have consented to this law or obligation through myself or my representatives. A democratic regime, therefore, is that regime, that, in principle, is willed by each individual. This is because a democracy defines itself as, and seeks to be, that regime that is willed by each individual. With this starting point in mind, how could anyone want anything but democracy? It is quite striking to observe that totalitarian regimes, even during the period of their greatest strength, officially deferred to the principle of consent by organizing elections. This is also what the Islamic Republic of Iran does today.

In other words, once the principle of consent has been brought to light, even its most resolute adversaries spare no effort in extorting from their populations formal signs of the most unanimous possible consent.

The present essay, which originally appeared in French in the fall 1996 issue of *Commentaire*, first appeared in English in *The Journal of Democracy*, April 1997, and is republished with permission.

In a certain sense, an opponent of the principle of consent is always in self-contradiction: by choosing a principle of action different from consent, he in effect wills not to will. We see here the intrinsic and invincible superiority of democracy over all its competitors. Democracy finds a supporter, indeed an accomplice, in the will of each man as man. The moral prestige and irresistible political strength of democracy derive from its "universalism": man's humanity is the sole "hypothesis" of a democratic regime, and this hypothesis is always verified by us as human beings—unless, of course, we deny outright the humanity of certain people. This is exactly what the totalitarian regimes did, explicitly in the case of Nazism, implicitly or "dialectically" in the case of communism. Nazism subjected or exterminated the "naturally" inferior races; communism subjected or exterminated the "historically" condemned classes.

But how can one fail to see the humanity of another human being? How can it be denied in this terrible way? How could the totalitarian denial of the unity of the human race seem plausible to so many otherwise intelligent people, not all of whom were deliberately evil? I believe that it is because this project was based on certain aspects of being human that are also constitutive of our humanity, on differences that define man as much—or almost as much—as his universal humanity. I speak of the two great differences of nation and class.

Indeed, the contemporary victory of democracy coincides with the weakening in the West of these two differences of nation and class, a weakening due partly to the discredit totalitarianism cast upon them. Today universal humanity tends to overwhelm difference so much that it sometimes seems that between the individual and the world ("we are the world") nothing intrudes except maybe a void where various ethnic, religious, and sexual "identities" float, each demanding "respect."

It thus seems to me that our feeling about the present situation combines—in different proportions depending on the time, place, and person—satisfaction at the triumph of the democratic principle and anxiety about the disappearance or at least the weakening of all forms of the political articulation of the world, in particular of the nation-state. This last subject will be the focus of the remainder of this essay.

The Rebirth of the Nation

A historian might say that Europe had already found itself in an analogous situation, one characterized by homogenization. Over two centuries ago, Jean-Jacques Rousseau observed, "Say what you like, there is no such thing nowadays as Frenchmen, Germans, Spaniards, or even

Englishmen—only Europeans. All have the same tastes, the same passions, the same customs, and for good reason: Not one of them has ever been formed *nationally*, by distinctive legislation. Put them in the same circumstances, and man for man, they will do exactly the same things."[1] The Enlightenment—the advent of commerce, of the sciences and arts, and of what soon came to be called "civilization"—produced an initial homogenization of Europe. The French Revolution and its military and ideological consequences, in particular the enormous Napoleonic enterprise, both prolonged the movement toward homogenization and unleashed a contrary movement of particularization and national separation. "I speak for Germans simply, of Germans simply," the philosopher Johann Fichte could declare in 1807, without the enormity of this remark shriveling his tongue in his mouth![2] To be sure, European nations had existed for a long time, but their particularity now burst forth with a new intensity and energy. They had almost died, or so they felt, but now they believed themselves reborn. And in fact, as a result of the Napoleonic enterprise and its ultimate failure, they *were* reborn. No longer were they merely nations in some passive sense, now they wished *to exist* as nations.

The decisive point to underscore in this context is that democracy and the nation henceforth had a common existence; or, rather, democracy, as we understand it came into being within the framework of the nation. The nineteenth century is thus simultaneously the century of democratic expansion and the century of the emergence of nationalities, marked not only by the unification of Italy and Germany but also by various nationalist excesses. On the one hand, democracy multiplied the power of the European nations, whose extraordinary energy was evident in colonial conquests, as well as in the intensity and length of the First World War. On the other hand, the nation provided a concrete context and gave "flesh" to the democratic abstractions of the sovereignty of the people and of the general will. It is this people here who wish to govern themselves, who wish to be represented by a parliament elected by universal suffrage, and so on.

These well-known historical realities lead us to the discussion of a problem of great theoretical and practical interest, a problem that also happens to be the most difficult of all.

Modern democracy, as distinguished from ancient democracy, is not immediately political. It is a principle of legitimacy, that of consent, which was first demanded and which first prevailed in the political order, but which applies to all associations or communities, and thus to all human actions. Alexis de Tocqueville most clearly captures this singular aspect of modern democracy:

In the United States the dogma of the sovereignty of the people is not an isolated doctrine, bearing no relation to the people's habits and prevailing ideas; on the contrary, one should see it as the last link in a chain of opinions which binds around the whole Anglo-American world. Providence has given each individual the amount of reason necessary for him to look after himself in matters of his own exclusive concern. That is the great maxim on which civil and political society in the United States rests; the father of a family applies it to his children, a master to his servants, a township to those under its administration, a province to the townships, a state to the provinces, and the Union to the states. Extended to the nation as a whole, it becomes the dogma of the sovereignty of the people.

Thus in the United States the generative principle underlying the republic is the same as that which controls the greater part of human actions.[3]

For example, the principle of consent is applicable in the family no less than in the polity, as the evolution of democratic societies attests. In ancient politics, however, democracy presupposed the city, that is, a form, a specific framework, a definite circumscription of humanity. It was the city as city—as a relatively small, homogeneous civic body capable of being taken in at a glance with one's own eyes ("synoptically," as Aristotle put it)—that made ancient democracy possible, and in a way called it forth. The political problem of modern democracy remained largely unrecognized as long as its national framework or context was taken for granted, which has been the case since the French Revolution. It is worth noting, however, that in the eighteenth century the democratic principle did not appear under its own name, precisely because the word democracy seemed indissolubly bound to this ancient political form, which long had been considered dead and worthy of little regret.[4] When the authors of *The Federalist* defended and explained the "popular" constitution of the United States, they presented it as a "representative republic" in precise contradistinction to "democracy."[5] Now that the nation has lost its self-evidence, at least in Western Europe, we are rediscovering, although in a different form, the problem that the American founders faced at the dawn of the democratic nation.

The practical political difficulty can be summarized as follows: the democratic principle does not define the framework within which it operates. For example, a vote for self-determination, a democratic act par excellence, takes place within a framework previously established by undemocratic means and principles, generally by tradition, corrected or confirmed by force. Before the French, considering themselves a nation, could take "sovereignty" for themselves in 1789, "forty kings" (as the monarchists said) had first "made France" through marriage and war.

The Ambiguity of Europe

When the nation is weakened and declines as the community of belonging par excellence, the framework in which democracy (and especially popular sovereignty) operates is consequently weakened. One might say that the democratic principle, after having used the nation as an instrument or vehicle, abandons it by the wayside. This would not be worrisome if a new vehicle were available or clearly under construction. This new political form, however, is nowhere in sight. Of course, some might suggest that "Europe" is this new political framework. In a certain sense this is true. After the Second World War the European idea and its accompanying institutions facilitated the reconstruction on solid foundations of the European nation-state, while also making plausible, imaginable, and even desirable the withering away of this supposedly antiquated political form. But does "Europe" mean today the depoliticization of the life of peoples—that is, the increasingly methodical reduction of their collective existence to the activities of "civil society" and the mechanisms of "civilization"? Or does it instead entail the construction of a new political body, a great, enormous European nation? The construction of Europe, from the Common Market established in 1957 to the European Union today, has made progress only because of this ambiguity, and as a result of combining these two contradictory projects has taken on its character as an imperious, indefinite, and opaque movement. Yet this initially happy ambiguity has become paralyzing, and threatens soon to become fatal. The sleepwalker's assurance with which "Europe" pursues its indefinite extension is the result of its obstinate refusal to think about itself comprehensively—that is, to define itself politically.

Europe refuses to define itself politically. What precisely does this mean? A political order is a political or public thing, and therefore a certain way of "putting something or having something in common." The first thing a political order puts in common is a certain territory and a certain population. Democracy requires that the population consent to the political structure proposed to it. But what population should we ask for consent—in this case, whether it wishes to belong to Europe? Why ask, for example, the Swedes, but not the Moroccans, who, after all, are more familiar to us French?

The political vacuity of Europe was harshly brought to light by the war in the former Yugoslavia. The territorial "unconsciousness" of our Europe, its refusal to take seriously the problem of territory and population as a political question, finds its counterpart—and its nemesis—in the other Europe, where the ethnic cleansers worked with utmost savagery to make population and territory coincide. Refusing to consider the territorial question as important in itself—incapable, in fact, of seeing, feeling, and conceiving its own territory—Europe understands passionate attachment to a place as folly, which is exactly what the behavior of the ethnic cleansers confirms. Europe does not understand that if it wants to think and to act politically, it first must think and will a definite territorial arrangement, both within and beyond its borders. After much lost time, such an arrangement was finally imposed in the former Yugoslavia by the United States, the "imperial" power, that is, the political power par excellence. As we know, in order to achieve this result, it was necessary at the Dayton peace talks to reproduce the "virtual" image of the *territory* of Bosnia-Herzegovina!

I do not think it necessary to multiply examples in order to confirm the importance, even today, of territory and more generally of political forms and parameters. Yet however numerous these examples may be, they do not forestall an objection that comes immediately to mind: politics, as the putting of things in common, or giving form to what a certain number of people have in common, is outdated. The network of "communications" is now so dense and extensive that humanity as a whole possesses a *sensorium commune* sufficient for all its legitimate needs. In this network, each one can find his place at the intersection of a multiplicity of identities—familial, local, sexual, and so on—that can be almost indefinitely combined. There is little doubt that this is the direction our world seems to have taken. It is not absurd to think, therefore, that political attachments (foremost among them, national passions) are deplorably archaic ways for individuals and groups to select their identities. Moreover, do not the various nationalisms of today, which, even when they are violent, tend to be defensive rather than expansive, seem to confirm that they belong to the past?

The recollection of an older Europe (a homogeneous Europe, and one without passports!) that nevertheless exploded into furiously inimical nations ought to move us to prudence. "Communication," in itself, does not create a true bond among people. It is like an amorous encounter reduced to the "kiss" of two telephone numbers on a computer screen. Today's popular term *identity* is a terribly impoverished substitute for the older term *community*. Among the communities that make up the human world, the political community was traditionally considered to be the community par excellence, the "supreme" community, as Aristotle famously noted in his *Politics* (1252a–b). The question is thus inevitably raised: Do people necessarily need a "community par excellence"? And supposing that they can and want to do without such a community, would their lives as a result be freer and richer, or rather the opposite? I do not have the space here to respond to these questions other than by a series of assertions.

Man as a free and rational being cannot fulfill himself except in a political community, with all the consequences (not all of them pleasant) that this entails. It is in the political body, and only in the political body, that we seriously put things in common. And we are obliged "to put things in common" in order to realize our membership in the same species, in order to concretize our universal humanity. Why? Why not be content with the family—whether nuclear or extended—supplemented by the local community, and perhaps by the new "family" that individuals today find in their business or workplace? Without insisting on the fact that the family today is less and less a community, I would observe merely that, however one might conceive of the family's vocation or purpose (if it has one), the family is rooted in the particularity of bodies, in the needs and desires of our animal nature. Its law is love; its emotional tone is one of unmediated identification. It therefore leaves the individual short of justice, which presupposes or requires rational deliberation. The political community is thus irreplaceable as the framework for deliberation over justice. This deliberation is serious because it has real consequences: the taxes I pay, the laws I obey, perhaps even the war I am obliged to fight. In short, the meaning of the city is precisely not to be the family. In the city all of the individual's faculties come into play. In the city people "put in common actions and reasons," as Aristotle puts it in his *Nichomachean Ethics* (1126b11–12).

Identity versus Identification

It is for this general reason—and not primarily to provide a rationalization for my own national passion, which is undoubtedly quite real—that I argue that we should show more respect not for "identity," which is a passive, lifeless notion easily manipulated by demagogues, but for the political bodies that are the political contexts of human action. In Europe, this means the nation. Let me add that if one thinks of the nation in political terms, as the political context of action rather than as a "cultural identity" to be defended, then its relationship to the "European project" ceases to be as conflictual as either stubborn nationalists or fervent supranationalists believe.[6]

Instead of speaking of "identity," which is passive and passé, let us speak of "identification," which is active and, I dare say, a call to action. Europe cannot construct itself meaningfully (i.e., politically) unless Europeans in the various nations identify themselves with a common

European political action, and for the foreseeable future that means with the common action of European nations. Someone might say that this proposition is tautological. I do not think so. It acknowledges these two characteristics of real life: first of all, politics is about action; and second, the motive of action is the future or a view of the future. Here one may object that I am only reformulating the old saw of "political voluntarism," which condemns us to the kind of pious exhortations that are received with more and more irritation by European peoples. However, by refraining from defining the European identity and by calling for political action, we do not opt for something arbitrary and condemn ourselves to impotence. There already exists a certain tradition of common European action to which we can appeal. The moral-political root of the construction of Europe was the decision taken by France and Germany in the 1950s, and later ratified and deepened by Charles de Gaulle and Konrad Adenauer between 1958 and 1963, to consider each other as partners, allies, and even friends. This politically decisive decision was made by nations and not by a supranational institution. It in no way required any previous accord on some "European cultural identity." This is not the place to develop this point in terms of political objectives or programs. I merely want to suggest that to speak of common political action by European nations is a proposition that is quite meaningful, one that invites us to extend into the future what Michael Oakeshott would have called an "idiom of conduct." If we do not succeed in tightening the dangerously loosening bonds in the Western world between human communities and the political action of their governments, the divorce between the nation and democracy will be no less dangerous for the latter than for the former. What is a democracy without a body, a democracy deprived of what psychologists call the sentiment of one's own body? To repeat: With respect to the principle of democracy, its territorial framework is external, contingent, and thus arbitrary. That is why as democracy today grows more and more self-aware and self-confident it so tranquilly bids farewell to the nation, the framework that seemed natural to it for two centuries. Democracy punishes the nation for the follies it caused it to commit but also, one fears, for the services it rendered it (which reveals a more than royal ingratitude). Modern democracy, which is founded on the will, wants to be self-sufficient, but it cannot do without a body. Yet how can it give itself a new body, a body that would not be the necessarily contingent and arbitrary legacy of the predemocratic age, a body of which democracy would be the sole author? Therefore, democracy has put on this abstract body called "Europe." But in order for this body to become real, and to be able to produce and circumscribe an awareness of itself, it must have height, length, depth, and dimensions—that is, limits. But since every limit would be arbitrary from the point of view of the democratic principle, democracy gives itself a body without limits: a Europe of indefinite extension, a Europe contradictorily defined as indefinite extension. How many nations, in fact, belong to it? Twelve? Twenty? Thirty? Does Turkey, for example, belong? Why not? Or why? The European political class has not even seriously begun to ask these questions, let alone answer them.

The world of democratic nations was formed when the principle of consent was adopted by political bodies that had been constituted in accord with other principles, both political and religious. Now that the principle of consent has banished every other principle, it is not clear how a new body could form and then subject itself to the principle of consent that constituted the democratic nation. The political molds are broken, and democratic vigilance inhibits their reconstruction. Instead of vigilance, it would perhaps be better to speak of arrogance and immoderation. Indeed, democracy may be starting to suffer the consequences of the immoderation that has characterized it for the last generation. Perhaps the political impotence I have tried to describe is the punishment inflicted on Europeans for accepting only the principle of consent as legitimate, for using the principle of freedom in a tyrannical fashion. The European wanted only what he himself willed; he rejected as arbitrary and outdated the nation, the political instrument that allowed him, by giving him limits, to exercise his sovereignty or will. Now his will finds itself increasingly without an instrument, without a framework of formation and action, alone and politically impotent. Even with the meticulously guaranteed democratic right to will everything, the European as a citizen finds himself able to accomplish less and less.

I have spoken of democracy's "punishment" of the nation. One might prefer another word. For the point of view I am defending here is not the moral or religious one that reproaches modern man for having rejected natural or divine law. Rather, my perspective is political. What ever man's latitude to define and to produce his conditions of existence, he is not the sovereign author of the human world. It is therefore dangerous, and above all logically contradictory, for him to act as if he were its sovereign author—which is precisely what he does when he grants exclusive legitimacy to the principle of consent. We do not reflect enough on the singular fact that we are the first people who wish to submit all the aspects of the world to a single principle. Even though this principle is that of liberty, the project itself nonetheless has something tyrannical about it. Two and a half centuries ago, when religious rule was burdensome and even in certain ways tyrannical, the great French liberal political philosopher Montesquieu, perhaps the most judicious defender of modern liberty, wrote, "It is strange to say, tho' true, that virtue itself has need of limits."[7] Today, the true friends of liberty are inclined to think, even if they do not yet dare to state, "Who would say it! Liberty itself has need of limits." These limits include those of the political body, for only within the political body can liberty be truly effective.

One might say that if man is a political animal (as is obviously presupposed by my remarks), his political nature will not allow itself to be rendered impotent. It inevitably will find some way of asserting itself in an unprecedented manner. I believe this too. But in a world where the principle of consent increasingly is becoming a principle of political impotence and paralysis, the only other principle capable of constructing political institutions, or at least of producing political effects, will be the unprincipled principle of pure force. This is a principle that lacks any spiritual dimension and completely disregards consent. (By the way, it is because force disregards the principle of consent that, in certain circumstances, it obtains it most easily.)

A political body always combines force and justice in variable proportions. As soon as there is a political body, justice is never wholly without force. But if we completely leave behind political existence, we must fear that, despite all the cultural, commercial, and technological artifices of a perfected civilization, justice and force might find themselves completely separated, with justice becoming perfectly pure or impotent and force merely strong or unjust. Our old nations, it is true, are tired, unwieldy, slow to move, obtuse, and pretentious. But they are also substantial and enduring; they are infinitely precious "condensations" of thoughts and actions; above all, they are still the only political entity that we have between us and "the state of nature" or, rather, between us and this state of civilization without justice. It is not by ceaselessly denigrating these nations but only by employing their energy, dormant but still capable of being roused, that we have the possibility of elaborating a new political body, a political "Europe" that will not succumb to the first storm over monetary or defense policy.

The Particular and the Universal

If the preceding might be seen as a defense of the nation, it is of the nation as a political body and not as an expression of particularity. To defend the nation in its particularity is ultimately to condemn it as only a region, a territory, or (even less than a territory) a "culture." Thus understood, the nation has only the ineffable but paltry charm of "the people from here," and about the people from here one can only say, in the words of a popular French song, "They're from here, the people from here." On the other hand, as a political body the nation in Europe has succeeded, in a manner comparable only to the ancient city, in realizing the articulation of the particular and the universal. Each great action and each great thought produced by one of our nations was a challenge to and a proposal for the other nations, a proposal by humanity for humanity. Centuries before the efforts of Europeanists like Jean Monnet to construct a "united" Europe, there was a vibrant and dynamic "common European home." But our nations, like the Greek cities, ended up succumbing to the intensity with which each asserted its part in what Shakespeare called the "great quarrel."

Today the nation's power to articulate the universal on the basis of the particular is weakening, and the two are coming apart. On one side, we see the particularity inseparable from all real human things; on the other, the universal is becoming the general, that is, this unreal "communication" that pretends to be real, as if the unity of humankind had already been realized through such superficial ties. I am told that in Switzerland the great "national" languages, especially German, are less and less in use among the young because they have lost their prestige in favor of the local dialect on the one hand and worldwide "English" on the other. The concrete universal of the national-cum-universal language has given way to the sterile juxtaposition of the patois of the "people from here" and the abbreviated, brutal language of people from nowhere. If things continue in this fashion, the phenomenon will soon extend throughout Europe. A national language cannot be preserved and reanimated unless it is the instrument by which the nation proposes something for humanity at large and, first of all, for Europe. It must be an instrument for larger national and political purposes. It cannot merely serve the subpolitical task of promoting commerce and communication. I am sure that these remarks will appear to many enlightened minds to be excessively emotional. My hope, however, is at least to have shown that today one may still "defend the nation" out of concern not for the particular but rather for the universal. The nation remains the indispensable form that gives concrete expression to our common human nature and aspirations.

Translated by Daniel J. Mahoney and Paul Seaton, with the assistance of Brian C. Anderson

Notes

1. Jean-Jacques Rousseau, *The Government of Poland*, trans. Willmoore Kendall (Indianapolis: Hackett, 1985), 11.
2. Johann Gottlieb Fichte, *Addresses to the German Nation*, trans. R. F. Jones and G. H. Turnbull (London: Open Court, 1922), 3. See Rousseau: "It is of man that I must speak, and the question that I examine tells me that I am going to speak to men"; *The First and Second Discourses*, ed. Roger D. Masters (New York: St. Martin's, 1964), 101.
3. Alexis de Tocqueville, *Democracy in America*, ed. J. P. Mayer, trans. George Lawrence (New York: HarperPerennial, 1988), 397.
4. See Pierre Rosanvallon, "The History of the Word 'Democracy' in France," *Journal of Democracy* 6 (October 1995):140–54.
5. James Madison, Alexander Hamilton, and John Jay, *The Federalist*, ed. Jacob E. Cooke (Middletown, Conn.: Wesleyan University Press, 1961), no. 10, 56–65.
6. I would note in passing that the notion of "cultural identity" is, in this context, both inconsistent and violent. It erases the articulations of the human world by jumbling together religion, the arts, principles of government, mores and private manners, and the like. To be sure, it is legitimate to think that these diverse elements, variously combined, give to each political body a "general spirit" that the legislator should respect. This is Montesquieu's position, and it contains nothing inconsistent or violent. But these elements, from which the "general spirit" of the nation is distilled, are ultimately held together by its political form. Once this form is effaced—whether or not it is replaced by another—the distillate evaporates like perfume from a broken bottle. If, for example, we suppose that France were to disappear as a political body, then a serious French Catholic would no longer have any "metafamilial" tie except to the Catholic Church—and certainly not to the abstraction called "French culture"!
7. Montesquieu, *The Spirit of Laws: A Compendium of the First English Edition with an English Translation of "An Essay on Causes Affecting Mind and Characters,"* ed. David W. Carrithers, trans. Thomas Nugent (Berkeley: University of California Press, 1978), book 11, chapter 4.

Part Seven

Reflections on Strauss, Nature, and History

As his opening intellectual autobiographical statement made clear, Manent's introduction to the work of Leo Strauss by Raymond Aron was a decisive encounter. The two pieces in this section show the twin sides of this encounter. In "Strauss and Nietzsche," Manent clearly sides with Strauss's Socratic posing of commonsense questioning over against Nietzsche's perfervid, "moralized" thinking-as-action. In "On Historical Causality," on the other hand, Strauss's quest for a sempiternal idea of nature appears to Manent to fail to account for the permutation in the human world introduced by the Christian church and then intensified in the modern world with its dynamic historical logic. Manent carves out a theoretical position faithful to the phenomena of both continuity and change, to the evidence of a permanent human nature and of its "mutated" modern version, a position that is neither simply naturalistic nor historicist. Manent believes that such a position, rather than being derived from dogmatic tenets, forces itself on the attentive observer of the Western political experience.

Strauss and Nietzsche

Pierre Manent

1988

As a reader of Leo Strauss, I continually have the same, contradictory experience. On the one hand, I feel that he sheds great light on certain major junctures of the history of political philosophy and on certain essential authors. But at the same time, when I turn to the source of this light, Strauss himself, obscurity abruptly appears, and I find myself before an enigma. Today, having the responsibility to speak of Strauss's interpretation of Friedrich Nietzsche (i.e., an author to whom Strauss devoted, in addition to some brief remarks, only one, unfinished text[1]) I must somehow imagine or reconstruct what he would have said, or more precisely the context within which the little that he said acquires its meaning. This is what I am going to try to do, with the sincere conviction of the sketchy and inadequate character of my remarks.

Let us begin with the author Nietzsche "resembles" the most according to Strauss, and to whom Strauss devoted detailed studies. Let us begin with Jean-Jacques Rousseau.

The movement of Rousseau's thought can be characterized in two formulations: a return to antiquity and a radicalization of modernity. It is obviously the *and* in this formulation that carries the main weight: the effort to rediscover the authenticity of political life beyond the corruption of modern life leads to a definition of man even more remote from the Greek conception than is the case with early modern thought. Now, this rhythm of thought, this Rousseauian motif, provides the key to the *movement* that will carry modern philosophy along in the nineteenth and twentieth centuries. (Please note, I say the key to the movement or dynamism of modern thought, not the key to all its aspects.)

This text was originally presented to the Collège de Philosophie in Paris on 23 April 1988. It was first published in French in the *Revue de metaphysique et de morale* 94 (number 3, July–September, 1989): 337–45 and appears here with permission.

This same motif will be found at work in Nietzsche and Martin Heidegger: a "return to the Greeks" and a simultaneous exposition of the limits of the thought and humanity of the Greeks, which entails the promulgation of a new determination of man's being.

But why did Strauss choose to study this motif in Rousseau, rather than in Nietzsche or Heidegger? We put the question more precisely, although in appearance more superficially, if we ask, Why did Strauss stop at the French Revolution? Why did Strauss not devote any of his more important works to any of the great authors who wrote after the French Revolution? A passage from *Thoughts on Machiavelli* will show us our way:

> The conditions of political thought were radically changed by the French Revolution. To begin with, we cannot help reading earlier thinkers in the light afforded by the changed condition or the novel situation of political thought. All serious errors in the interpretation of the thinkers in question can be traced to a failure to grasp the parochial character of the 19th and 20th century outlook which inevitably pretends to be wider than that of any earlier age.[2]

The conditions of political philosophy were "radically changed" by the French Revolution. With that event, philosophy, for the first time in its history, accepts a *revelation*, even if a revelation of reason. For the first time it left its element, and Strauss suggests that it never returned to it. From this derives the specific value that Strauss attributes to Rousseau: Rousseau is the last modern who posed the human problem in the original terms of philosophy, as a problem of nature and convention, as the search for nature beyond convention, for the life according to nature.

But someone might object that until now, I have only mentioned Rousseau, Nietzsche, and Heidegger—authors who are clearly "extremists." Why does Strauss appear to be only interested in such limit-case authors, so to speak? I have already given a part of the answer: it is in these authors that the source of the movement that characterizes modern philosophy best reveals itself. Here one finds what one might be called the source of modern philosophy's historicity. But it would be false to think that Strauss says nothing about the other, "nonextremist" authors, whom many think are the greatest and most interesting of modern thinkers. Strauss does say something about Hegel at least, during his dialogue with Alexander Kojève in *On Tyranny*:

> Syntheses effect miracles. Kojève's or Hegel's synthesis of classical and Biblical morality effects the miracle of producing an amazingly lax

morality out of two moralities both of which made very strict demands on self-restraint. . . . Hegel's moral or political teaching is indeed a synthesis: it is a synthesis of Socratic and Machiavellian or Hobbian politics. Kojève knows as well as anyone living that Hegel's fundamental teaching regarding Master and Slave is based on Hobbes's doctrine of the state of nature. If Hobbes's doctrine of the state of nature is abandoned *en pleine connaissance de cause* (as indeed it should be abandoned), Hegel's fundamental teaching will lose the evidence which it apparently still possesses for Kojève. Hegel's teaching is much more sophisticated than Hobbes's, but it is as much a construction as the latter.[3]

Here we have a text that is deceptively clear and deceptively brief. I will pass by, for the moment, the rather banal remark, that Hegel attempts to achieve a synthesis between Hellenism and Christianity or biblical morality. Let us concentrate on the second proposition, that Hegel's teaching is founded on Hobbes's doctrine of the state of nature and fundamentally is only worth as much as the latter. This is what I believe Strauss means to say in this passage.

Let us take *The Phenomenology of Mind*. The work's development and conclusion are inseparable from its beginning. What beginning? It is a question of the difference in the respective attitudes toward death of the master and the slave. This is the difference between the ignorant courage of the master and the knowing cowardice of the slave, the latter destined to be ever more knowing, and finally absolutely knowing. It is the slave who simultaneously determines the beginning, the development, and the end of history as Hegel conceives it. In short, Hegel's philosophy fundamentally amounts to what his analysis of the state of nature is worth, that is, of his analysis of the fear of death. Now, the main point or pivot of this analysis is his formulation of the virtues and the limits of warrior courage. But, of course, there are other possible analyses of courage. There are, for example, those of Socrates, Plato, or Xenophon; there is also Blaise Pascal's. They differ among themselves, and with Hegel's analysis. Philosophy's task is to distinguish them clearly, then to compare them, in order to discover the one that is most exactly adequate to natural human experience in its totality. Thus, Strauss thinks—or at least I believe he thinks—that before interpreting Hegel, and perhaps instead of interpreting Hegel's system (or construction), one must begin by asking, What is courage?

As soon as one suspects that Hegel's interpretation of the original human experiences is a synthesis or mixture of the Greek and the Christian interpretations, the task is to free each one in its native authenticity. Only in doing so will the clear awareness of the fundamental problems be recovered. Then the double polarity—nature and convention, philos-

ophy and revelation—will come to the center of attention. Goethe, whom
Strauss said was the last great man to retain in a vital way the original
idea of philosophy, wrote: "The true and unique theme, the most profound theme of the history of the world and of men, to which all the
others are subordinate, remains the conflict between unbelief and belief."[4]

Thus, what appears to modern man as the progress of self-understanding (and modern philosophy aims to be self-understanding) appears to
Strauss as the obscuring of the fundamental problems.

I now can attempt to formulate the contrast between the ancients and
the moderns.

The Greek city is the site of natural experiences (or of natural consciousness) in their highest degree of intensity and variety. (After all,
Hegel said pretty much the same thing.) This natural consciousness is
inseparably a self-interpretation: it includes moral and political opinions,
it also includes poetry and religion. Philosophy is the endeavor, at once
heroic and unobtrusive, to keep one's distance, to refuse one's adher-
ence to all these interpretations by interposing between them and oneself the small question, What is? Between oneself and the laws, one
interposes, what is law? Between oneself and poetry, for example, the
one that recounts the courage and wrath of Achilles: What is courage?
What is wrath? Philosophy refuses to succumb to the authority or charm
of any of these interpretations, while recognizing that they have a natural, that is, partially natural foundation. In this view, philosophy is essentially *skeptical*. It is therefore essentially not a doctrine, system, or
view of the world, but a *way of life*. Philosophy shows that one can live
without resorting to or appealing to these interpretations, which means
that one can live according to nature. But philosophy also shows that
only the philosopher can live in this way, that only the philosopher's
life is fully in conformity with nature. It is in this sense that philosophy
is its own or proper object, that it is self-understanding. It is the original meaning of self-understanding or self-consciousness.

For the moderns—and modernity in a sense begins with Christianity—these experiences have been covered over or have become dangerously remote.

On the one hand, the religious interpretation of the world has taken
a more elaborate, rigorous, and extreme form with the revealed religions.
On the other hand, because of the extraordinary posthumous success of
the apology of Socrates, of Xenophon's and Plato's justification of the
philosophic life, philosophy was received as an authorized and even noble
activity, and thus as nonproblematic. (This is true at least in the Christian world—the case is different in the Islamic world and with the Jew-

ish people.) What in the Greek city was the immediate proximity—problematic and conflictual, to be sure—of nature and law, and philosophy and religion, appears now in the form of a polarity between two cities, between two established authorities clearly separated, each one the result of a long effort of elaboration and abstraction.

It is in this context that the modern project properly named intervenes. It is a polemical project. But against which enemy? Is it Christianity or classical philosophy? Strauss sometimes suggests one and sometimes the other. What is certain is that the project is directed against what the two have in common: it is a matter of renouncing the vain and corrupting search for "imaginary principalities" dreamed of by both philosophy and religion and of assuring the actualization of the just or satisfying social order. To achieve this, one must lower the goals of human action, and one must conquer chance and establish man as the master of nature and thus of his own nature.

This project is a construction. It takes as its materials or elements aspects of Greek experience, aspects of Christian experience, and in amalgamating them neutralizes them, by pitting one element against the other. It makes them serve in a construct contrary to the two original experiences or interpretations. One example will make this clear.

Pride, which Christianity sees as its most implacable enemy, invincible if God does not lend His aid, is transformed by Thomas Hobbes into *vain glory*. This passion, always redoubtable, now can be mastered by human art, by the "Leviathan." Soon it will become docile and give its content to a new citizenry. All that is required is to see the good aspect of vain glory, or perhaps to invent an artificial light that causes a new good side of vain glory to appear. For example, one can interpret it as the "desire for recognition." The sin of the Christian, once neutralized, becomes the right of man.

In this sense the modern project presupposes and attests to the victory of the Christian point of view: who would dare to prefer his vain glory to his neighbor's, who would dare truly to claim an unequal or superior right? Thus, if nature no longer succeeds in making itself heard and no longer makes itself heard even when one no longer believes in Christianity, it is because it is a weak or insufficient determination of man. This victory of Christianity is not one of Christianity in its strength because it died in its triumph, because its "realization" produces ever more deleterious effects. Nature is impotent; grace is degrading. It appears to be as futile to return to Greek contemplation as to continue to act as a Christian. What is to be done? This is where Nietzsche enters our picture.

The history of Christianity (i.e., the history of modern peoples) proves the power of a weak or base will. It is the weakness of modern man that best proves the strength of willing. This revelation of the strength of willing invites one to hope for and to prepare an affirmation of the strong or high will. We find ourselves before the alternatives of the supreme exaltation or the ultimate degradation, of the overman and the last man.

Beginning with his youth, Strauss was powerfully attracted to and remained attracted to Nietzsche. Why? I do not believe he has ever explained why. It is easy to conjecture, however, that he was attracted by the Nietzschean *psychology*, by the importance Nietzsche accords to human *types* (the philosopher, the religious man, the saint, the scholar), by his way of capturing the ultimate consequences of the different vital possibilities.

It is more clear what separated Strauss and Nietzsche. This can be summed up in a word: historicism. Nietzsche explicitly and emphatically adopts the historical or genealogical point of view. But he sees that if this point of view remains what it was initially (i.e., theoretical), it injures life. The historical point of view cannot provide motives for action. Moreover, even though it represents progress, the sole progress of modern consciousness, it also witnesses to a specific weakness of modern peoples: they lack being or substance, they are not self-sufficient, which is why they surround themselves imaginatively and in fact with the products of every place and epoch. In Nietzsche's view, one must reestablish the possibility of action while preserving historical consciousness.

Nietzsche finds himself before a problem that is, at bottom, technically similar to Hobbes's. One must think of human action in the context of a theoretical interpretation of the world that appears to deprive it of meaning or motive: in Hobbes's case a mechanistic science of nature, in Nietzsche's the historical point of view. And both have recourse to the notion of power. For both thinkers, man is a quantum of power. But in Nietzsche the will to power is emancipated from natural limits, limits posed by the laws of natural causality, which Hobbes still acknowledges. In Nietzsche, the will to power "creates values." Strauss remarks that Nietzsche understands himself poorly when he shows such disdain for English philosophy.

I suggested earlier that the idea of the will to power does not emerge solely from a conceptual necessity, that is, from the critique of theoretical historicism. It also comes from the historical experience of Christian peoples. It is thus inseparable from an extreme valorization of religion, in particular, biblical religion. Nietzsche is thus the philosopher—as a philosopher he is an atheist—who maintains a doctrine (i.e., the will to power), that until now has found its best illustration, and its truth or verification, in the Christian religion.

Thus, what Nietzsche indicates to Strauss is the ambiguity, equivocation, and fragility of his character as a philosopher. He is incomparably closer to religion, more intertwined with it than the Greek philosophers, on the one hand, and the modern philosophers until Rousseau, on the other. The "free spirit" of the future, the "philosopher of the future" of which Nietzsche speaks, is he a philosopher—or a novel version of *homo religiosus*?

> In the preface he intimates that his precursor par excellence is not a statesman nor even a philosopher but the *homo religiosus* Pascal (cf. aph. 45). . . .
>
> After having tempted some of his readers (cf. aph. 30) with the doctrine of the will to power Nietzsche makes them raise the question as to whether that doctrine does not assert, to speak popularly, that God is refuted but the devil is not. He replies "On the contrary! On the contrary, my friends! and to the devil, what forces you to speak popularly?" The doctrine of the will to power—the whole doctrine of *Beyond Good and Evil*—is in a manner a vindication of God (cf. aph. 150 and 295 as well as *Genealogy of Morals*, Preface Nr. 7). . . .
>
> Could atheism belong to the free mind as Nietzsche conceives of it while a certain kind of non-atheism belongs to the philosopher of the future who will again worship the god Dionysos or will again be, as an Epicurian might say, a dionysokolax (cf. aph. 7)? This ambiguity is essential to Nietzsche's thought; without it his doctrine would lose its character of an experiment or a temptation.[5]

Is not the foe of the crucified the secret friend of the crucified? Is not Dionysos in some way the mask of Christ? It seems to me that there is no doubt that in Strauss's eyes Nietzsche remains a modern to the extent that he does not succeed in recovering the original idea of philosophy, and these two formulations are equivalent to the extent that he remains Christian.

As Strauss writes in his autobiographical "Preface to *Spinoza's Critique of Religion*":

> The most profound change which the human soul has hitherto undergone, the most important enlargement and deepening which it has hitherto experienced, is due, according to Nietzsche, to the Bible. . . . Hence, the overman is "the Roman Caesar with Christ's soul." Not only was Biblical morality as veracity or intellectual probity at work in the destruction of Biblical theology and Biblical morality; not only is it at work in the questioning of that very probity, of "our virtue, which alone has remained

to us"; Biblical morality will remain at work in the morality of the overman. The overman is inseparable from "the philosophy of the future." The philosophy of the future is distinguished from traditional philosophy, which pretended to be purely theoretical, by the fact that it is consciously the outcome of a will: the fundamental awareness is not purely theoretical, but theoretical and practical, inseparable from an act of the will or a decision. The fundamental awareness characteristic of the new thinking is a secularized version of the Biblical faith as interpreted by Christian theology.[6]

Modern atheism, atheism motivated by conscience or probity—we see that Nietzsche explicitly connects his own revolt against the Christian God to his Christian conscience—represents in a certain way the ultimate victory of biblical morality, that is, of the moral attitude as such over the philosophical attitude as such (and this is not less true when the consequences or contents of this attitude are shockingly immoral in the eyes of common moral conscience).

The ultimate alternative is finally that between the moral and philosophic attitudes. In their project to conquer chance, to realize the ideal, to subject or to replace religion, the moderns progressively have effaced the fundamental distinction between theoretical reason and practical reason. They, in fact, have absorbed theoretical reason in practical reason, or rather in a practical attitude that no longer can or wishes to be reason. They have ended by replacing philosophy with a new sort of thinking that, like Christian faith, is both intelligence and decision. Moreover, Nietzsche with his "historical point of view" retains something of the "provincialism of the nineteenth century." It is Heidegger in Strauss's eyes who best illustrates this new thought. According to Heidegger, to think is also to will as well as to pray, and all this is at the same time the supreme action, which does not go beyond itself. Immediately after the lines I cited earlier, Strauss continues:

> What is true of Nietzsche is no less true of the author of *Sein und Zeit.* Heidegger wishes to expel from philosophy the last relics of Christian theology like the notions of "external truths" and "the idealized absolute subject." But the understanding of man which he opposes to the Greek understanding of man as the rational animal is, as he emphasizes, primarily the Biblical understanding of man as created in the image of God. Accordingly, he interprets human life in the light of "being towards death," "anguish," "conscience," and "guilt"; in this most important respect he is much more Christian than Nietzsche. The efforts of the new thinking to escape from the evidence of the Biblical understanding of man, that is, from Biblical morality, have failed. And, as we have learned from Nietzsche, Biblical morality demands the Biblical God.[7]

The greatest threat to thought or to philosophy according to Strauss is the moral point of view as such. With its rather ostentatious critique of morality modern thought frequently hides from itself that its initial impulse is essentially moral. And even those, like Nietzsche, who know how to ask, "To what extent are we too pious?" want nothing more than to institute a new morality, ever more anti-Christian in its content but ever more Christian in its form.

Now certainly Strauss acknowledges that one must act morally. But precisely, one must *act* morally, and not think morally. Nietzsche and Heidegger think morally and invite us (without being aware of it—how could they, since according to their philosophy, they only know to will?), they invite us to act immorally from time to time. The only human life capable of living morally without thinking morally, of overcoming the "human, all too human," of living according to nature, is that of the philosopher, of Socrates.

That is why we find Strauss's true criticism of Nietzsche (who reproached Socrates for having corrupted Plato's beautiful nature), his true criticism of Nietzsche and Heidegger, in his decision to devote the last and most important part of his work to rediscovering the authentic figure of Socrates. I do not know if he succeeded in this task. But if we wish to appreciate Strauss's work, *en pleine connaissance de cause*, this is what we most of all must know.

Translated by Daniel J. Mahoney and Paul Seaton

Notes

1. See "Note on the Plan of Nietzsche's *Beyond Good and Evil*" in Leo Strauss, *Studies in Platonic Political Philosophy* (Chicago: University of Chicago Press, 1983), 174–91. I say "unfinished" because this text, as interesting as it is, does not have the density of Strauss's "polished" writings.

2. Leo Strauss, *Thoughts on Machiavelli* (Chicago: University of Chicago Press, 1958), 231.

3. Leo Strauss, "Restatement on Xenophon's *Hiero*," in *What is Political Philosophy?* (Chicago: University of Chicago Press, 1988) 111.

4. Leo Strauss, *Persecution and the Art of Writing* (Chicago: University of Chicago Press, 1988) 107. Strauss states that "one cannot recall too often this remark of Goethe."

5. Leo Strauss, "Note on the Plan of Nietzsche's *Beyond Good and Evil*," 176–79.

6. Leo Strauss, "Preface to *Spinoza's Critique of Religion*," in *Liberalism Ancient and Modern* (Ithaca, N.Y.: Cornell University Press, 1989), 236–37.

7. "Preface to *Spinoza's Critique of Religion*," 237.

On Historical Causality

Pierre Manent

1994

The problem that I seek to illumine is the one that beginning in the nineteenth century became central in European awareness: how is one to explain, and first of all to define, the singular movement that carried Europe, and its American colony, on a completely unprecedented moral and political, scientific and spiritual path, a path on which the rest of the world in turn seems irresistibly drawn? How are we to understand and to explain what the German historians call the *Sonderweig* or "separate path" of the West?

Not only is this problem so central and so complex that it mobilized all the disciplines, but one can say that it occasioned the birth of the reigning science of the modern period: sociology. In truth, what are the foundational works of sociology, whose peak moments Raymond Aron traces in *Main Currents in Sociological Thought,*[1] if not primarily a reflection on the definition and genesis, and the static and dynamic, of modern society? Even if Karl Marx defines the latter by capitalism, Alexis de Tocqueville by democracy, Auguste Comte by industry, and Max Weber by rationalization, these fathers of almost all of our thoughts and ideas have in common the fact that they question themselves about the specificity and the genesis of the modern difference.

Here is the particular difficulty I encountered. Of these great authors the one who seemed to me to describe best the original characteristics

This is a translation of the first part of "De la causalité historique" (*Commentaire* 67, Autumn 1994). In this article, Manent clarifies his reflections on the "modern difference" that he had developed in his book *The City of Man* (Paris: Fayard, 1994; Princeton: Princeton University Press, 1998) and responds to criticisms of his book raised by Alain Besançon and Philippe Raynaud (*Commentaire* 66 [Summer 1994], 419–31). We have reproduced only the first section, "The Cause of the Modern Movement," and not Manent's specific responses to Raynaud and Besançon. It appears here with permission.

of modern society and modern man is also the one who explains the least well its genesis—one might go so far as to say that he did not concern himself at all with explaining it. Tocqueville admirably describes democracy; he does the same for its counterpoint, what he calls aristocracy; he adds, in an enigmatic, unsettling formulation, that they form as it were "two distinct humanities." And the grand master leaves us there. It is there that I have camped for the past twenty years.

I thus ask myself about this process that is our modern development. I seek *the cause of a movement.* In this sense I am first of all a historian and, one might suggest, a physicist who is looking for a "dynamic formula." But it is a matter of a movement of a particular sort; it has, or appears to have, a particular radicality. It is a movement during the course of which, and because of which, *man changes.* This is at least what the man who changes says about himself: he becomes modern, ever more modern. But who precisely says this? It is said by the modern men who generally are the most competent, that is, the learned, and first of all those special learned men, the philosophers, who give themselves the task of understanding, with the greatest amplitude and exactitude, the human situation. Modern philosophy desires this change; it promotes it; it recognizes it and proclaims it. Giving expression to his humanity in the terms of modern philosophy—human beings are free beings who have rights—philosophy is both the expression of and the condition for modern man's self-understanding.

In this way philosophy, which poses questions, itself becomes a part of the question I ask. Where am I, and who am I, so to question those who ask the questions? I am neither a philosopher nor not a philosopher. But if I am thus divided, so is philosophy itself. It is inevitably double or divided from now on: it is both ancient philosophy and modern philosophy. Philosophy divides itself and it does not cease self-dividing; it critiques itself, and it does not cease so doing: what it initially said about man, it no longer says; it, in fact, rejects it as something no longer worthwhile. From a certain date philosophy, having become modern philosophy, discovers that the point of view previously considered to be the most lucid about man—that of philosophy (which has now become ancient philosophy)—is revealed to be full of prejudices and even, in a sense, the source or the support of all the most pernicious prejudices. Aristotle, after having been for so long "the father of those who know," is denounced as the father of those who are ignorant, the father of all error. But to break with Aristotle and with ancient philosophy is to break with the original expression of human universality, with the thought that knew how to see and to say "man," defining him as the political and rational animal. Does this rupture somehow allow us to attain a more universal universality? But what is more universal than "man"? In any case, there are henceforth two different, successive, and incompatible rational ways of affirming human universality. And if philosophy is characterized by the effort to arrive at self-understanding, we must note that there are from now on two possible self-understandings. How can the rational animal find rest before having overcome this division or before having understood why it is insurmountable? We ought not to act as though we do not see this scandal of reason divided against itself. We must not be philosophers whom nothing astonishes.

Martin Heidegger and Leo Strauss are, in my eyes, the philosophers who have meditated on this scandal with the most perseverance and radicality. They never stopped thinking in the light of this wonderment. They gave the most coherent solutions to the problem of the cause of the movement that I have sought to resolve. I willingly would have followed one or the other, devoting the rest of my life to understanding better all the things that remained unclear to me in their thoughts, if their two solutions had not been strictly contradictory.

We can summarize Strauss's solution in this way. Because there is a nature, and because this nature as such remains sempiternally the same, man does not change. If there nonetheless is a change or a rupture in the modern period, it is because modern man conceived the project of mastering nature, including his own nature. The source of the modern movement is in this effort to master, and thus to change, the nature of man, which, in truth, cannot be changed. This enterprise necessarily has all sorts of effects, but it cannot change anything fundamental in the human order. For example, it cannot change anything about the order of the human soul. Modern man constructs windmills and takes himself for a giant.

To be sure, such an interpretation assumes that the experience of the modern movement, or the modern experience of history, is entirely illusory. Heidegger, to the contrary, believes that this experience, by its novelty and profundity, obliges us—if we want to understand it and ourselves—to "deconstruct" and redo the most fundamental categories of traditional philosophy, of "essentialism," and above all, the idea of eternal truth. Thus, in 1922 he writes to Karl Jaspers:

> The old ontological separation between essence and existence is insufficient, not only in its content—but because it has an origin in a domain of meaning in which today's experience of the being of life (to put it briefly: the "historical") and of its ontological significance is not possible. The old ontology . . . must be fundamentally revised—if we seriously want to understand and master our own life and present in its fundamental intentions.[2]

The modern development is only the refraction, on the superficial plane of politics and of culture, of an incomparably more profound history that one can call the history of Being. Heidegger thus takes seriously— and he is perhaps the only one really to take seriously—the rather banal affirmation, the obsessive slogan of our democracy: "Man is a historical being." In order for man to be a historical being, it is necessary for Being itself to be history.

These two positions appeared more and more clearly to me as simultaneously rigorous and untenable, like the positions of the Eleatics and the Heracliteans on the question of "physical" motion. Strauss is the Eleatic, Heidegger the Heraclitean. To understand the modern movement, I had to depart both from the Straussian "nothing changes" and from the Heideggerian "Being itself changes." To be sure, I did not allow myself to be governed simply by the physical analogy, since on this question the political and moral contents of our history necessarily play a decisive role.

As for Heidegger, let me briefly say the following. The movement I seek to understand has its location in the element of politics. Even more, its generative principle belongs to the political order, or at least it is reflected and inscribes itself primordially in this order. But there is no place for this element in Heidegger's thought, except as something derivative and subordinate. But I am able to read and understand Aristotle's *Politics* no less than his *Physics* and *Metaphysics*. It would be arbitrary for me to consider his exploration of man's political condition and his analysis of political regimes, as the weak and vulgar residue of a forgotten order of Being. Both modern experience and the reading of ancient things equally tend to persuade me that the future, like the present and the past, will be, insofar as it is human, political, and to the extent that it is political, human.

Rejecting the history of Being, am I therefore going to find refuge and an explanation in the nature that Leo Strauss, with the aid of the ancients, seeks to recover? The answer is no. But I must stop for a moment.

I certainly do not believe that it is possible to understand the human world without having recourse to the notion of human nature. I am even ready, in order to defend this notion, to brave the jests and sarcasm of the learned. But it seems to me that the very description that Strauss gives of the modern movement, and in particular of its propensity toward radicalization—of its accelerated movement, of a movement ever more in motion—poorly fits with this idea of nature. Why does modern man get carried farther away from his nature? His political regime is ever more contrary to nature because he desires, by means of this regime, to elevate himself ever more above his nature. But *why*? If the discovery of nature above and beyond convention is the very definition of philosophy, how could modern philosophy, which abolished the idea of nature, forget itself to this extent? There is something unnatural about this movement away from nature described so well by Strauss.

The causal perplexity in which Strauss leaves us can be stated more precisely. Sometimes he suggests, and even affirms, that the modern movement was decisively unleashed and motivated by "antitheological ire"—by hostility toward and a revolt against Christianity. Sometimes he suggests, more forcefully than if he affirmed it, that the modern movement can be understood without any mention of Christianity. At least he helps us to gain some distance from the widespread interpretations of the modern movement in terms of the "secularization of Christianity." This last notion presupposes that Christianity was the cause of political, moral, and even scientific effects and that these effects are now and henceforth independent of their cause. But one of two things is true: either "Christianity" was the cause of these effects, and the latter can never become independent of it; or these effects truly are independent, and "Christianity" cannot be their genuine cause.

My work, described in the most general terms, thus consists in interpreting the modern movement, the condition of modern man, in accordance with a triangularization that takes seriously the ancient, modern, and Christian poles. And it is by taking seriously the Christian pole that I am able to escape from the alternatives of Straussian "naturalism" and Heideggerian "historicism," while preserving the phenomenon of nature and that of history. Such in any case is my intent.

The terrain my book surveys then appears a bit like this. There is a natural order that the Greek city and philosophy allow us to bring to the light of day. This order contains and manifests a tension, even a conflict, between the city and philosophy, a conflict to which Strauss always drew our attention. Man is the political animal who realizes his nature in the city: he realizes his universality in the particularity of the city. Philosophy is necessarily in conflict with the city because it reveals the city's limits.

The decisive novelty brought by the Christian church is the church herself, which is a real universal community. Henceforth man is divided between the city and the church. The philosopher himself is divided: as a philosopher he is with the citizen against the Christian because he only wishes to know what is accessible to natural reason as such. But as a philosopher he is with the Christian against the citizen, because he is for the universal as against the particular. Here we see the dynamic of our situation. Philosophy comes to play a decisive and absolutely unprecedented political role. It is a role situated at the interface of the city and the church. It legitimates the city before the church; it affirms the human virtues; it maintains the legitimacy of human affirmation.

At the same time it affirms, if not the church, at least the universality of the church against the particularity of the city; it provides a critique of the pride that marks this particularity; it displays a skepticism toward every human self-assertion that remains particular. In this sense modern philosophy is the place where the mutual critique of the city and the church most clearly is accomplished.

Translated by Daniel J. Mahoney and Paul Seaton

Notes

1. See Raymond Aron, *Les Étapes de la Pensée Sociologique* (Paris: Gallimard, 1967). This work is available in two volumes in English as *Main Currents in Sociological Thought* (New Brunswick, N.J.: Transaction, 1998). Volume 1 treats Montesquieu, Comte, Marx, Tocqueville, and the sociologists and the revolution of 1848. Volume 2 analyzes the thought of Durkheim, Pareto, and Weber. See Manent's essay "Raymond Aron and the Analysis of Society" in part 6 of this volume (editor's note).

2. See Heidegger's letter of 27 June 1922 in *Martin Heidegger/Karl Jaspers Briefweschel 1920–1963* (Frankfort-sur-le Main: Klostermann/Piper, 1990), 27.

Part Eight

Liberalism and Conservatism Today

Originally presented as a lecture at the University of Chicago in May 1997, "Liberalism and Conservatism: The Transatlantic Misunderstanding" did not need to be translated for this volume: it was written in English for that occasion. Manent's discussion is conducted by way of a comparison and contrast of the American and French views of liberty.

The two countries have in common a dedication to liberalism or the system of individual liberty. Both are modern societies, with modern governments. However, liberty, while truly a predicate of man and political life, is not wholly or simply true: liberty must have credible motives of action, it must be able "to give an account" of itself if it is to be humanly satisfying. Manent's account of the two countries explores the various understandings of liberty that distinguish them as well as the complements they propose to guide and humanize their basic commitments to liberty.

Manent suggests that man's political nature is precisely such a complement to and frame for the exercise of individual liberty. Man's actions and thoughts, goods and goals, are not fully human until they are "politically inscribed" in some form. On the basis of this thought, Manent is able to suggest to American conservatives that "hierarchical systems of command" that they tend to denigrate as state paternalism provide modern liberty and modern men and women with a much needed public affirmation of goods other than their cherished liberty.

And lest contemporary liberals gloat too much at this dart tossed at their opponents, Manent is quick to chasten them, too. Human liberty must be *rational* liberty and thus willing to look outside itself to the complex human world and to enter into a dialectical consideration of this variegated world. Liberals, one might say, should practice political philosophy. And liberals must stop confusing rational liberty with authoritarian systems of command, or state collectivism, that undermine the dynamism and capacity for renewal of modern societies.

215

Liberalism and Conservatism: The Transatlantic Misunderstanding

Pierre Manent

1997

In what is perhaps the weightiest sentence in the weightiest modern work of political philosophy, Hegel writes as follows: "The principle of modern states has prodigious strength and depth, because it allows the principle of subjectivity to progress to its culmination in the extreme of self-subsistent personal particularity, and yet at the same time brings it back to the substantive unity, and so maintains this unity in the principle of subjectivity itself."[1] It is good to ponder these pregnant phrases, at the same time obscure and illuminating; they will help us to confront coolly a number of our public squabbles. To begin with, the quarrel between liberalism and conservatism, that is, between the party of the state as the sovereign agency responsible for peace and justice, and the party of society as an association of equal, free, and accordingly responsible individuals, will appear to us as the inevitable but somewhat meretricious quarrel between two equally necessary moments or aspects of the same political contrivance—our good and great contrivance, the modern democratic regime.

I do not mean to suggest that there is no substantial bone of contention between the parties or that the arguments they exchange are just the products of two opposite and equally paranoid imaginations, although paranoia plays a considerable and legitimate role in the workings of modern liberty, as Montesquieu saw so well two centuries ago.[2] But since modern society needs a sovereign and representative state, and the modern state needs a free society, the two protagonists are condemned to tinker along as they have done until now. However eloquently liberals blast Wall Street greed unleashed, however persuasively conservatives lament the decline of the sturdy spirit of personal responsibility, I can not bring myself to join either choir, although I will admit that when I have to take sides—when push comes to shove—my deck is slightly but neatly stacked toward the conservative camp. But my considered judgment is that the Gordian knot of our present condition is not tied around the points that divide liberals and conservatives. Since I am able to neither contribute to this current debate nor authoritatively propose some new full-fledged interpretation of our situation, I will only try to describe a few salient features of the world around us, without aiming at more order and coherence than I can see.

The most sketchy account of our present circumstances requires a return, however brief, to our arché, that is, to the latest decisive event to mold these circumstances. The collapse of communism is this decisive event, an event now as reluctantly considered as it had been poorly anticipated. Nevertheless, on one point there is widespread agreement: the end of communism is identical with the triumph of democratic legitimacy. The lofty idea of the science of history had to give way to the more pedestrian principle of the consent of the people, a consent produced through the free institutions of a free citizenry. At long last democracy evolved out of its typical predicament. For most of its adult life, it had to sustain the two-pronged attack of two very dissimilar—but at the end very similar—enemies: on the one hand, the partisans of an antidemocratic regime, whose enmity climaxed in the Nazi challenge that was decisively disposed of in Dresden's and Berlin's fire and rubble; on the other hand, the partisans of a more than democratic regime—that is, more democratic than democracy—whose challenge suddenly and gently disintegrated as the Berlin Wall was nibbled away by souvenir hunters. However different the processes, the outcomes add up: democracy now has no serious ideological challenger in the western world, or even in the world simply. On that score, Francis Fukuyama's thesis holds good.[3] But what does it mean?

The expression "the victory of democracy" is doubly ambiguous. First, the event or process we are talking about was more a collapse of communism than a victory of democracy—to be truly victorious you ought to desire victory, to crave it. Second, it was more a victory of democratic legitimacy and principles than of democratic countries or regimes. As a victory of democratic countries, as a political victory, it was nearly exclusively (as a European, I regret to say it) an American victory. Let us consider for a moment the strange demise of communism, one of the strangest phenomena in human history.

If communism led an atrocious life or made life atrocious for its slaves, at least it managed to pull off a hugely successful death. It died drowning under the applause of the whole Western world. The point is not that an average communist bully like Mikhail Gorbachev was everywhere lionized and in some places canonized, however distasteful the whole thing was. The point is that as a result of such a process, the incredibly criminal enterprise of communism was not condemned, it was not even judged by ordinary politicians and the citizenry at large. People recoil from thinking about communism further than to agree that "it does not work." So communism is just one of many things that admittedly do not work—somewhat like the squaring of the circle. But because man is a moral and political animal, and even a thinking being who cannot live too far away from truth, there is, as a result of this failure to confront the nature of communism, a festering sore at the heart of Europe. Even discounting the American and European pundits who wittily and hopefully noticed that the end of communism meant the end of anticommunism, we have to admit that it was not a famous victory.

But it was an *American* victory. As a political victory, it was an American victory. The bulk of the weaponry was American, the strategy American, as was the unity of resolve within the politically decisive class, and the president who had the vision and courage to say loud and clear that the communist empire was evil, and that it was crumbling, and to act according to both judgments. It was not a European victory simply because the European countries did not really want it, with the notable but ambiguous exception of the German political class, which wanted it as a means to the reunification of the fatherland. As far as European countries wanted something, they wanted the preservation and continuation of the status quo, at most its improvement through the construction of a union of Western Europe.

When communism collapsed under its own ignominy and nullity, Western Europe did exactly what Gorbachev was doing: it put the best face on it—it even indulged a few firecrackers on Pariser Platz and that was it. If the then French president, François Mitterrand, could have saved communism in the USSR, he would have done it. As a matter of fact, he tried his best to do it, flying to Kiev to encourage Gorbachev to resist Chancellor Helmut Kohl's resolute move toward German reunification. I recount all this more in sadness than in anger. If we discount an undercurrent of moral obtuseness, and occasional bursts of malignancy like the one to which I just alluded, European equivocations were largely determined by situation and history, as was America's simplicity of purpose. There have been instances of European resolve and American hesitancy. And some of the most acute analysts of communism as an intrinsically perverse regime were European. But the larger picture is clear: the victory of democracy is an American victory.

As far as the political realm is concerned, this means that European nations have been more enfeebled than strengthened by this victory and that the political gap between each European country and the United

States has grown, that the Atlantic community—yesterday an alliance with a paramount leader—is becoming more and more of an empire in the traditional meaning of the term. The political units at the periphery have a diminished capacity to act according to their best judgment, and the main body of the empire is increasingly disinclined to let them do it when they are so disposed. The organs of sense of the American body politic, if you allow me the expression, are less and less able simply to distinguish between what is within and what is without American provenance. Why use another language when the American one is so commodious, why govern oneself by other laws than those passed by the American congress? And, of course, no case is settled before it comes before an American court. This time, I am speaking more in anger than in sadness, because hopefully we have time amicably to stem the tide.

The end of communism has made the relationship between America and Europe not only more politically unequal but also more problematic. When both were under the same menace, what we have in common had pride of place; now that the danger is gone, the differences come to the fore. And one has to admit that we are not always very nice toward each other. Americans tend to feel that Europeans are complacent and lazy—and if moreover they happen to be French, they are afflicted with a very specific and apparently incurable distemper that goes by the clinical name of "delusions of grandeur"; Europeans tend to think that Americans overwork themselves if not exactly to death, at least to a degree where there is not much point in continuing to live. I have to admit that, personally, I am evenly split between exasperation at the European way and consternation at the American one, or vice versa. Many travelers or observers have tried to encapsulate in a formula, or to explain through many volumes, what makes our societies, or regimes, or ways of life, so different despite their evident similarity. Here is one more try.

Without telling anew the speculative feats of the founding fathers of our modern regime—or, if you prefer, without rounding up the usual suspects—I will only summarize the principle of modern liberty, the principle of human rights: each human being is the best judge of what is most conducive to his or her own self-preservation, whether the latter be considered strictly as the security of mere life, or more extensively as comfortable self-preservation, or even more extensively as the pursuit of happiness. Liberty is just a means to this end, but a means so necessary, so pervasive, so paramount, that it most resembles an end in itself. This ambiguity of modern liberty—this oscillation between end and means—may be a theoretical liability or weakness, but it largely accounts for its prodigious dynamism. The Americans are the ones who take this ambiguity in stride. If the end is a means and the means is an end, there is no motive ever to stop, no place to rest, no old family seat to retire to, no genteel name to buy or earn, no leisure with or without dignity to enjoy. You have to do things, to do things your way. Under the spell of this ambiguity, some abstraction and simplification of human motives necessarily enter. It is not so much that money becomes all-powerful or that Americans peculiarly worship money—a trader in junk bonds is not necessarily more cupiditous than a Venetian gondolier. Rather money becomes the most socially explicit thing: it proves that you have done things; it registers your doings. The abstraction of money nicely fits in with the abstraction of "doing things."

Certainly Europeans feel uneasy with this simplification, not necessarily because they are more subtle; rather it could be because they are more hesitant or confused. Anyway, they tend to consider liberty more as a means for something "substantial." On this point many Europeans would agree among themselves. But as a means to what end? On this score they disagree among themselves, and there is even disagreement within each European breast.

Liberty can be a means to security and well-being. But if the state can guarantee these objectives, you have no need to bother very much about economic liberty. You Americans will say that the state as such is utterly unable to deliver the goods. Nevertheless, the European brand of state-sponsored economic liberty has produced performances that in the long term are not visibly inferior to the American one, although in these past few years Europe has undoubtedly been lagging.

Liberty can be a means to culture, in the old Latin meaning of *cultura animi,* or to *Bildung.* Then you have to admit that *Bildung* has flourished under less than free institutions. Racine flourished in Versailles, Goethe in Weimar, and these were less than democratic settings. Even Athens—the most democratic body politic ever, but at the same time the most exclusive club of white males—fell far short of the hoped-for marriage between high culture and equal liberty. Thus *Bildung* is a worthy objective, perhaps better taken care of by the state, or by the church, or by a tiny circle of distinguished individuals.

I have just mentioned the church. The purpose of the church is not properly *Bildung* but salvation. And it is obvious that the motive of salvation is even less amenable than the motive of *Bildung* to the general and genial recommendation of doing one's own thing. More often than not, your way, including my way, is not the Lord's way.

Liberty can be a means to Liberty, that is, to this new and exalted condition in which man—until then a slave to the dead—breaks forth as a really living and sovereign creature, a law unto himself. This transformation, this self-overcoming, is supposed to take place in this most fear-some of European deeds, which is called a revolution. Revolution sus-pends the working of every mundane motive: self-preservation becomes utterly unintelligible since there are no more selves to preserve, and all are one. I need not stress that European revolutions did not exactly de-velop according to plan. As a Frenchman, I ought to know. But the idea of revolution, now unable to stir Europeans to real action, remains po-tent enough to bring some discredit to the prosaic liberty of modern democratic society. How paltry the prospect of doing your own thing seems when the shapeless but sublime image of a new society—of a new man, even of a new earth—is still hovering around!

It appears that the relative strength of America depends on its suc-cessful synthesis of human motives—again, bought at the price of *some* simplification. Conversely, the relative weakness of Europe follows from the remaining heterogeneity of motives. Motives other than prosaic lib-erty retain just enough strength to enfeeble what is necessarily, in Eu-rope no less than in America, the mainspring of human action in a modern democratic setting.

The synthetic motive, which has had in America such an extraordi-nary career, at the beginning was a discovery of the Europeans, an elab-oration of European experience. As you well know, during the eighteenth century, in England, Scotland, and France, perceptive observers felt able to describe the workings of a new social bond, which went by the ge-neric name of *commerce,* not rarely qualified as *doux commerce.* Com-merce then is not just a human activity among a number of human activities; it connotes a new regime of human action itself, and its de-velopment gives the axis of human progress. The radical newness of commerce in this comprehensive meaning consisted in this, that people were now linked to one another without commanding one another, and without necessarily sharing a common way of life.[4]

To better understand our present situation, we have to take a full view of the radicality of this revolution. Ancient politics—that is, pre-modern politics—employed two great means to make people relate or hold together within a social body. The main one was the institution and preservation of a fundamentally unequal relationship between the few who are entitled to command and the many who are obliged to obey as a matter of conscience. This iron law of human obedience and in-equality had been very rarely broken, only, and most eminently, by Greek cities and the Roman republic but also by such Italian cities as Venice and Florence. The Greeks, the Romans, and the Florentines proved that men could live in liberty and equality—that is, that they could rule and be ruled in turn—but only by belonging to the same body politic in the full sense of the verb "to belong"—that is, by "putting in common their actions and reasons" (an Aristotelian phrase)[5] by sharing a way of life, by forming an exclusive community. The radically new relationship that comes by the name of commerce consists in this, that the link between persons is now the result of what they *severally* do—with no one explicitly commanding anyone, nor with everyone sharing a common way of life.

During the eighteenth century, moralists and philosophers, no less than economists and calculators, explore in awe, as if contemplating a miracle transforming human life itself, the strange properties and hidden causality of this new dispensation. Interest, sympathy, and benevolence are the new and invisible rulers of this new society that prospers best when it is least commanded.

These things happened two centuries ago. What prevented the definitive triumph in Europe of this commerce that Europeans had invented and were the first to celebrate? As everybody knows, the fact is that this first expansion and generalization of commerce—of what Adam Smith called "commercial society"—did not spell the end of political command. After all, the eighteenth century was followed by the nineteenth and twentieth centuries, the era of pacific and pacifying commerce by the era of national wars and total states. And it is precisely this succession that makes you wonder and ponder.

At the end of the eighteenth century, European peoples, first among them the French people, at the time by far the most numerous and considered to be the most civilized, decided that they no longer needed an absolute prince reigning by right of birth, that they could and should govern themselves as a unitary and sovereign nation. This decision entailed a tremendous strengthening of the feeling and means of "being together." Thus, the French Revolution, with the storms that soon followed in its wake—that is, the huge Napoleonic enterprise and the surge of national self-assertion all across Europe—meant an intensification of command, a reaffirmation of a collective and common bond (we could call it, in Platonic terms, a reaffirmation of The One).

The nineteenth and early twentieth century nation-state—that is, *the* nation-state—was a very strange political creature. As for what interests us here, it was a *coincidentia oppositorum*. On the one hand, at least within its borders, it freed commercial society from its shackles. Civil equality meant that you had a right to whatever position you could attain through your own efforts. French novels evoke with much gusto talented and ambitious young men who bolt from their cramped circumstances: these go-getters do not go west but up, toward the yawning heights of the new society. Indeed, and this second aspect is inseparable from the first, the nation-state embodies a reaffirmation of command and hierarchy not only at the political center where the people make their will known and effective but in the great institutions making up the body of the nation: first of all, the army and the administration, of course, but also the university, the church, and soon the industrial enterprise. The democratic and commercial nation is at the same time, to put it colloquially, very much a "top-down" structure. By the way, it is the reason that it could accommodate what the French called *le grand monde,* or simply *le monde:* the top brass of these great masculine and exclusive institutions met in the salons of beautiful or elegant hostesses where the impotent remnants of aristocracy fancied they still reigned and the sturdy commoners dreamed they were welcomed among the deities of Olympus.

I do not want to suggest that these imposing masculine institutions, these potent structures of command, were an exclusively European feature. I do not doubt that there was, and still is, some hierarchy for instance in the American military or the American business enterprise. It remains that this hierarchical structure of command played a much larger role in Europe. True, the tone of command varied according to the country: with more dependence on social deference in Britain, with a distinctive bureaucratic regularity in France, with an indelible Prussian heavy-handedness in Germany, to name only the three biggest European powers at the time. But it is a common trait, and it certainly contributed to the fateful stiffness and inflexibility with which our countries dealt with one another in their rivalries and to the mad obstinacy with which they carried on their quarrel after war had broken out in August 1914.

We are thus powerfully tempted to distinguish the "system of liberty"—another Smithian coinage—that leaves people free to act according to their interest as they conceive of it—that is, that lets people have *some* motive, however schematically conceived, and do things according to it; and the system of command in which people are supposed to act according to a specific rationality, but in which the mere weight of hierarchy tends to void this rationality of its free content. Because the system drains action of its congenial motives, it often incites citizens to do nothing or occasionally presses them to do mad things. (By the way, the communist system managed to make its slaves do both. In this light, indeed, communism comes to sight as the perfect realization of the system of command reduced to itself—that is, a regime in which all that remains is the system of command without any specific content: there is not much difference left between the army and the university, the university and the factory, the factory and the police, and so on. It was *only* from-the-top-down, and with a more than Prussian heavy-handedness.)

What is the purpose of these remarks? Their drift seems to run counter to what I stressed at the beginning, when I said that state and society in modern circumstances are two sides of the same coin. Now, I have just distinguished sharply the system of command—of which the state is the paramount structure—from the system of liberty, which is another name for commercial society. To clear things up, or at least to try to do so, I must enter the last part of these considerations, the most adventurous part of an assessment already too ambiguous for an honest citizen.

To begin, it seems clear to me that the two systems developed together. No serious observer would content himself with saying that the system of command is just a legacy of the *ancien régime*. It grew with the growth of modern civilization and society. When the individual breaks free from the old unequal communities of birth—thus begetting the new system of liberty—he must find his place within the new community, which now appears as the paramount community. I am speaking of the nation-state. The modern individual must become part of it. He best accomplishes that by attaining through his merits a well-regarded position—indeed, the highest possible position—within one of the great organizations through which the new body politic articulates itself. The organization is neither a society as the realm of freedom nor the political state as such; it is the link, the *tertium quid,* without which state and society would risk breaking apart. For all practical purposes, that is the point of the Hegelian statement I read at the beginning of these remarks.

European nations have generally followed Hegel in favoring mediating institutions between state and society. Americans have generally judged that they could dispense with this dangerous supplement to the original design of the liberal polity, even if, for all practical purposes many huge organizations bind state to society and society to state in America also. I have heard it said that not so long ago, there was a "military-industrial complex" there, which, with such a forbidding name, could not be small beer. However, Americans seem to have less need of vertical inscriptions of the pecking order of the great social body. This could be because the evaluation in dollars of every accomplishment offers sufficient guidance, or because the immensity of American society precludes such common hierarchies, or because American men and women, leading more natural lives, have less vanity than their European contemporaries. Whatever the reason, Americans have to settle for less social precision than Europeans have long been disposed to accept.

Even if we have no taste for Hegelian synthesis, the enmity between the system of liberty and the system of command cannot be such as liberal philosophers make it out to be. (Of course, here I am using the term "liberal" in its original European meaning.) There is more in common between the two systems than meets the eye. Both have to deal with—both are an answer to—a certain indetermination of human motives. And as I have suggested before, the second is meant to supplement the first on that score. The system of liberty is summarized in the formula "Do your own thing"—within the limits of the law, it goes without saying. However you conceive of it, such a maxim leaves much to be desired, in every sense of the expression. The system of command could be encapsulated in a formula like this one: "Do as you are told because what you are told comes through the hierarchical order that embodies the higher finality of the institution." You will easily agree that this maxim also leaves much to be desired. But what, exactly?

In a manner, this maxim is only common sense and good—that is, Aristotelian—philosophy. Specific hierarchies enable the end of each activity to govern that activity. Thus, specific hierarchies protect the free content of the corresponding activities. As a matter of fact, and to take an example familiar to me, what in France came to be called *le lycée napoléonien*—the Napoleonic high school—with the undertone of military discipline and marching in step, has long been indeed the citadel of the most perfect intellectual and personal liberty for teachers and pupils alike. But generally, the hierarchical logic tends to outstrip the logic of the corresponding activity. It is not only because men like to command and restlessly desire power after power, a desire that "ceaseth only in death," as Thomas Hobbes famously put it. It is also, more to the point, that contrary to plausible expectations, the separation of hierarchical functions, so characteristic of the modern state, weakens the several activities after it has strengthened them, or even as it strengthens them. As soon as each activity frees itself, asserts itself, and, to organize itself, takes on a specific hierarchical structure, it loses somewhat the sense of its place in the human world as a whole: it is relatively stronger, but on shakier ground. We can observe this contradictory process in many aspects of the modern European development.

The formal structure of command came to the fore, not only because considerable numbers of men had to be accommodated but also, paradoxically, because the intrinsic spirit of the institutions began losing some of its natural vigor even as it was exacerbated. The obsession with hierarchy and the intensification of organization have to do with some loss of substance in what Karl Marx called the "contents of life."[6] For instance, the Catholic Church took on its extreme hierarchical structure, with the pope deciding on everything of any importance, when it came in danger of being cut off from the nations of Europe after the French Revolution and its subsequent upheavals. Analogously, the transformation of the army into a huge bureaucracy encompassing with conscription the whole society not only meant a progress of democracy in state and society—this progress that transformed peasants into Frenchmen, to borrow an apt phrase—not only an answer to the intensifying rivalry between European nations, but also coincided with *some* weakening of the martial spirit in the society at large, the appearances to the contrary notwithstanding. Karl Polanyi coined a very evocative expression to describe this development when he spoke of the new crustacean type of nation—very hard on the surface, awkwardly soft inside. After August 1914, war transformed itself into something very different: *total* war. (By the way, as everybody knows, the model for the Leninist command economy was the German war economy as administered by Walter Rathenau.)[7]

Without underestimating its accomplishments, we are obliged to recognize that the system of command cannot supplement the system of liberty in a durable and satisfactory fashion. But conversely, I am not convinced that we can live only within the system of liberty. It is not only because you need the state to take care of those who for whatever reason are unable to do their own thing. (As Simonde de Sismondi, the great Swiss economist, put it, "If I don't oblige myself to employ my village's cripple, nobody will hire him or her." The welfare state is the instrument of this self-obligation.) It is not only because the unity of society must have some vertical—that is, political inscription—and the political inscription makes necessary use of the state. It is, perhaps more essentially, because what we do cannot be accompanied only by the bland commentary that we have the right to do it and that we hope we will do even better next time. It is by any measure an insufficient public account of what we do. If we stay within the confines of this point of view, we necessarily fail the paramount human obligation of *logon didonai*. For instance, it is not sufficient, for justifying or defending this lecture, to say that my offer met your demand, or the other way around, and that I will try to do better next time, if there is one. But if I stay within the confines of the system of liberty, I am not authorized to say much more.

The principle of subjectivity—my right, my way—is not self-sufficient. It must find some socially objective expression and inscription. It has to be brought back to the substantive unity, as Hegel said. You cannot leave it at the consideration that my action and its reasons are best judged by the market, because the market does not sanction the *specific* requirements of any human activity as such. It is a prodigiously effective rule of thumb, but nothing more, if nothing less.

Because it works by rule of thumb, the system of liberty leaves much indetermination in its wake. The glorious indetermination of liberty(!), many will enthuse. Not only that. The necessary metaphors of the mind say something: much liberty means much free space, much free space means much void. The system of command is an admittedly brutal and ill-tempered effort to fill this void, but it is not just an arbitrary imposition on an otherwise self-sufficient human reality. Even left to itself, the system of liberty is busy producing its own devices to fill its own void, to give itself the determinacy it necessarily lacks. With some frenzy it multiplies the representations of itself, through statistics, polls, PR, generally speaking through what now comes by the name of *communication*. The growing self-sufficiency of the market—at least, it is what is hoped for—gives birth to, and is conditioned by, a growing number of artifacts that produce and multiply the self-presentation of goods, products, and services. This self-presentation aggravates the indetermination it is intended to abolish or to attenuate. You have to propose the thing—that is, its anticipatory image—well before you are sure it even exists or could exist. And, of course, this same thing has to be bought, and commented upon, again before one is sure it exists or could exist. We gravely ponder the trends. Just imagine now Martin Luther the day after posting his theses at Wittenberg: TV, e-mail, the pundits, *Larry King Live*, Oprah Winfrey . . . the Reformation is over before it has begun. It is easy, when poking fun at the phenomena of communication, to invoke vanity and greed; but the deep cause is in the abstraction and simplification of human motives inseparable from the system of liberty.

The collapse of communism meant the end of the most complete, the most iron-clad system of command, of a social and political organization reduced to the mere system of command—with the most perverse system of mendacity to boot.[8] The system of liberty, with America at its center, has won the day; and we have every reason to rejoice at the outcome. Nevertheless, I would not counsel Americans to push too hard for the swift dismantling of every system of command, particularly in Europe, where they still fulfill many worthy social tasks in a civilized manner. In Europe, old motives still linger on, without much strength, indeed, perhaps devoid of sincerity. But people are thus reminded that there are ends that are desirable by themselves, because they are simply good or noble. Under what conditions these insubstantial longings could become the principle of meaningful public actions or individual expressions of high art, I do not know, and I admit that the prospects do not seem good. But you have to leave something to the gods or to nature, without always sacrificing the possibility of doing things to the right of doing them.

Notes

1. Friedrich Hegel, *Principles of the Philosophy of Right*, paragraph 260.
2. Montesquieu, *The Spirit of the Laws*, book 19, chapter 27.
3. See Francis Fukuyama, *The End of History and the Last Man* (New York: Free Press, 1992).
4. One has in mind such perspicacious observers as David Hume, Adam Smith, Adam Ferguson, and Montesquieu. On commerce as a new regime of human action see especially Montesquieu, *The Spirit of the Laws*, books 20 and 21 and chapter 1 of my book, *The City of Man* (Princeton: Princeton University Press, 1998).
5. Aristotle, *The Nicomachean Ethics*, book 4, chapter 3 (1126b11–12).
6. See Karl Marx, "On the Jewish Question," in *The Marx-Engels Reader,* ed. Robert C. Tucker (New York: Norton, 1978), 45.
7. On the rise of total war and the total state in the twentieth century, see the remarkable analysis of Raymond Aron in *The Century of Total War* (Garden City, N.Y.: Doubleday, 1954).
8. For a particularly penetrating analysis of the role of the lie in communist theory and practice, see Alain Besançon, *The Rise of the Gulag: Intellectual Origins of Leninism* (New York: Continuum, 1981), especially 243–91.

Index

absolutism, 109–10, 111
Adenauer, Konrad, 192
agnosticism, 98–99
America: command structure, 228–29; communism and, 219; democracy and, 10–11, 67, 69, 188, 219–20; liberalism and conservatism, 215–29; relations with Europe, 220; relations with France, 181–83; religion and, 105, 107
Anglicanism, 110
animal rights, 157
Appel du 18 juin, 176, 179–80, 182–83
appropriation, ontology of, 57–58
Aquinas, Thomas, 18
Arendt, Hannah, 139, 181
aristocracy, 11, 38, 67, 224; character of, 69–70; liberty and, 74
Aristotle, 18, 49, 51; human regime and, 68; impartiality of, 60–61; ontology of, 53, 57–60; partisans and, 4; as philosopher, 210–11; political community and, 191; politics and, 45, 101–2, 212
armistice, French, 174–75, 180–81
Aron, Raymond, 1, 2, 23, 209; on French armistice, 174–75; death of, 169; democracy and, 38; influence on Manent, 16–18; Machiavelli and, 36; modern society and, 167, 169–71; philosophy of, 16–18

art, socialist conception of, 85
artificialism, 119, 120–22
atheism, 85–86, 98–99, 206
Austen, Jane, 165
autonomy, 6–7

Bastiat, Frédéric, 14
Being, degrees of, 55–56
Belle Epoque, 79
Berthelot, 86
Bible, 205–6
Bildung, 221
birth right, 223
Bloom, Allan, 1, 19, 24, 149, 161–65
Blum, Leon, 178
Bolshevism, 141
Borgia, Cesare, 5, 52
bourgeois ideology, 6, 7, 127, 130
bourgeois society, 84–85, 123–24
Burke, Edmund, 104

capitalism, 13, 171
Catholic church, 63n.13, 97–98; command structure, 227; de Maistre and, 126; democracy and, 100–101
Catholicism, 86, 91
Céline, Louis-Ferdinand, 152
Christian church, 213
Christianity: democracy and, 79, 97–115; history of, 203–4; man's limitations and, 87–88; nature and, 203; Péguy's view of, 90–

92; political aspects of, 93–94; representation and, 128; secularization of, 40–42, 213; significance of, 50

church, 112, 114–15, *see also* religion

church and state, 98, 105–8, 113–14

Churchill, Winston, 178, 179, 181–82

The City of Man, 13, 17–18, 19–23, 42

civil society, 7; character of, 171; democratization and, 128–29; liberty and, 128; power and, 122; representation and, 14, 133n.3; state and, 122–26, 130–31

civilization, 153, 156, 187, 189

Combes, Émile, 94n.1

Combism, 82

command structure, 224–29

Commentaire, 2, 23–26

commerce, 222–23

commercial republicanism, 14

common good, 156

Common Market, 189

communications, 190–91

communism, 154–55, 171; collapse of, 218–20, 228; critique of, 16–17

community, 154–55, 190–91

Comte, Auguste, 171, 209

consciousness, 22

consent, principle of, 185–86, 188, 193, 218

conservatism, 143–45, 215, 217–29

conspiracies, 53

Constant, Benjamin, 14, 39, 65–66, 103–4, 164

constitutionalism, 7

contents of life, 2, 126–30, 226–27

contracts, 158–59

Corneille, Pierre, 92–92

cultural identity, 191–92, 196n.6

Dante Alighieri, 3, 103

de Bonald, Louis, 99

de Gaulle, Charles, 1, 26, 55, 167, 173–84, 192; French armistice and, 174–78; honor and, 179–80; policy of, 180–83; relations with French, 183–84; Roosevelt and, 182; Third Republic and, 177–79

de Maistre, Joseph, 2, 99, 104, 110, 126

Débat, 33

democracy: America, 10–11, 67, 69, 188, 219–20; aristocracy and, 67; art of, 70–73; Catholic Church and, 100–101; character of, 9–12; Christianity and, 40–42, 79, 97–115; communities within, 152; consent principle and, 185–86, 188; effects of on humans, 2; enemies of, 11–12; expansion of, 187; friends of, 11–12; historical interpretation of, 40–42; legitimacy of, 167, 218; liberty and, 73–75; Manent's view of, 167; nature of, 70–73; nature/history relationship and, 68–70; origins of, 37–39; religion and, 71; representation and, 6; spirituality and, 75; Tocqueville's view of, 9, 65–67, 105–8, 171, 187–88, 209, 210; without nations, 185–96

Democracy in America, 10–11, 67, 77n.5, 151

democratic process, ambivalence of, 126–28

democratization, 128–29

democrats, 60–61

Descartes, René, 89–90

despotism, 10–11, 15, 106

Discourses, 53, 58, 60

Dreyfus Affair, 82–84

Eastern Europe, 156

eclecticism, 171

Ecole Normale Supérieure, 94n.2

Elizabeth I, Queen of England, 109

Emile, 163

England, 128, 180–83

Enlightenment, 34, 98–104, 187
Europe: civilization and, 156; communism and, 219; homogeneity of, 187; identity vs. identification, 191–93; liberalism and conservatism, 215–29; politics, 24–26, 189–93; relations with America, 220; uniting of, 195
European Union, 189

faith, 79–80, 81–96, 105
family, character of, 11
The Federalist, 188
Ferguson, Adam, 135
France: Catholics, 111; command structure, 226; Dreyfus Affair, 82–84; history, 173–78; liberalism and conservatism, 215–29; politics, 200; relations with England, 180–83; Revolution, 84, 103–4, 131–32, 200, 223; Third Republic, 177–79; Vichy regime, 174–76
freedom, 170–71
friendship, 149, 161–65
Fukuyama, Francis, 218
Furet, François, 1, 2, 65

Germany, political class, 181–82, 219
God, 41, 63n.13, 102; democracy and, 98; relationship to man, 88–89
gods, man's awareness of, 88
Goethe, Johann, 202
goods, appropriation of, 57–58
Gorbachev, Mikhail, 218, 219
Government and Opposition, 24
the Great, 56–60
Greece, 69, 87–88
Gregory XVI, 79–80
Guizot, François, 6, 65
The Gulag Archipelago, 1

Hayek, Friedrich A., 10, 15, 23
Hegel, G. F. W., 7, 34, 39, 200–201;

concept of will, 101–2, 103–4; modernity and, 217; politics and, 53–54; state and society, 225; substantive unity and, 227–28
Heidegger, Martin, 39, 137, 200, 207; modern man and, 211–12; philosophy and, 34–35, 206
heroes, existence of, 173
Herr, Lucien, 82–83
heteronomous domination, 6
historians, 87–88
historical methods, 87–89
historicism, 13, 19–23, 52, 197, 209–14
history: democracy and, 68–70; experience of, 52; nature and, 20, 61; Péguy's view of, 86–87; socialist view of, 86–87
Hobbes, Thomas, 35; artificialism and, 119–20; command structure and, 226; constitutionalism and, 7; nature and, 201, 204; politics and, 53–54; pride and, 203; religion and, 41; representation and, 120, 121, 122, 133n.1; role of man, 146; role in modern movement, 36–37; social contract, 74; view of sovereignty, 5
Holocaust, 154
homogenization, 186–87
honor, 179–80
Horace, 21
human nature, 19, 212–13; analysis of, 142–43; existence of, 100; Péguy on, 91–92; philosophy and, 202–3, *see also* individualism
human relationships, 156–57
human universality, 210–11
humanitarianism, 14–15, 157
Husserl, Edmund, 143

identify vs. identification, 191–94
Imitatio Christi, 20
individual rights, 2
individualism, 171; effects of, 2, 149; Manent's view of, 5–8;

modern, 151–59; reactions to, 7–8; Tocqueville and, 8–13
industry, 171
Innocent XI, 109
Inquisition, 106–7
An Intellectual History of Liberalism, 2, 4
Italy, history, 48

Jacobinism, 131–33
Jaspers, Karl, 211
Jaurès, Jean Léon, 82–83, 85
Jefferson, Thomas, 49
"On The Jewish Question," 117, 123, 131–32
Judaism, 154
justice, 60–61, 69–70, 194

Kant, Immanuel, 101, 120, 157
Kempis, Thomas à, 20
Kierkegaard, Sören, 34, 154
Kohl, Helmut, 219
Kojève, Alexander, 200–201
Kolnai, Aurel, 1, 117, 135–49

labor, 84–85
The Labor of Machiavelli's Work, 47–48
Lamberti, Jean-Claude, 2
language, national, 195
Lefort, Claude, 1; Machiavelli and, 45, 47–63; Strauss and, 48–51
Les Libéraux, 15–16
Leviathan, 146, 203
liberalism, 2, 6; character of, 13–16; *Commentaire* and, 23–24; evolution of, 7–8; Manent's view of, 3; religion and, 18
liberty, 7–8, 61; ambiguity of, 220–21; art of, 11–12; basis of, 86–87; character of, 215; civil society and, 128; command structure and, 227–28; consequences of, 106; democracy and, 77n.18; equality and, 222–23; fear of, 105–6; limits and, 194; positive aspects of,

221–22; religion and, 105–7; Tocqueville and, 45, 73–75, *see also* liberalism
Locke, John, 7, 13–14, 35
Louis XIV, 109
love, 149, 161–65
Luther, Martin, 52

Machiavelli, Niccolò, 3, 107; denial of common good, 4; Lefort's view of, 45, 47–63; paganism and, 42; religion and, 41; view of political life, 4
Mahoney, Daniel, 1–29
Main Currents in Sociological Thought, 169–70, 209
man: aspects of, 119–20; definition, 210–22; limitations of, 87–88; nature and, 213; politics and, 191; power of, 69; property and, 129; rights of, 125; self and, 38–39; Tocqueville's view of, 65–78; will and, 104, *see also* utopian mind
Mandel, Georges, 179
Marcel, Premier dialogue de la cité harmonieuse, 84–85
the market, 13, 228
Marsilius of Padua, 3, 103
Marx, Karl, 2, 3, 209; bourgeois ideology, 5–7, 127; civil society and, 131; conceptual system, 66; contents of life, 226–27; Jewish question and, 117, 123, 131–32; philosophy and, 34; representation, 131–32; totalitarianism and, 129
materialism, 85–86
Memoirs (Aron), 174–75
Memoirs (de Gaulle), 175, 183
metaphysics, 85
Metaphysics, 212
Mitterrand, François, 219
modern difference, 19–23, 33
modern man: character of, 89–90, 211–12; human nature and, 19–23; Manent's view of, 20–22;

Péguy's view of, 84–90, *see also* man

modernity, 7, 103–4; character of, 8, 13, 36–37; chronology of, 35–37; definition, 34; necessity and, 4; origin, 52; Strauss's view of, 45; traits of, 35; utopian mind and, 137; will and, 21

monarchies, 108–9

Monnet, Jean, 195

Montesquieu, Charles de Secondat, baron de, 8, 14, 18, 23, 167, 217; liberty and, 74–75; science and freedom, 170–71; virtue and, 194

moral life, 7, 179, 200–201, 206, 207; Constant's view of, 39; nature and, 18–19

moral philosophy, 135–36, 143–44

motives, human, 222

nation-states, 223–25

nationalism, 190

nations: character of, 194–95; definition, 195; democracy and, 185–96; identity vs. identification, 191–94; nation–states, 223–25

natural order of things, 13

naturalism, 3, 19–23, 212–13

nature: democracy and, 68–70; history and, 20, 61; Hobbes and, 201, 204; moral life and, 18–19; ontology of, 53–54; society and, 85; state of, 152

Nazism, 139, 154–55, 186

necessity, modernity and, 4

Nichomachean Ethics, 191

Nietzsche, Friedrich, 90, 101, 137, 162, 170; Enlightenment and, 34; Manent's view of, 197, 199–207

Notre Jeunesse, 83

Oakeshott, Michael, 137, 143, 192

oligarchs, 60–61

paganism, 42

Paine, Thomas, 14

partisans, justice claims, 4

Pascal, Blaise, 90–92, 201

Péguy, Charles, 1, 21; Christianity and, 90–92; Dreyfus Affair, 82–84; eminent cases, 48; faith and, 79–80, 81–90; modern world and, 84–90; overview of works, 81–82; theology-politics relationship, 92–94

the people, 4–5, 56–60

people's desire, 58–60

Pétain, Marshal, 55, 174–76

The Phenomenology of Mind, 7, 201

philosophers: character of, 205; Christianity and, 213–14; political, 117, 135–49; role in modern-movement, 36

philosophy: character of, 50, 202, 210–11; human nature and, 202–3; nature and, 201–2; origin, 51; as origin of modern difference, 33–34; politics and, 213–14; religion and, 205–6; as teaching, 49–50; threat to, 207

Physics, 212

pity, 157–58

Pius X, Saint, 98

Plato, 51, 68, 165, 201

Plutarch, 20

Pocock, J. G. A., 62n.3

political philosophy: character of, 52–53; France and, 200; origin, 51; overview, 42; people's desire and, 59; reflections of Manent, 1–29; Strauss's view of, 48–49, *see also* philosophy

political science, 17–18, 45

Politics, 60, 101–2, 212

politics: character of, 53–55; closed, 4–5; Europe, 24–26, 189–93; man and, 191; Manent's view of, 23–26, 167; moral philosophy and, 135–36; ontology of, 53–54, 56–57; origin, 51; parts of, 56–57; people's desire and, 59; philosophy and, 213–14; religion and,

41; Strauss's view of, 5; theology
  and, 3–5, 92–94, 102–3, 111, *see
  also* church and state
Polyeucte, 92–93
Popper, Karl, 143–44
power, society and, 122
"Preface to Spinoza's Critique of
  Religion," 205–6
pride, 203
Prince, 58, 60
*Principles of the Philosophy of
  Right*, 34
privacy issues, 113–14, 125–26
private property, 128–29, 154, 171
progressivism, 12–13
protestantism, 110
Proust, Marcel, 152
public opinion, 15
puritanism, 71, 110

reading, principle of, 49–50
religion: America, 105, 106–7; democracy and, 71, 112; liberalism
  and, 18; liberty and, 105–7;
  Péguy's view of, 86; philosophy
  and, 205–6; political history of,
  108–12; privacy issues, 113–14;
  representation and, 128; Tocqueville's view of, 105–8;
  transformation of, 130; utility of,
  107, *see also* church and state
religious freedom, 6, 97–98
Renan, Ernest, 87, 88
Renaudet, A., 48
representation, 65, 66, 76–77n.5;
  ambivalence of, 126–28; artificialism and, 120–22; character of,
  121; Christianity and, 128; civil
  society and, 13–14, 123–24,
  133n.3; democracy and, 6;
  England, 128; forms of, 120–21;
  Hobbes and, 133n.1; Locke's
  view of, 13–14; Marx and, 131–
  32; spiritual aspects, 124–26;
  totalitarianism and, 117, 119–33

Revue Blanche, 82
Reynaud, Paul, 174, 178
Robespierre, Maximilien, 133
romanticism, 162–64
Rome, 54
Roosevelt, Franklin, 181–892
Rousseau, Jean-Jacques, 3, 35, 101–
  2, 146, 157; homogeneous nations
  and, 186–87; political philosophy and, 199–200; representation
  and, 120–121; romanticism and,
  162–63; Strauss's view of, 199–
  200

Schmitt, Carl, 2, 3
science, 170–71
Second Vatican Council, 99, 113,
  152
Shakespeare, William, 164, 165
Shakespeare's Politics, 164
Sismondi, Simonde de, 227
situation, notion of, 55
Smith, Adam, 223
Social Contract, 102, 163
social divisions, 60
social sciences, Manent on, 2–3
socialism, 85
society. *see* civil society
sociology, 66, 169–71, 209
Socrates, 201, 207
Solzhenitsyn, Aleksandr, 1
Sonderweig, 209
Sparta, 54
The Spirit of the Laws, 14
spiritualism, 85
spirituality: dissolution of, 75;
  representation and, 124–26
state: civil society and, 122–26, 130–
  31, 225–26, *see also* church and
  state
Strauss, Leo, 1, 2, 4, 5, 36; influence on Manent, 18–23; Lefort
  and, 48–51; Manent's view of,
  197, 199–207; modern man and,
  211–12; nature and, 197, 209–14,

212–13; Nietzsche and, 197, 199–
207; political philosophy vs.
modern thought, 45; religion and,
205–6
Summa, 61
supernaturalism, 3
Symposium, 165

Taine, Hippolyte, 87–89
teaching, 49–50
temporal power, 103
territorial consciousness, 156
territorial unconsciousness, 189–90
theology, 206; politics and, 3–5,
92–94, 102–3, 111
Thermidor, 132–33
Thoughts on Machiavelli, 200
Thucydides, 51, 68, 69
Tocqueville, Alexis de, 1–2, 104,
209; aristocratic party and, 11;
Commentaire and, 23–24; conceptual system, 65–68; democracy
and, 38, 45, 65–78, 105–8, 171,
187–88, 209, 210; humanity and,
151; individualism and, 8–13;
man and, 65–78; Manent's view
of, 8–13; religion and, 105–8;
role in modern movement, 36–37;
sovereignty and, 14

*Tocqueville and the Nature of
Democracy,* 8–9, 12–13
totalitarianism: character of, 15–16;
definition, 122–23, 130–31; individualism and, 7; Marx and, 129;
representation and, 117, 119–33;
utopias and, 138–40, 145–46
traditionalists, 142–43
On Tyranny, 200–201

United States. *see* America
utopian mind, 117; character of,
140–41; leftist ideas and, 137;
modernity and, 137; positive
aspects of, 146; rightist ideas
and, 137; value content of, 136
utopias, 137–40, 145–46

Viviani, René, 79

Weber, Max, 170–71, 209
welfare state, 15, 227
Western Europe, 219
will, 21; concept of, 101–2, 103–4;
emancipation of, 105–6; representation of, 121

Xenophon, 201

Zangwill, 48

About the Authors

Pierre Manent, one of France's leading political philosophers, is a professor at the Ecole des hautes études en sciences sociales in Paris.

Daniel J. Mahoney is an associate professor of politics at Assumption College in Worcester, Massachusetts. He is the author of *The Liberal Political Science of Raymond Aron* (1992) and *De Gaulle: Statesmanship, Grandeur, and Modern Democracy* (1996).

Paul Seaton is a doctoral candidate in political science at Fordham University in New York.